the heart of things

Green Balloon Publishing

"And that night the cold stars made a constellation from the
pieces of my broken mind."
(Jeanette Winterson, 2011)

"... the possibility of emotional trauma is built into the basic
constitution of human existence."
(Robert D Stolorow, 2007)

the heart of things

understanding trauma –
working with constellations

Vivian Broughton

Green Balloon Publishing

First published in the United Kingdom in 2013
by Green Balloon Publishing

© V. Broughton 2013

Green Balloon Publishing
Steyning, West Sussex, BN44 3GF UK
www.greenballoonbooks.co.uk
info@greenballoonbooks.co.uk

ISBN 978-0-9559683-4-1

Book production by The Choir Press, Gloucester

Contents

Contents

Foreword

I have known Vivian Broughton since 2005, and this co-operation has been very fruitful, as is documented here in Vivian's new book. She has taken up my theory of the multi-generational psychotraumatology, and my particular use of the constellation method, in a profound way and worked it through to its "heart".

Vivian adds some new elements to my approach, coming from her own psychotherapeutic background, and her own perspectives on that complex field of the client-therapist interaction.

The "Constellation of the Intention" offers new opportunities for working with trauma, where words alone cannot help us to access the split-off experiences of helplessness and being overwhelmed, especially in the period of our early childhood. It offers a chance to come into contact with traumatic experiences without the danger of retraumatisation, and Vivian has brought her own particular thinking to this practice.

Franz Ruppert
Munich, May 2013

Preface

"Nothing arrives on paper as it started, and so much arrives
that never started at all.
To write is always to rave a little."
Elizabeth Bowen, The House in Paris 1998

This book is about trauma, its impact on the individual and on
subsequent generations. It is also about the intimate processes
of early attachment for the infant, and how he or she is
impacted by the traumas of others earlier in the family through
bonding with the mother and father. And it is about the
methodology of the constellations process as a means for
finding resolution of trauma, healing the psychological splits
that are the result of trauma, and the personal journey from
symbiotic entanglement to autonomy and healthy relationships
with others. In my view trauma lies at the very heart of things.

For the last eight years I have immersed myself in the
study of trauma based on the work and practice of German
professor of psychology, Franz Ruppert. Already three of
Ruppert's books have been published in English,[1] and while
these cover his theories and ideas about practice very well, my
hope is that another perspective can find its place. I aim to
elaborate on his ideas and offer my own interpretations and
thinking, none of which I think conflicts with his. I aspire only
to add another perspective and approach.

---

[1] With a fourth currently being translated.

In order to work with a set of ideas developed by someone else, I think one has to find a way of making them one's own. It is not enough to follow and copy without putting heart and mind into the adventure, and 'adventure' is what it has been for me. Over the past eight years I feel as though I have been on an extraordinary adventure of self-discovery and professional development. This 'development' now finds me in a somewhat unique place: I am a psychotherapist, trained in the Person Centred work of Carl Rogers and Gestalt psychotherapy, having practised as a psychotherapist since 1989. But I have also been involved with the Constellations work originated by Bert Hellinger in Germany since the mid-1990s, and worked with Family Constellations from 2000 to 2010, by which time I was well into my journey of study with Franz Ruppert. In 2011 I finally realised that I couldn't work with Family Constellations any longer; the work being developed by Ruppert, and my journey with it, were showing me quite clearly that there was a stark and irreconcilable difference between the two (for more on this see Chapter 11).

I would describe myself as a Gestalt Trauma Constellations psychotherapist. My psychotherapy background is Gestalt, and I now only work with what I would call 'trauma constellations', what Ruppert has termed the 'constellation of the intention', where the central focus is the impact of trauma as a personal and trans-generation phenomenon. I do not 'fit' in the regular 'constellations community', and in a way I don't fit in the regular 'psychotherapy community' either. There are subtle and profound challenges in the work that I do to both Family Constellations and conventional psychotherapy. In my view, one of the main challenges to psychotherapy is that trauma, generally speaking, does not occupy nearly a central enough position in the perspective of most therapists, particularly early attachment trauma, and neither does a transgenerational perspective, sometimes over three, four or even five generations. My working assumption is that unresolved early attachment trauma and the resulting transgenerational entanglement with the trauma of others underlie *all* psychotherapeutic issues. The psychological splits resulting from early trauma are the foundations of our internal conflicts and our external difficulties. This early situation may well be obscured by later childhood abuse and trauma, but work with this later trauma will need, at some point, to address the former.

The other challenge is that working with the methodology of the constellation does not require the client to attend therapy on a weekly basis, but leaves him to find his own pace and frequency. The work does not hold the relationship between therapist and client as the crucible for change, and so does not necessitate weekly contact. Clients' attendance may vary from once a month or six weeks to a much more sporadic basis. On a very practical level this presents a formidable challenge to the conventional psychotherapist, since it completely reconfigures one's basic regular income framework. (For more on the relationship between the work I do and psychotherapy generally see Chapter 12.)

It is a considerable challenge to write about another's work, and in doing so to find a place that doesn't just repeat, but offers something else, not anything greater, but perhaps something that can sit well alongside. I attempt it out of respect and gratitude to Franz Ruppert, because my connection with him and his work has extended my competency as a practitioner, and increased my personal clarity. Both give me a sense of peace and stability, and also an excitement and sense of purpose in my life.

Unresolved trauma influences our lives quite beyond what we generally think. For many there are personally experienced traumas that they know about and can recount the details of, events that happened within the range of memory. But we do not know, and it is difficult to know, the impact on us of the very early moments of our lives when in the intimate symbiosis with our mother, and slightly later with our father. From the moment of our conception it is very likely that we are affected by many things, but the possibility of recalling and recounting such things seems impossible. The idea that we may take on the effects of unresolved traumas of others in our family through the early attachment process with our mother and father is novel, and since seemingly impossible to access in therapy, usually is not a topic of focus. It is an unusual psychotherapist who enquires into his client's family history beyond the time of the client's own life, let alone two, three, four or even five generations back.

In most cases, the later, describable, traumatic event is in fact, in part, a retraumatisation relating to something much earlier, which perhaps explains the troubling phenomenon of different personal reactions to similar events that most trauma therapists find in their work. The current formal diagnosis of Post Traumatic Stress Disorder (the only formal diagnosis that specifically refers to trauma in the American Psychiatric manual, the DSM IV) covers traumatic events that are recallable, and has no criteria for the inclusion of earlier, pre-verbal trauma.

A look at the history of trauma study, which I recount briefly in Part I, shows that trauma has suffered primarily from an avoidance of study, rather than being given a central place within psychotherapeutic investigation. As a psychotherapist of some 23 years practice, at times it still shocks and surprises me how little the topic of trauma featured in my training, and indeed in the first fifteen years of my psychotherapy practice. It isn't that psychotherapy and its educational institutes were deficient or wrong; at that time in the late 1980s trauma just wasn't a topic many were giving much attention to. It has taken a lot to get trauma properly on our agenda, and for many, even now, it still isn't.

I am interested in engaging a wide audience on this journey of investigation of the dynamics and effects of trauma. I think it so central to our lives that to downplay it, or specialise it into a professional-only topic, is likely to play into our unconscious fears and strategies of avoidance of trauma. I believe we all can benefit from informing ourselves and understanding the dynamics of trauma better. It isn't just a topic for professionals: it helps me understand myself of course, and be less easily triggered by others' behaviour. It also helps me understand others and make sense of behaviour in partners, friends, relatives and co-workers that otherwise could annoy or distress me.

I hope to encourage others to become interested in resolving their own trauma, to believe that this is possible and to strengthen the innate healthy desire for integration, wholeness and fulfilment of potential that is in all of us. To know that someone else thinks a thing possible, at the very least may give another the courage to investigate it for him- or herself. And it is helpful to be informed enough to make good choices about how to do this, who to work with, what to look for to assist one on one's journey.

Part I looks briefly at the history of the study of trauma, contextualising what follows. I then set out Ruppert's theory of Multi-Generational Psychotraumatology, making reference to other current and historical thinking on trauma and early attachment. I make references to conventional attachment theory, and finally put the theories of trauma and attachment together in an exploration of what Ruppert has termed symbiotic trauma and its companion, symbiotic entanglement.

Part II looks at the practice of the Constellation of the Intention, the form of the constellations process Ruppert devised specifically to work with the intra-psychic splits resulting from traumatisation. The methodology of Family Constellations emerged in Germany as the work of the psychotherapist and philosopher Bert Hellinger in the late 1980s. It focused on ancestral entanglements and consequent systemic disturbances as disrupting the ability of family members to have real loving relationships. Since the early 1990s Family Constellations has spread rapidly worldwide, generating enthusiasm and interest amongst many different peoples.

The 'trauma constellation', or Constellation of the Intention as Ruppert has termed it, draws only on the method Hellinger devised of using group members to represent people or elements relevant to a client's presented issue, but not the underlying ideas of Family Constellations. There are reasons for this that I set out in Chapter 11.

Part III (which includes Chapter 11) looks at the relationship between 'trauma-oriented constellations' as discussed in Part II and psychotherapy generally and family constellations particularly.

This book represents where I am at the moment. I think it is the best I can do for now, and it sits in a stream of the development of thinking on the topic of trauma, and in the stream of my own professional and personal development. It doesn't end here; it isn't definitive, and there may be reference to work and authors that I have missed. Also I may develop different ideas and arguments in the future. The very best I could hope is that this book stimulates others to think further and join the debate.

Note on terms

In my previous book I used the term 'facilitator' to describe the person who works with the constellations process as I thought it more appropriate in Family Constellations. Since moving more into the realm of working with trauma I find I am back to using the term 'therapist' since in many ways the work that I now do is closer to the work of psychotherapy than the work of traditional constellations, and the term 'therapist' seems more accurate. So at times, when I am talking about Family Constellations I have used the word 'facilitator' more, but generally when talking about trauma constellations I have used the word 'therapist'. The reader can think of them as interchangeable.

For the person who comes to do a constellation I use the word 'client' rather than 'patient'. This is traditional in the UK psychotherapy world, and in the absence of a better word, I prefer the term 'client' to 'patient'. Regarding the usage of gender terms I have varied these in an ad hoc manner.

Acknowledgements

This book would not have come into being without the help and contribution of many people. Any work such as this must be a culmination of what the writer has become at the time of writing; whatever the topic, the writing comes from the agglomeration of all one's life of experience and learning from others. Among those many people, there are those who appear in this book by their particular contribution. My thanks to them for their loving support and critical courage; for being willing to engage with me in long conversations and passionate debate, and for putting up with my obsessive need to talk about these topics until I, temporarily, ran dry. Such discussion, challenges, arguments and friendly repartee helped me immeasurably to solidify and gain confidence in my thoughts. The challenges from my colleagues, while sometimes painful to me, often in the end proved their point, and make perhaps the greatest contribution to the end result by encouraging me to think further.

In particular, of course, I thank Franz Ruppert for his persistent commitment to understanding and researching trauma and attachment, and his willingness to deal patiently with my challenges and arguments as I attempted to keep up with him and his developing ideas. And to his wife, Juliane von Krause, for putting up with Franz's many absences from home demonstrating his work throughout the world, in part for his visits to the UK which have been so valuable to me.

My profound appreciation also goes to Professor Kim Etherington for her patient and professional supervision of my work and my writing, and for her openness to what, for her were sometimes new and challenging ideas, and sometimes new versions of old ideas. She always generously offered me the benefit of her long experience, interest and considerable knowledge about trauma, and demonstrated her commitment to me and my work in quite extraordinary ways.

Others include: Liz Martins, Kirti Wheway, Tony Glanville, Kathie Murphy, Jude Higgins, Pam Smallwood,

Philip Smallwood, Judy Scott, Natasha Morgan, Tore Kval, Clare Kavanagh, Dimitrina Spencer, Vanja Orlans, Claudia Schmidt, Frankie McGibney and Josie Eckholdt, all of whom have provided their time to listen to me, challenge my thinking, support my efforts and offer contributions of their own. My thanks also to those students of this work, and those students of Family Constellations, whose questions and arguments have been endlessly stimulating, challenging and fascinating.

A particular thanks to John Mitchell as my most helpful and supportive critic, my formal editor, proofreader and, as the director of Green Balloon Books, my publisher. My thanks to John McClean for his meticulous proof-reading; and finally to Miles Bailey and all at The Choir Press for their help in bringing the book to a physical reality.

My deepest gratitude, however, goes to all those clients and students who were willing to put their trust in me and what I do, from whom I have learnt more than from anywhere else, and whose lives and stories touch mine more deeply than they can ever know.

Prologue

"What I want does exist if I dare to find it ..."
(Winterson, 2010)

The room is quiet. Sun filters in through the leaves of an old oak tree just outside. The group sits attentively, and I wait. The woman next to me, I shall call her Beth, is also quiet. She looks at the floor a few feet in front of her, her head hanging slightly, a bit slumped in her chair but, even so, leaning slightly forward, her hands clasped between her knees. Her breathing is slight, but there. The damp tracks of recently shed tears still show on her cheeks. It is the first time she is quiet since she came to sit next to me. I wait.

I was the last one to speak. For about fifteen minutes Beth had recapped her life in some detail, telling about events from her teenage years, her childhood, slimly disguised complaints about her mother... and her father, her alienation from her brother, a year younger, and her sister a year older. She knows that the focus of the workshop is trauma so she tells me about what she knows... about herself... about various things that happened in her life that she thinks might come under this term. At times her anger and resentment are barely concealed, and the tears emerge somewhat reluctantly from years of suppression, a habit from times when to cry didn't help, perhaps even made things worse. And every now and again, when she can meet my eyes it is only for a moment, and I see the faint flickering of fear, terror even, behind a protective veil of distance; it is as though she comes and goes. . . a moment of connection and then she's gone.

I had asked a simple question: "So what do you want, for now, from a constellation?"

Over the years I have learned to ask this question gently, in different ways, and not to expect a clear answer. Of course there are times when a clear answer is there, but more often I know that sitting with a client in this way, with the proposal that she takes a step towards something new, is a process of enquiry, a journey towards herself in the presence of another. I have learned that few of us dare let ourselves really wonder: What do I want? Asked in this way it is a heart-stopper. At best it brings a person into a gentle and focused inner alignment. But often it confuses. "I don't know" is a frequent answer. And for some even to admit that not-knowing is too much; instead they will go back over the problem, re-telling the story in a different way, with further examples, perhaps with a slight increase in awareness and understanding. For some it is a question to avoid, because, quite simply, it will put us in touch with our trauma.

Trauma is always close, and as Beth struggles to find an answer to my question she, too, struggles with the inner conflict between a desire for health and integration, and a terror of what that might entail, because trauma is always potentially traumatising, and terror is always potentially terrifying. It is exactly the present state of Beth that will determine what is possible right now, inform her ability to answer the question, and the progress and outcome of the constellation she will do.

It is a question I may ask a couple of times during this initial stage of the constellations session, thereby allowing a growing familiarity with this notion that she may really be able and allowed to want something for herself. And then there is always the tension with what is possible now, at this time, this moment.

As Beth and I continue to sit together I can see her deepen her experience of herself. In the quiet moments between us she connects more with herself. I see her breathing deepen; her body relax a little more. I can see the moment she moves away from this intimacy with herself, perhaps in that moment too much to contemplate, and begins to talk again as a way of distracting herself. A while later she is quiet again. I see her breath deepen again, and that she is now once more involved in herself. Perhaps in that moment I don't even exist for her. I don't disturb her. She is in some communion with herself. That is fine with me.

After a few minutes she looks up, takes a breath and turns to face me. And she says what she wants, for now. It's clear. Now she can set up the constellation and see what emerges.

It's always different, but eventually there is always that moment. A moment however small and fragile where clarity shines through, as much as is possible right now. To gain this clarity in the face of the closeness of one's trauma is no small thing, and is itself of immense value.

The leaves in the trees outside rustle and the sun shines through the windows, and Beth chooses a representative for her intention for the start of her constellation.

Introduction

"Trauma is perhaps the most avoided, ignored, belittled,
denied, misunderstood, and untreated cause of human
suffering." (*Levine, 2008*)

"... individuals in all their messy complexity should remain at
the heart of psychological study and practice."
(*Grogan, 2012*)

In 2004 while attending a conference on Systemic and Family
Constellations in Germany, I went to a presentation and
workshop facilitated by Professor Dr Franz Ruppert. Although
I had been deeply involved in Family Constellations since the
mid 1990s when I first saw its originator, Bert Hellinger,
working in London, and had organised a training in the UK on
the work since 2000 (mainly as a way of learning for myself),
I had never heard of Franz Ruppert. I can't remember what the
title of his presentation was, nor why I was drawn to that
particular presentation from some thirty others, but it changed
my life.

The room was quite large and there must have been two
hundred or so people squeezed into it. I managed to get in the
door but no further. Over the heads of people, some fifteen to
twenty yards away was a small clearing with about four people
standing up as the demonstration constellation, and a youthful
looking man standing to one side.

It's difficult to say now exactly what impacted me most,

but the comparison with the facilitation of Family Constellations that I had seen so far (and done myself) was startling. Ruppert as the 'facilitator' stood well outside the group of people forming the constellation; he hardly made any interventions, and when he did so it was in a quiet voice, and always in response to something one of the representatives in the constellation had said. He seemed to initiate nothing. There was a genuine feel from him of collaboration rather than management, of engagement with a process rather than authorising that process, and an understated respectfulness that was compelling.

Up to this moment, while being fascinated and greatly drawn to the work of Family Constellations I had always had secret reservations about *how* those facilitating them worked. Those readers who are familiar with the constellations work originated by Bert Hellinger may have some sense of what I mean.

Over my time of working as a psychotherapist I have come to believe that the client always knows better than I about themselves, often more unconsciously than consciously for sure, but even so I believe that the task of the therapist is to wait on that emerging knowing in the client. I believe that if the client can experience that trust in him from the therapist, then he will begin to feel that same trust in himself. I saw most constellations facilitators at that time as, to a varying degree, authoritative and managerial, where the 'truth' of the constellation often emanated from the facilitator, not the client, and where what happened in the constellation was frequently choreographed according to the facilitator's hypotheses rather than allowed to emerge and reveal its own truth. Hellinger's own stated position was phenomenological – respectful of the emergent reality – and his original exploration of the constellations process theoretically did depend on his willingness to experiment and learn from the constellation rather than try and manage the process. Nevertheless, my experiences of his work at times, and much of others' work, often did not support this. My own family constellations work at that time also, in moments of uncertainty, veered far too close to the managerial and directive than I really felt comfortable with.

I had rather batted these concerns away, as a nuisance that I could ignore in the face of this absorbing work, but as I watched Ruppert facilitate this constellation everything I knew that I had been attempting to overlook fell into alignment. I knew this man had something very important to offer me, just in the way he stood and interacted with the people in the constellation, in the quiet and understated manner in which he spoke to them. At once I understood exactly what had disturbed me about constellations work generally, and my own work with Family Constellations to that point.

At the end of the presentation I went straight up to Ruppert, and with little introduction asked if he would come to the UK to do a workshop. Somewhat bemused he agreed, and so began my studentship of trauma and attachment, and a friendly collaboration that continues to the present day. At the time I knew nothing about his research and study into trauma and bonding, I just intuitively liked the man and his style. However, as I began to learn from him I became increasingly interested and absorbed with his theories as well as his practice. I suggested having his first book translated into English,[2] which I then edited, and subsequently his second and lately his third. Currently his fourth is in the process of being translated.

Ruppert was originally an employment psychologist. In the mid 1990s he came across the Family Constellations work of Hellinger, which made a great impression on him and, like many others back then, he began to facilitate constellations workshops alongside a growing psychotherapy practice. (Broughton, 2010b) In his work with constellations he saw that everything seemed to come back to issues that were traumatic, and that the most crucial relationship in the bonding system of the family was always that between child and parents, particularly the mother. He began to study the work of the English

[2] *Trauma, Bonding & Family Constellations*, Green Balloon Publishing, UK (2008).

psychoanalyst John Bowlby who had made his particular focus early attachment and bonding, and texts on trauma. He began to find in the constellations method a useful research tool, a means of studying and understanding trauma and bonding with each constellation that he facilitated. This is not dissimilar to Hellinger's original use of the constellations method in order to study and understand loving relationships. Ruppert has said that the constellations process is the most effective way of giving access to the unconscious and inaccessible parts of ourselves, and since the main thesis of his work is the relegation to the unconscious of the intolerable trauma experiences, the combination of his theory of a Multi-Generational Psychotraumatology and the method of constellations form a coherent model for understanding and working with trauma. It is this combination of theory and practice that forms the basis of this book.

I find myself now in a very different place from my beginnings as a psychotherapist. I think unresolved personal and systemic family trauma is at the very heart of our difficulties in life. It is at the heart of who we are... and who we aren't, and of what our life can be – and what it isn't, and what it cannot ever be. Unresolved trauma sits, frozen and split off, waiting for redemption, spurned from consciousness, ignored, unloved and lonely. It diminishes our ability to love and care, and to be loved and cared for, compelling us to choose partners similarly compromised, because real openness and intimacy are likely, in the moment of loving feelings, to surface the frightening emotions associated with the unresolved trauma.

The traumatised person struggles with life, and often sinks into desolation and loneliness. Our survival of a trauma does indeed allow us to survive, but split within ourselves, unknowing of who we really are, isolated from our true self, often hugely compromised by strategies of dissociation, distraction, avoidance and compensation. The current proliferation of addictions, disorders and compulsions, from the most serious to the mild, all in my opinion are likely to originate in a survival of trauma. They are the means of avoidance and

4

control, and also the means of compensation for the absence of good feelings. It makes no sense to me to work behaviourally with, for example, someone suffering from an eating disorder, without considering the case in relation to trauma, particularly early attachment trauma.

I also believe that real love and integrity are at the heart of things. Our desire for truth, reality and wholeness, to be fulfilled, social, dignified and loving beings fires in us the will to carry on, to survive traumatic events, and also the will to risk change. Facing unresolved trauma requires courage, determination and steadfastness, and I believe that these qualities, along with the potential for a real love of ourselves and our integrity, also lie, often dormant, at the heart of all humans. Such belief in ourselves, that we *can* transcend our difficulties, is the force of life that is at the heart of us, side by side with unconscious trauma. As much as we may be the victim of trauma, we are also the hero of our life, the rescuer of ourselves; we are our own knight in shining armour fighting our own dragons for the lost and imprisoned parts of ourselves.

Until we understand just how endemic trauma is in our society, and how much it influences people at all levels, from governments to families, in the decisions and choices they make, we will inevitably continue to re-create and repeat these unconscious trauma situations privately and publicly, locally and globally. The transgenerational nature of unresolved trauma, where the split off and dissociated feelings of the traumatic event are passed on to the subsequent generation through the intimate process of bonding, makes certain that trauma will never just 'go away'.

Two of the biggest social trauma issues that have demanded our attention over the past 30 years have been domestic trauma – violence and abuse, including sexual abuse and rape within the family; and combat trauma, the traumatisation of those trained to serve in violent situations, combined with the traumatisation of ordinary people in combat zones. Perhaps one could say that these topics alone provide the most urgent and comprehensive social foci for us globally at this time, particularly if we consider the effect on children of having traumatised parents.

However, no one can heal anyone else's trauma, so it has to start with the individual. The politician cannot make good the trauma of the combatant, and the social worker cannot heal the trauma of the abuse survivor. But they can help by understanding the significance, endurance and influence of trauma; and those working with the effects of trauma can best equip themselves by working to heal their own trauma, so that their perception and comprehension when working with others' trauma is clear.

In order to heal one's own trauma, we need to know the possibility of such healing ... that it is there. Much trauma work today is avoidant, tending to help the client manage their trauma rather than seeing the possibility of real healing and resolution. It isn't enough just for professionals to understand these things, we *all* need to take responsibility for ourselves individually, to find the means to face our own trauma in order to integrate the unintegrated, allowing us to become whole and truly ourselves.

Most of the intentions people have when they come to work with me are quite ordinary, simple and understandable. . . and yet to the person they often seem impossible, too much to ask, unattainable and at times not even worth risking wanting or saying. Disappointment breeds resignation, and resignation is so hard to bear that we give up daring to want at all, until we feel trapped in a life of limits.

Generally we want to feel good, happy and safe in our lives, at ease within ourselves, able to be in good relationship with others, to enjoy intimacy with a few: a partner, our children, our closest friends. We want to be able to have a primary intimate relationship, to share our life, have a family, achieve success in whatever arena we choose. We want to feel fulfilled, to use the gifts we have as far as we are able. We want to be able to manage the difficulties of our lives without feeling overwhelmed. We want the fast beating of our heart to be because of something that is recognisable and real in the here-and-now, whether it is love or fear, rather than reaching back into some confusing and unresolved past. We want to feel whole, when we know we feel fragmented. I believe it is possible to heal the psychological ravages of traumatisation, and to disentangle ourselves from the unresolved traumas in our families.

Trauma

"[This] subject (the traumatic neuroses) has been submitted to a good deal of capriciousness in public interest. The public does not sustain its interest, and neither does psychiatry. Hence these conditions are not subject to continuous study, but only to periodic efforts which cannot be characterized as very diligent." *(Kardiner & Spiegel, 1947)*

In my view trauma is endemic rather than exotic; that is to say that if we start to understand the possibility of very early, even in-utero trauma, and the impact on the new child of the traumas of the parents, grandparents and even great grandparents, there is likely to be the residue of trauma in all of us. Trauma in the sense in which I will discuss it in this book is not an exotic thing that happens to just a few people who experience terrible things in their lives. That isn't to discredit the impact of these awful experiences, but it is to understand that we are all likely to have a prior vulnerability, sometimes from very early in our lives. To confine ourselves to what we remember, or even what others remember about us on our behalf, leaves aside a whole time of our lives that was our original coming into being. Who is to say how this was for us, what we experienced and how it has affected us as we grew up?

At the same time we may manage, often very well. We may not have all of the things we would like in our lives, we may not always feel whole, integrated, healthy and happy, but we do often manage. And sometimes we don't. Sometimes the events in our lives may suddenly overwhelm us, seemingly inexplicably. During my years as a psychotherapist it has so often been the case that a person comes into therapy at that

7

point in their lives when externally everything seems to be going well. Perhaps they have found a partner, established a home, and even had their first child. Everything looks good. And yet their inner experience is otherwise. It seems that getting all the external things right just doesn't change the internal state, even though we think it will; in fact it often makes it exquisitely clear by contrast that internally all is not well. No longer can we devolve responsibility for our inner chaos and confusion onto external conditions.

Psychoses, emotional and psychological breakdown, increasing obsessions and anxieties, sometimes physical illnesses, all indicate that our trauma management is not working. Some of us make our lives overtly supremely successful through exactly the means that we have used to manage the less conscious disturbances in our psyche. How many of our successful corporate executives have gained success and privilege through the grim determination of their trauma survival tactics, and how in some does the trauma dissociation involved allow them to persecute and bully their way to the top at the expense of their colleagues, friends and family? And much of our lives is constantly influenced by the decisions such people make, particularly those who reach government. Are we governed by the traumatised? Are the wars and combat situations our countries get involved in the work of men and women who, because they are traumatised, make decisions that affect us all from a partly dissociated and traumatised state? You only have to think of the persecutory selfishness and greed exhibited by those in the financial world that left global economics in such a mess at the beginning of this century to find an answer in understanding trauma to the question: how could they (or we, because we too have a part in this) have done this?

Understanding trauma takes a trick of mirrors: in order to see the truth sometimes we have to start by seeing it reflected back and forth many times in several different mirrors. It is as if we cannot look directly at the thing itself in the beginning, like the Gorgon of ancient Greek myth. It was said of the

Gorgon[3] that one must not look directly at her face, for any human who did would be turned to stone. If we look directly at trauma too soon we are likely to freeze with terror, be "turned to stone", an unhelpful retraumatisation.

It takes a tenacity on the part of the person wishing to understand, because if I am right, and trauma in the sense I will be discussing it here is endemic, then we all employ the strategies for trauma survival, strategies of dissociation, distraction, the creation of illusions, secrets and deluded beliefs, and a collective collusion to avoid trauma. Like Alice entering through the looking glass,[4] it seems, when dealing with trauma, that as much as we try to go in one direction, we find ourselves going in exactly the opposite; or like the Red Queen who says: "It takes all the running you can do, to keep in the same place." How else could it be that psychotherapy, a discipline that aims to help the psychologically and emotionally frail, has successfully evolved over the last century and a half of its existence with so scant attention to trauma? Even Sigmund Freud and his colleagues, as we shall see later, turned away from trauma. And in that sense we live in a world of illusions and mirages, of strange creatures and illogical premises, until we are not sure what exactly reality is, what or whom we can trust, and whether or not we can really trust ourselves.

Method

> "One of the issues that all therapists of 'traumatic neuroses' continue to grapple with is how and whether to help patients bring unconscious traumatic material into awareness." *(van der Kolk, 2007a)*

As we come to study trauma an important question, and one which is currently the subject of much debate in the wider

---

[3] The word Gorgon comes from the Greek 'gorgós' which means dreadful.
[4] *Alice through the Looking Glass, and What she found there*, Lewis Carroll.

psychological community, is how to work with trauma. The broadest terms of this debate involve understanding the fragility of the traumatised person, and the potential for retraumatisation, and from there the question comes: is it better to teach the person skills to enable them to manage and permanently avoid the chaotic and turbulent feelings involved, or can the person re-visit the trauma experience in a controlled and safe way in order to resolve the experience? This latter is a kind of safely contained retraumatisation in the present that then becomes, not a replica, but an overlaid experience that includes the novel here and now experience of support and safety.

Freud and other pioneers of psychotherapy understood that talking, with increasing awareness and understanding, to a sympathetic other, the analyst or therapist, seemed to help people feel better, and more in control. Essentially this was the start of the psychotherapeutic movement. However, if we include in our thinking the possibility of very early birth and bonding trauma, and the unconscious systemically inherited effects of unresolved trauma from previous generations, these means are limited, simply because these trauma phenomena are beyond conscious recall. They apply to pre-verbal and pre-brain-memory experiences, and our potential unconscious connection to the trauma of earlier others. Most current work with trauma largely deals with symptoms that relate to trauma that can be remembered and described, but this omits any idea that all later traumas, remembered traumas, are likely to have roots in much earlier pre-verbal trauma. This is where the methodology of constellations is crucial, because in the constellations method we find an access to these earlier times of life in a way that is self-regulating, safe and easily integrated.

The Constellations Method

Constellations has its methodological roots in the psychodrama work of Jakob Moreno and the family reconstruction work of Virginia Satir, culminating in the original work of the German psychotherapist and philosopher Bert Hellinger. All of these methods use group members in a group, or abstract markers in a one-to-one session, to represent parts of the self, family members and other necessary elements in order for the person to understand themselves and the dynamics of their family better. However, the difference between these methods is profound. In psychodrama and family reconstruction work the representatives are usually required to play a role, often being given specific information about the person represented and how they should be portrayed.

Hellinger dispensed with this character portrayal, giving the representatives in the family construction very little, and sometimes no, personality information at all. He required the representative to connect only with her moment-by-moment phenomenological experience. Probably no one was more surprised than he at what then happened; it seemed to produce some formidable and extraordinary results. He found, again and again, that the information given by representatives in the constellation was not only more often than not factually accurate, as corroborated by the client, but seemed to go to an entirely different level of reality. The experiences of the representatives when placed in a constellation, devoid of information, seemed to reach to a level where the issue became the dilemma of existence within the system of one's family, sometimes over many generations. The more Hellinger worked in this way, the more he came to trust the process of the constellation as having its own innate wisdom and form and, at times, even the ability to find its own conclusion without any intervention by the therapist.

It seems to me that Hellinger stepped further out of the way of the natural forces of life in the client than psychotherapy generally has. The psychotherapist helps... that is, he or she is generally configured as a 'helper'. To call someone a 'helper' already gives them a task: helping. Over its history, psychotherapy has developed dozens of different ways of thinking about helping: techniques, aspirations, diagnoses, categorisations, strategies, treatment plans, ideas about the stance of the therapist, philosophies, values, ethics, and all the intellectualisation and academicisation that currently is such a feature of psychotherapeutic training. (Academically trained and qualified psychotherapists don't automatically make good therapists; they may, but it cannot be assumed as so.)

What we have done much less is stand back and see what happens. In psychodrama for example, the role-players are given a role. It seems no one asked "what if we just place them and see what happens." Our difficulty of trusting that anything would happen on its own, and our sensitive ego that needs to produce good results, impelled us to do *something*, say something, interpret something, organise something, suggest something. Even if just reflecting back to the client what we have heard him say in order to convey my empathy and under-standing, or the idea that I must approach the client with 'unconditional positive regard'[5] already gives us a task. Hellinger's great contribution in my view was to have the courage to wait and listen ... and I have watched him wait and listen, sometimes a *very* long time, to see what happens. It is simply the hardest thing for a therapist to do: trust that the process itself may actually achieve something without therapist intervention; tolerate the confusion, uncertainty and not-knowing and wait it out. One of the originators of Gestalt therapy, Fritz Perls, said, "the person most in control is the person who can give up control".

From his work Hellinger learned some things about loving relationships in families, principles that he considered the underpinnings of good relationship, that he called the Orders of Love. This produced the foundations of a framework of thinking that became what is known today as Family

---

[5] As in the client-centred tradition.

Constellations or Systemic Constellations.[6] The dilemmas in Family Constellations are seen as coming from the distortions of love that the Orders of Love, if enacted, are seen to rectify.

In this book, however, trauma is central, not principles of love, although the vicissitudes of love are there right through our endeavour. The contention here is that love can only really exist in a psyche that can perceive clearly, and such clarity of the psyche is dependent on its integrity, its wholeness. A psyche that is fragmented and paralysed by trauma has a diminished and compromised clarity. So our primary focus here is trauma and traumatic entanglement as underlying the distortions of love, and the understanding that you cannot impose principles of loving relationship if the underlying traumatic split is not addressed.

We use the constellations method to help us understand how trauma works, and the resultant theory can then be tested out in the next constellation: the theory and the method then are in a continuing open dialogue.

The basic methodology of the constellation will work without the theory of trauma or The Orders of Love. That is, if you have a topic and you choose people to represent elements or people related to that topic, placing them in some kind of relationship to each other in a room, the people will have experiences that seem to relate to the topic at hand. In fact you will find that the representatives will often have a lot to say! Hence many people working with family constellations are working without thinking in terms of trauma; but in my view trauma is always there. If it isn't clearly present in the therapist's thinking and approach it keeps its head down. The natural instinct we all have to avoid the frightening forces of trauma makes us shy away from explicitly naming it. Our exploration of the survival strategies evoked by trauma later in this book will show how shy trauma can be, and how easy it is for a collective collusion to dissociate and distract from it.

---

[6] For more on Family Constellations refer to my first book, *In The Presence of Many*.

Work can be done for sure, but just how useful this work is in the end without understanding the underlying trauma dynamics involved is, in my opinion, limited, and the potential for dangerous retraumatisation of the client (and sometimes the therapist) is heightened if the therapist does not understand trauma. So I suggest that the value of the work presented here is that by making trauma central, and attachment trauma particularly, we are in effect going to the source, the roots of our being and the heart of our difficulties and dysfunctions.

Principles for Practice

"Be like a polished sword, free from tarnish.
Work to become a polished mirror, free of rust.
Cleanse yourself from all the attributes of the self, so that you may see your own pure and untarnished essence!
Behold in your own heart all the knowledge of the prophets, without books, without learning, without teacher."

(Rumi)

The journey for practitioners of this work is a journey of the self; it is challenging and involves a commitment, above all, to oneself. The practitioner is only able to travel with their client to territory they have explored within themselves. The natural tendency to avoid trauma is as strong in the therapist as in the client, and the therapist can only avoid this pitfall by making a primary commitment to herself above all else.

For the moment, I would like to sum up with the following four principles for good psychotherapeutic work with trauma:

1. Have a good theoretical framework, such as that proposed here, that makes sense to you of what you experience and observe with your clients... and always keep this frame open to adjustment and ongoing learning as you proceed. It does no good just to adopt someone else's framework without deep and persistent questioning so that it makes sense and works for you. Anyone really engaged in any work must in the first instance adopt a theoretical

framework, but also, in time, must bring their own understanding to it. This keeps the frame open, and keeps us as practitioners alert and alive. Never think that those who came before you knew it all and that there isn't something new to learn. Perhaps you too may discover something no one else had quite seen before.

2. Understand comprehensively the physiology and psychology of trauma processes (including the emerging developments of neuroscience and neurobiology) and PTSD symptomatology. It will not do to present yourself as working with trauma if you cannot recognise, understand and know what to do in a situation of potential retraumatisation.

3. Recognise that you also carry unconscious and unrecognised trauma and work with it – do your personal work. When a client enters his or her own trauma field we need to aim to be able to remain present and not succumb to dissociation and deflection ourselves because our own unresolved trauma is re-stimulated. Our clients have a right to expect this of us: that we continually and persistently work with ourselves.

4. Practise working with the method of constellations as a therapist, representative and client long enough to be able to trust yourself, your client and the constellations process. . . not just intellectually but deeply in your body, so that it is as natural to you as breathing. A student once asked Franz Ruppert how long he thought it took to become accomplished in this work. His answer was ten years. The implication here is not that it takes exactly ten years to become accomplished in this work, but that it takes time, and ten years indicates something of the time scale involved.

In researching for this book I became very interested in the historical context of trauma study, together with the historical traditions of certain terms that we commonly use. I would suggest that committed students of trauma will contextualise their practice better if they too have a reasonable sense of the journey taken by researchers and therapists to the present day and so I have included this material. At the same time the reader who is simply interested in understanding Ruppert's theories and my work may quite easily choose to skip over these sections.

Part 1

A Multi-Generational Psychotraumatology

"For clinicians attuned to the transmission of trauma, one sees its operation and its effects with great frequency."
(*Gerard Fromm*, 2012)

When Franz Ruppert first developed his theory he called it a multi-generational psychotraumatology (MGP). This then is a study of the psychological effects of traumatic events and how they affect bonded family members across generations.

There are four basic components to understanding this subject:

1. A definition of trauma.
2. The dynamics and processes of trauma as defined.
3. Dynamics and processes of early attachment and bonding.
4. The relationship between these attachment processes and trauma processes.

1

Trauma

Introduction

> "The real voyage of discovery consists not in seeking new
> landscapes, but in having new eyes."
> *(Marcel Proust, Remembrance of Things Past)*

Unresolved personal and systemic (prior family) trauma is
likely to influence every moment of our lives: how available to us our mothers were to us as infants, which in turn
influences how available we are able to be to those we love,
our partner, friends, children and grandchildren. It surfaces
surreptitiously whenever we have a decision to make and
feel torn between options. It influences our ability to feel
confident, whole, happy, loving, effective and successful. It
underlies any internal conflict we may feel at any moment.
It influences our choice of partners and forces us to manage
our relationships instead of allowing ourselves to be fully
present, honest and intimate. In fact unresolved trauma
makes true intimacy impossible, because feelings that go
with intimacy will also always draw to consciousness the
more problematic and disturbing feelings related to the unresolved trauma, which surface as acute anxiety or panic,
immediately forcing us to deflect, dissociate and withdraw.
This is the primary cause of so-called 'oscillating relationships', also described as 'co-dependency'.

We manage our lives with more or less rigidity and often with an underlying subtle terror of losing control... because losing control means that all those dreaded, unexplained and seemingly unexplainable emotions and experiences we dimly know are there will take us over. The more extreme examples of this controlling come in what are termed the 'personality disorders' of the psyche, such as 'obsessive compulsive' disorder at the more rigid end of the scale, or 'borderline personality disorder' at the more chaotic end;[7] and the myriad of other disorders that have, as their central theme, control: anorexia, bulimia, alcoholism, addictions, self-harming practices and so on. At the extreme end of the loss of control pole we find psychosis and psychotic disorders such as schizophrenia or bi-polar, clinical depression and other serious psychological diagnoses. But in the terms we are to discuss here these are all really attempts to manage unresolved trauma, to keep the terrifying perceived chaos of extreme feelings out of consciousness. We can also consider many of our daily activities, if the underlying purpose is to control our environment and those around us, to be a form of attempting to maintain control over our unresolved trauma.

Traumatic events have a very long reach, transmitted across the generations through the intimate and profound experiences of parent/child bonding, as one generation connects to the next. From genetics we are familiar with the idea that we inherit physical characteristics and some illnesses, and even some psychological disorders such as schizophrenia and depression are considered to be inheritable. However, we are less likely to consider the more subtle, hidden, never discussed traumas of families to be passed from one generation to the next.[8] What is the effect likely to be on a grandchild of the fact

---

[7] The American Neuro-Psychologist Dan Siegel posits two diagnostic categories that indicate a person is not in harmony (health), on the one hand chaotic and the other rigid. I would term these the prioritised survival styles adopted in the face of trauma.

[8] It is debatable in my view as to how helpful it is to think in terms of an alcoholic gene, for example, as if it is unrelated to individuals' experiences.

that her grandmother lost her own mother when she was a baby? Of course we don't know; every situation is different, but we might now expect there to be something rather than nothing. This essentially motherless child became a mother having lost her own mother when she was very young. Even from the perspective of attachment theory we already know that she does not have personal experience of what it is to be mothered, and thence how to be a mother herself. If we only consider this from a behavioural perspective, she has no behavioural model experience for 'good mother'.

But this concept alone does not plumb the depths of what such a trauma means to a mother's ability to be psychologically and emotionally present for her child. We don't know how the bereaved father coped, and who, then, took care of the motherless child, how the bereavement of the child was managed. Did the child in fact also lose her father to his bereavement? Was the child left to her own devices? How did this impact on the child? This is a different dimension. What might the effect be on her ability to bond with her own child? Might she on some unconscious level fear that she might die as her mother did when she was born? Might the birth of her child re-stimulate her own trauma of abandonment and loss, perhaps even her fear for her survival when the warm, known, safe, loving and protective body and being of her mother was suddenly taken from her? Or might she unconsciously see the child as offering her another chance to connect symbiotically with her own lost mother, thereby condemning their relationship to confusion and inversion – the child as the mother of the mother. How does this affect how she takes her child into her arms? Does she hold her child away from her because the feelings that surface are too painful, her child, in time, becoming for her the source of these turbulent

---

The question remains unanswered as to what comes first, the gene or the traumatic event that perhaps causes a person to turn to alcohol, and whether over time this alters the genetic structure. It is certainly likely that once this is encoded it creates a tendency in subsequent generations, but to see it only in terms of genetic inheritance encourages a sense of helplessness and lack of responsibility for one's life.

feelings? Or does she hold her child tight to her for fear that she might be lost to this child or that the child/mother be lost, again, to her? And how does the child experience these things? Might this invoke a trauma of attachment in the child? And how does this affect this child's ability to bond with her own child later when she becomes a mother?

What makes trauma a much more central topic than so far thought is exactly the consideration of these very early stages of our lives, the time in the womb, and after birth, the time before words and cognitive memory, when, paradoxically the conditions are ripe for trauma. During this time we are helpless, vulnerable, incapable of doing anything much for ourselves, and must rely completely on another, our mother. These conditions render the infant particularly susceptible to trauma. And in our non-separateness from our mother, we are also non-separate from our ancestral family and the unresolved trauma from there. Through her, our mother, we potentially connect helplessly to the unconscious, unresolved forces and residues that each bonded family member holds.

Our current diagnostic category of Post Traumatic Stress Disorder (PTSD) limits us in our thinking about trauma to events that happened to us that we can recall. It has no scope for understanding very early trauma, before the brain's neural connections for ordinary memory are formed, nor for under- standing the impact of systemic trauma, where the far less conscious impact of major events in families across the gener- ations remain operant but impossible to verbalise. Within the DSM IV,[9] the commonly used diagnostic manual of psycholog- ical disorders in the west, out of 300 diagnostic categories trauma is mentioned in only 30, and in the title of only one, Post Traumatic Stress Disorder. And yet if we looked at all the other DSM IV diagnoses in terms of what we are about to study here regarding trauma, we would come to quite different conclusions as to the likely causality. Trauma is likely to be implicated to an extent in all of them.

---

[9] *DSM IV, American Psychiatric Association Diagnostic and Statistical Manual.*

In addition PTSD has no framework for including an underlying vulnerability to the later, remembered trauma, because of earlier, pre-verbal trauma. Later trauma is always rooted in earlier trauma in the sense that, if there is an earlier (primary attachment) trauma any later traumatic event will to an extent always involve a re-triggering of the earlier trauma. Sigmund Freud understood when working with his very early clients in the late 19th century, that the presented event which seemed to have set in train a 'hysterical neurosis'[10] in the client as an adult, which often seemed a fairly insignificant one, was always linked to an earlier, more devastating event.[11] But even so, again, he was thinking in terms of what the client, sometimes with "the most energetic pressure of the analytic procedure", could relate – something remembered. (Freud, L'Hérédité et l'étiologie des névroses, 1896)

Not until the appearance on the scene of John Bowlby, the English psychoanalyst of the mid 20th century, did we begin to understand something about these very vulnerable early, pre-verbal stages of life (Bowlby, 1958, and Holmes, 1993). Bowlby appalled the established Freudian community at the time with his paper 'The Nature of the Child's Tie to His Mother' (1958), in which he declared as crucial to the child's development the attachment and emotional bonding of the child to his mother, thereby calling into question Freud's followers' mainstream thinking that the child only looked to his mother for the gratification of his 'id' needs.

We know from the work currently emerging from the neurosciences that the neural connections for explicit memory (or declarative memory: that which allows us to be able to recall experiences) do not start to be made until approximately

---

[10] This was the common diagnosis that we would now mostly interpret as post traumatic stress disorder (PTSD). See later in this chapter the brief History of the Study of Trauma.

[11] "[Freud's] theoretical position, often expressed, was that hysterical symptoms in latency (after the age of eight) or in adolescence almost invariably represent the effects of a much earlier sexual assault." (*Masson, 1984*)

two years of age (ibid.). However it seems that we still have much to learn about the nature of our memory before that.

The notion that we also have a cellular memory, a memory of our life from the beginning, that is embedded in our cells, while considered pseudo-scientific by the more conservative scientific community, is a commonly held understanding amongst many others. For example, the biochemist and neuro-scientist, Professor Candace Pert: "the body is the unconscious mind" (Pert, 1999); Deepak Chopra: "the mind is non-local" (ibid.). Many involved in the study of organ transplants, particularly heart transplants, are frequently confronted by situations where the recipients of organs have experiences that seem to be to connected to their donors. An organ recipient found that after her operation she started to act and walk differ-ently, in a more masculine way, and craved foods that she had never liked before. She also began to have dreams about a man with a particular name. Later she discovered that her donor had the name she dreamed of, was male and liked the foods she had started to crave (Linton, 2003). I am sure that many prac-tising body-workers such as osteopaths, chiropractors and therapeutic masseurs would have no problem with this concept of cellular memory. It would not only support the notion that we can have a memory in our bodies that precedes our normal cognitive memory, perhaps back to the moment of conception, but it would also support the idea that unresolved trauma can be transmitted across generations as the new baby is formed from cells that belong to the mother, and father. It certainly calls into question when exactly life and consciousness in the human being begin.

Trauma is always a collective phenomenon, a systemic event, never confined just to the obvious victim. Traumatic events affect those who are closely bonded to and love the trau-matised person, often including their descendants. When combatants returned from the Vietnam War their reception by their family and community was often confused, and their own reactions often those more appropriate to war situations: aggression and violence (Shay, 2002). A family who has one member who has experienced trauma in war is never the same again.

Under the usual circumstances of people's lives trauma is rarely 'resolved', since our primary instinctual way of managing trauma is psychologically and emotionally to dissociate from it, split it off and render it unconscious, to keep away from such disturbing feelings whatever the cost. Add to this the fact that the re-experiencing of the original event by bringing the dissociated experiences and feelings into consciousness is also potentially traumatising, and you can get a sense of why trauma has been a difficult subject of study. Indeed, as we shall see, the history of trauma study has been as fragmented as the state of the individual who has suffered trauma.

1.1 History

"The study of psychological trauma has a curious history – one of episodic amnesia. Periods of active investigation have alternated with periods of oblivion." *(Herman, 1992)*

"It is a deplorable fact that each investigator who undertakes to study these conditions [trauma] considers it his sacred obligation to start from scratch and work at the problem as if no one had done anything with it before."
Kardiner & Spiegel (1947)

It helps in our understanding of trauma to have a sense of the history of its study, and so what follows is a brief resumé of this history, for which I am indebted to the American professor of psychiatry at Harvard University, Judith Herman, and her book *Trauma and Recovery* (1992) and to an essay by Bessel van der Kolk, Professor of Psychiatry at Boston University and Medical Director of the Trauma Centre of the JRI, Massachusetts, entitled *A History of Trauma in Psychiatry* (2007a).

It is the fate of trauma, and its very nature, to be overlooked, ignored, forgotten, by-passed and sidelined. The natural human survival response is to put as much energy as necessary into avoiding such terrifying and overwhelming feelings and re-lived experiences; and as much as this is a natural response to personal experience, it seems, too, to have been the response to the research and study of trauma by professionals.

In her book, *Trauma and Recovery (1992)*, Herman opens with a chapter she calls 'A Forgotten History', in which she sets out a record of the study of trauma. She divides this history into three phases over the last hundred or so years, each separated by periods of time where trauma was forgotten, "periods of oblivion" (ibid.). Like personal trauma, where often we will only address it when the symptoms have become too much for us to manage, in effect when we have no choice, the phases of trauma study came about only because circumstances forced it to attention. Because the study of trauma is done by people who are likely themselves to be managing their own trauma, their approach to the study of trauma is always shadowed by ambivalence, unconscious dissociation and deflection. Why study something that perhaps at the time is not asking to be studied, and as well is likely to take one into rough personal waters? It's not a consciously thought through response, but a spontaneous, 'life-preserving' reaction.[12]

The three episodes[13] of trauma study over the last hundred years that Herman cites are:

- The study of the diagnosis known as 'hysteria' by the followers and students of the 19th Century French neurol-

[12] Recently I went to a 2-day lecture given by a prominent psychiatrist and neuroscientist with a particular interest in early attachment trauma. The material was interesting but delivered in a highly intellectual manner, utilising much technical jargon. At one point it struck me that one way to study trauma safely was to discuss it in technical terminology as a way of controlling the emotional impact on the presenter and the audience. At this event this may have been unconscious, or it may have been deliberate, I don't know.

[13] Van der Kolk, in his essay, includes phases of intense study during the Second World War.

ogist Jean-Martin Charcot, which included Sigmund
Freud, Pierre Janet, Joseph Breuer and many others.

- The study of shell shock or combat neurosis, which began
during the First World War in England, revived again
after the Second World War with the Holocaust, and
reached a peak during and after the Vietnam War.
- The growing awareness in the 1980s and 1990s of
domestic violence, the high incidence of violence,
neglect, rape and emotional and sexual abuse within the
privacy of the home.

'Hysteria' and Early Trauma Study

"As early as 1859, the French psychiatrist Briquet (1859) eluci-
dated an association between childhood histories of trauma and
symptoms of 'hysteria', such as somatization, intense emotional
reactions, dissociation and fugue states ... Sexual abuse of
children was well documented during the second half of the
19th century in France by researchers such as Tardieu (1878),
a professor of forensic medicine." (*van der Kolk*, 2007a)

Deeply engaged as I am in the subject of trauma, from my present
day perspective it seems quite extraordinary that science and the
discipline of psychotherapy have so successfully avoided for the
most part dealing with trauma,[14] particularly in light of the quote
from van der Kolk above. And yet, when we look at the roots of
psychotherapy, the psychoanalytic tradition based primarily on
Freudian principles, we can see that the whole endeavour was
founded to a large extent on an avoidance of trauma. Most
psychotherapies, and all the great innovators within the broad
realm of psychotherapy, whatever their philosophy and values,
were rooted in Freud's ideas, and their work was based on
Freudian principles, that essentially from the beginning tended
to avoid the issue of trauma.

---

[14] The diagnosis of Post Traumatic Stress Disorder and the concept of post
traumatic stress did not find official status until the late 1970s.

The diagnosis of 'hysteria'[15] originated over two thousand years ago in Greece, and stayed for the most part during that time as "a disease proper to women and originating in the uterus" (Herman, 1992). In the early stages of the development of psychotherapy 'hysteria' was understood by Freud and others to be the somatic symptoms that "represented disguised representations of intensely distressing events which had been banished from memory." (ibid.). Breuer and Freud, "in an immortal summation, wrote that 'hysterics suffer mainly from reminiscences'" (ibid.). Both of these statements could easily be current statements about trauma, except that, happily, we don't use the term 'hysteric' any more.

It is demonstrative of the tensions involved, and the need for a supportive social and political context for difficult phenomena to be tolerated, that when Freud presented his paper entitled 'The Aetiology of Hysteria' to his colleagues in Vienna in 1896, it caused such a stir, and was so challenging of the current ethics and perceptions of society, that just one year later it seems he quietly began to recant and move away from his published conclusions. Since many see it as a key point in understanding the modern history of psychotherapy and the study of trauma I will discuss it briefly.

In his paper Freud presented the thesis that "at the bottom of every case of hysteria there are one or more occurrences of premature sexual experience, occurrences which belong to the earliest years of childhood, but which can be reproduced through the work of psychoanalysis in spite of the intervening decades." (Freud, 1896, 1962). It is indicative of how important Freud thought this paper by a quote from him after his presentation: "I [have] shown them the solution to a more than two thousand-year old problem", referring to the hazy

---

[15] It is interesting to note that in parallel the study of physical trauma from a neurological perspective at the same time elicited the term "traumatic neurosis", first used by the German neurologist Herman Oppenheimer in 1889 (van der Kolk, 2007). The thinking in this stream of study was from the physiological and organic rather than the psychological perspective.

diagnosis of hysteria that had been in place for that long. This paper was based on twenty cases from Freud's practice. As Herman states: "A century later, this paper still rivals contemporary clinical descriptions of the effects of childhood sexual abuse"; I would agree. Despite the brilliance and importance of this paper, just one year later Freud withdrew his support of it.

Jeffrey Masson, in his book, *Assault on Truth (1984)*, offers a careful exploration of this paper, and the reasons behind Freud's eventual retraction. The assertion of Freud's paper was shocking and provocative at the time: that hysterical neurosis (trauma) symptomatology in adult life was founded on severe childhood trauma through inappropriate sexual activity, predominantly perpetrated by adult family members or other caretakers of the child (servants and nannies). It was founded on Freud's work with a number of clients who told him terrible stories of what we would now call sexual abuse and harassment (including violence) at the hands of prominent adults. It is hard for us looking from the 21st century to understand the impact of this assertion at the time. Most psychiatrists' client base then was the middle class bourgeoisie, and most psychiatrists were from this same class. To contemplate such a phenomenon amongst their own educated class was intolerable. One reaction by a colleague to his presentation was: "It sounds like a scientific fairytale." (Krafft-Ebing, in Masson, 1984). Freud was ostracised by his peers and colleagues for his paper, and in a letter to his friend, Wilhelm Fleiss, wrote: "I am as isolated as you could wish me to be: the word has been given out to abandon me, and a void is forming around me." A year later he retracted his support of his paper privately, and over the subsequent years increasingly publicly. In his Autobiographical Study twenty nine years later he wrote: "I was at last obliged to recognise that these scenes of seduction had never taken place, and that they were only fantasies which my patients had made up." (Freud, 1922). According to van der Kolk:

"... the relationship between actual childhood trauma and the development of psychopathology was henceforth ignored. In Freud's view, it was not the actual memories of childhood trauma that were split off from consciousness, but rather the unacceptable sexual and aggressive wishes of the child ... Real life trauma was ignored in favour of fantasy." *(van der Kolk, 2007a)*

In fact the knowledge of the prevalence of childhood sexual abuse was not new at the time. As van der Kolk says in the quote at the beginning of this section, the work of the French forensic scientist, Auguste Ambrose Tardieu was revealing through his work on dead children that sexual and physical violence to children was rife. Tardieu documented his findings in a publication in 1857,[16] and Freud, studying in Paris at the time, was very likely, along with his contemporaries, to have witnessed Tardieu's work and read his publication (Masson, 1984).

Additionally, in fairness to Freud, it is worth adding something more about the context at the time (1880s). There was already occurring fierce debate amongst the students and followers of the famed neurologist, Jean-Martin Charcot, at the Salpêtrière Hospital (with whom Freud also studied), as to the veracity or not of accounts of child sexual abuse; whether patients' accounts of their childhood abuse were real or a false memory, what Charcot termed a "hystero-traumatic auto-suggestion" (van der Kolk, 2007a). Freud was not alone in preferring to think in terms of "simulation and suggestibility" (ibid.) and fantasied imaginings, rather than the reality of the traumatic acts recounted. However, since the basics of all psychotherapy come from Freud's work, and the legend of Freud as the predominant author of psychological under-standing still dominates much thinking and study today, it does

---

[16] *Etude Médico-Légal sur les Attentats aux Mœurs*, 1857. In this publication Tardieu stated that over 75% of rapes or attempted rapes were on children under the age of sixteen.

not seem unfair to focus on his contribution to the years of subsequent avoidance of this truth.

The result has had far reaching effects for psychoanalysis and the whole of psychotherapy, and for the study of trauma. In effect Freud's withdrawal of his support for the idea that his clients were speaking the truth when they told him tales of sexual abuse and violence, set him and the development of psychoanalysis on a course of valuing the internal imagined, fantasy and dream world of the client, which the analyst or therapist could interpret for the client, over the external possibility of real traumatic events; in effect an avoidance of the reality of trauma. It also turned the child from victim of adult oppression and seduction into the fantasy seducer who could not be trusted, and the abusive parent/adult from perpetrator of violence on the child into the innocent and maligned victim of the child's subversive perpetrator fantasies and seductive nature.

This idea combined well with ideas about child-rearing that dominated at the time, many of which still persist to this day, what the Polish psychologist and renegade psychoanalyst, Alice Miller, explored under the term 'poisonous pedagogy'[17] (Miller, 1987). 'Poisonous pedagogy' was based on the idea that the child had to be controlled and disciplined by generally what we would see today as "mental cruelty" (ibid.), but also physical cruelty, at times to the extent of torture. The notion was of punishment by the parent as being for the child's own good,[18] with parents always being right and the notion that "every act of cruelty [by the parents], whether conscious or unconscious, is an expression of their love" (ibid.). In Germany particularly, at the time (late 19th century and early 20th century) these views were immensely popular and there

---

[17] The concept was first introduced by Katharina Rutschky in her 1977 work *Schwarze Pädagogik. Quellen zur Naturgeschichte der bürgerlichen Erziehung.*

[18] The title of this book by Alice Miller is *"For Your Own Good: The roots of violence in child-rearing"*.

was a flourishing literature on the topic of such brutal child-rearing techniques.[19]

This theme was repeated later when, in the 1980s, as clients again began to tell their therapists about their childhood traumas of sexual and violent abuse, the idea of 'false memory' took hold, which held that the memories of sexual abuse of a client were fabrications. (See below section on Sexual and Domestic Abuse) This was one of the sorriest episodes of our coming to terms with trauma, and a betrayal of the abused similar to that of Freud and his colleagues.

So psychoanalysis and psychotherapy were set along a path of mistrust of the client's ability to tell the truth. Everything the client said was to do with her sexual fantasies rather than the truth, which in light of the fact that the majority of the clients were women (although not all), set even more firmly the notion inherent in the age-old diagnosis of hysteria that women were malingerers and couldn't be trusted. Freud's female patients' disclosures of very real and agonising sexual trauma were interpreted back to them as their sexual fantasy desires for their fathers, and the Freudian tradition, indeed to an extent the whole of psychotherapy, subsequently took this as its underpinnings. One can only wonder at the potential for gross and tragic retraumatisation this has incurred in patients over the last hundred years in the therapy room as a result.

From the perspective of the study of trauma, all of this can be seen as an example of a collective unconscious avoidance of trauma, and in a sense from this moment trauma entered one of its periods of oblivion. Herman again: "Out of the ruins of the traumatic theory of hysteria, Freud created psycho-analysis", and what was lost was the good and careful study of trauma that was needed. Was the whole of the psychoanalytic tradition in fact born out of an unconscious survival tactic on the part of these pioneer analysts in order to protect themselves

---

[19] In the mid 1800s Moritz Schreber wrote a series of books on such child-rearing in Germany that were extremely popular. Miller relates this pedagogical climate to the childhood background of Hitler and the possibility of the massive support in Germany for him and his Third Reich.

from their own buried and unconscious trauma experiences? If the therapist remained the interpreter of the client's truth, then this 'truth' could be the therapist's safety net, protecting him from his own terrifying unresolved trauma.

Interestingly the current work of the psychoanalyst, Allan Schore,[20] (a forerunner in the work of linking psychotherapy with the findings of the neurosciences), is founded on the open empathic relationship between therapist and client. This means that the 'analyst' attends to his or her own emotional process whilst in relationship with the client, thereby, it would seem, potentially bringing the therapist's unresolved trauma more into the therapeutic framework.[21]

A further footnote to this account is the fact that Freud's great friend in later life, Sándor Ferenczi,[22] resurrected the issue of childhood trauma in a paper presented in 1932. Ferenczi became convinced that accounts of early sexual trauma given him by his clients *were* real rather than the fantasy wishes of Freud's theory. Ferenczi's paper on the topic was called 'Confusion of Tongues between Adults and the Child',[23] and in it he went further than Freud's original paper and implicitly criticised the current developments of Freud's theories. Ferenczi, for whom Freud was a father figure to look up to and revere, and from whom he always hoped to find support of his work, in fact received no support from Freud, and died not having retracted his devastating ideas, isolated

---

[20] Schore's work demonstrates the novel move within the psychotherapeutic profession to cross disciplines and sciences. His contributions are across such disciplines as psychiatry, neurobiology, behavioural biology, psychoanalysis, developmental psychology, clinical social work etc.

[21] The Humanistic tradition of psychotherapy has, of course, made the therapist/client relationship and the 'space between', the 'inter-subjective', the 'co-created reality' of both, and the therapist's own process central for many years. Additionally it would seem to me that at some point the analysts will have to re-name themselves, since analysis and interpretation are not the basis of an empathic, intersubjective, relational therapy.

[22] From 1913 until Ferenczi's death in 1933.

[23] In fact this was Ferenczi's third paper, a culmination of his earlier thoughts. Masson says of it that it was "in many respects, the twin of Freud's 'The Aetiology of Hysteria'".

and criticised by his colleagues and peers (Masson, 1984). His paper is very readable and immensely relevant today, as it should have been then. Here is an extract from Ferenczi's diary showing that it wasn't only the victims of abuse who were talking to him in analysis, but the perpetrators as well:

> "The obvious objection [to the thesis], that we are dealing with sexual fantasies of the child [as opposed to reality] . . . that is, with hysterical lies, unfortunately **is weakened by the multitude of confessions of this kind, on the part of patients in analysis, to assaults on children.**" (From Ferenczi's diaries, translated by Masson, in *Masson, 1984*. My emphasis).

When I first got involved in psychotherapy in the 1970s and trained in the late 1980s, the general atmosphere of therapy was in fact quite persecutory towards the client, with a "pervasive sub-culture . . . of the client being troublesome, resistant, defensive, stubborn, blind and manipulative" (Broughton, 2013). From my present perspective I would say this attitude is potentially extremely re-traumatising. There was a persecutory element in how what are known as transference and projection in therapeutic language were used, and may still be used. Many times did I hear, amongst my fellow trainees as we all endeavoured to learn from our trainers, someone accuse another of projecting unwanted psychological 'stuff'. These accusations always felt persecutory to me, as if I, as the 'projector' was not okay and should feel shame and guilt, which I did. This is subtle, but nevertheless has been a strong feature of the psychotherapeutic discipline.

There are two further points that I would like to make about this historical account: one is that the focus on the accounts of sexual abuse at that time, as important as they were, tended to deflect from other forms of childhood abuse, i.e. non-sexual violence, and emotional and physical neglect. Of course any form of inappropriate and/or non-consensual sexual activity is a violence whether to a child or adult, but it would seem that the idea of adult (parent)/child sexual activity was so horrific that violence and neglect as a traumatic stimulus on its own were for the most part missed. The second point I want to highlight is that if we hadn't deflected away from these topics, and moved away from traumatic reality as a central issue, it is possible that we could have come to understand the much earlier trauma of the attachment phase of the infant's life,[24] the 'symbiotic trauma' that Ruppert named, much sooner than we have (Ruppert, 2010). If the reality of traumatic events had been more within the domain of psychoanalysis than it was in the 1950s, it is likely that John Bowlby's work would have been much more oriented around the traumatic nature of very early attachment than it was.

War Trauma and the Trauma of Militarism

"... man is not by nature a killer." *(Grossman, 2009)*

Perhaps more than anyone else, the military have always known about trauma, but their relationship with it is complex. They have probably had a more consistent interest in it than any other section of society (Grossman, 2009, Shay, 1994, 2002). They have always had to grapple with the issue of how to get human beings to kill a member of their own species. No other species wilfully kills its own kind without severe provocation or under the pressure of evolutionary and ecological considerations, and even then will usually try all kinds of submissive and avoiding behaviours in order not to do so. Some animals, such as the male lion, when taking over the pride of another male who has died, may kill and eat the young of the previous male in the interests of evolutionary supremacy and survival, to make sure that the female's offspring have his genes rather than those of his predecessor. It is true that some of our human history of intra species violence has also at times had as its pressure securing or defending ecological security, but not all, and, as we shall see, even so there is an inhibition to killing our own kind. Interestingly the one species that we

[24] Even in utero trauma.

do know sometimes makes seemingly gratuitous attacks on another group of its own kind is the chimpanzee, perhaps not coincidentally the closest species to humans.

In addition to grappling with this issue of creating conditions in which humans will come to kill each other, the military have also always had to be concerned with how to keep personnel on the field in the face of the effects of their experiences in combat, i.e. when traumatised by their military experiences. In footnote 15 above we saw that in parallel with Breuer and Freud's explorations of hysteria, there was a study of trauma from the neuorological and organic (physical) perspective, which, according to Bessel van der Kolk was particularly appealing to the military:

> "When issues of cowardice and shirking are raised, ascribing post traumatic symptoms to organic problems offers an honourable solution: The soldier preserves his self-respect, the doctor stays within his professional role and does not have to get involved in disciplinary actions, and military authorities do not have to explain psychological breakdowns in previously brave soldiers." *(van der Kolk, 2007a)*

In other words symptoms that should be ascribed to trauma could be deemed as physical symptoms which allowed the military to avoid the sticky issue of the psychological damage of combat.

The military have a vested interest in two things: not talking about trauma, ignoring and trying to diminish its effects and consequences, but also in conditioning people to kill, which to an extent must involve traumatising them. It requires a degree of dissociation to be able to harm another, and traumatised people are always to an extent dissociated. As we discuss trauma further in this book it will become clear that the less severely traumatised person is able to see others clearly in a way that provides a strong prohibition to harming them. It seems worth proposing then, that it is the traumatised person who, because their dissociation confuses their clarity of perception, can cause trauma to another. They do not see clearly the humanity of the other. For the military this creates a very delicate, even impossible, balancing act. The training of combatants to kill must involve some degree of traumatisation, which produces the level of dissociation necessary to be able to perform their function.[25] At the same time, the traumatised combatant is also likely to be a troublesome liability for those in command.

In his book, *On Killing: The Psychological Cost of Learning to Kill in War and Society (2009),* the military psychologist Lt Col Dave Grossman devotes considerable space to gathered statistics and opinions of many authorities on war over the last hundred years or so of the 'firing rates' of soldiers in war; that is the number of combat soldiers who actually do or do not shoot to kill in a combat situation; the number who shoot to miss – above the head for example – or who find other ways of avoiding killing. Here is a quote, for example, from a Second World War veteran:

> "Squad leaders and platoon sergeants had to move up and down the firing line kicking men to get them to fire. We felt like we were doing good to get two or three men out of a squad to fire" *(ibid.)*

It is a relief to have someone from the military tell us that we have an innate resistance to killing another human being. At the same time we have faced two troubling developments in our recent war-making: one is that the military understood that in order to get combatants to kill, the training needed to involve the production of a degree of dissociation in their soldiers. In the period after the Second World War, through the Vietnam War and into the Iraq War, increasingly this was done by the cultivation of hatred.[26] From there combatants are

---

[25] A medical surgeon also needs to dissociate somewhat to be able to operate, however he or she knows that the operation is intended to be in service of the health of the other person, not the harm or even death of the other.

[26] One of the ways developed to achieve this is to make training more and more realistic. For example, instead of shooting at targets (bullseyes) soldiers were trained to shoot at cut-out figures of humans. . . and then these needed to become more and more realistic.

continually re-traumatised when on duty, their level of dissociation increasing each time.

A shocking statistic recently in the news (Los Angeles
Times, April 2012) was that 110,000 active duty US Army
troops in Iraq took anti-depressants in 2011. It has also been
reported that such medication is commonly issued as a preven-
tative aid – in my view to avoid combat soldiers becoming
vulnerable to the debilitating effects of traumatisation by
inducing a pharmacological pre-trauma dissociation.

A recent television programme on the BBC entitled "Are
you Good or Evil?" in part looked at modern military training policy in the US, which now understands that killing is
contrary to the human moral instinct. So military training
now has two elements: a learned embodied reactive ability
to kill, aimed to work alongside the natural human moral
instinct to only kill in order to "protect and defend life".
They realised after the devastating aftermath of the Vietnam
War and the Iraq debacle that training combat soldiers to
hate in order to get them to kill has awful, irrevocable
consequences. It killed their instinctive human morality,
causing the absolutely shocking behaviours of combatants
towards Iraqi captives that emerged in our news during the
occupation of Iraq after the fall of Saddam Hussein, and the
subsequent inability of combatants to re-integrate into
society.

The second development is war at a distance, which began
with distance bombardment and has become the more sophisti-
cated computer room war, where unmanned drones and other
remote military equipment are operated from a computer room
thousands of miles away. No longer does one have to face the
person one is about to kill; more and more war becomes like a
computer game, dissociated from reality.

The history of the Diagnostic & Statistical Manual of
Mental Disorders (currently the DSM-IV), which is the
American Psychiatric Association's manual of diagnosis and
categorisation of mental illness, in widespread use in the
western world, has a military background. Originally the

manual evolved from a census in 1840 that used a single category: idiocy/insanity (Wikipedia). At the time of the Second World War the American Military involved psychiatrists in the selection, processing, assessment and treatment of soldiers, and from this a team headed up by military psychiatrists developed a classification scheme called Medical 203 in 1943, and in 1952 the first DSM – DSM-I – evolved directly from this military document. The military were so in need of a means of assessing psychological conditions that they were the forerunners to what is now the psychiatric profession's established manual.

The Holocaust of the Second World War, probably the most known, but of course not the only, genocidal event of the 20th century, set in train its own particular study of trauma. This, followed by the Korean and Vietnam Wars, more than ever before brought war trauma and the trauma of persecution and victimisation to the forefront of our attention. In the social atmosphere in the latter part of the 20th century more people developed a sense of a right to their emotional life, to the exploration and expression of their emotional selves, as therapeutic resources became commonplace and a 'grin and bear it' attitude was no longer so much valued. This, along with the unprecedented number of servicemen who came home after Vietnam severely traumatised and found no good way of integrating back into society, made the reality of combat trauma harder to avoid. A society that had hoisted its flag in America (and to an extent in the broader western world) to the American dream, didn't want to know about the darker lives and experiences of these war-scarred men and women. This created an intolerable tension, and combat trauma was very much back on the agenda.

Sexual and Domestic Abuse and Violence

"The late nineteenth-century studies of 'hysteria' foundered on the question of sexual trauma. At the time ... there was no awareness that violence [was] a routine part of women's sexual and domestic lives. Freud glimpsed this truth and retreated in horror." *(Herman, 1991)*

"The acceptance of psychoanalytic theory went hand in hand with a total lack of research on the effects of real traumatic events on children's lives. From 1895 until very recently, no studies were conducted on the effects of childhood sexual trauma." *(van der Kolk, 2007a)*

"About 50,000 names are etched into the Vietnam War Memorial. If we made a memorial to children who have been sexually abused, it would be more than 1300 times the size of the Vietnam memorial. If we included other forms of child abuse it would be more than 7,500 times its size ... These are souls lost in a betrayal and wounding that is so deep that most are unable to heal and reconnect with self, others and God." *(Whitfield, 1995)*

In the late 1960s and early 1970s gradually the reality of many women's lives started to come to the surface. The dominant male trauma was war trauma (of course it was not only men, but predominantly men who suffered from war trauma), whereas the predominant female trauma was the hidden, private and shameful life of the home, where domestic sexual, emotional and physical violence played out, often on a daily basis:

"The cherished value of privacy created a powerful barrier to consciousness and rendered women's reality practically invisible ... Women were silenced by fear and shame, and the silence of women gave license to every form of sexual and domestic exploitation." *(Herman, 1992)*

A colleague of mine, who was a young social worker in London in the 1970s, tells me that domestic violence and sexual abuse were the most common issues that she had to deal with every day. The level of dysfunctionality that she witnessed and attempted to work with in families at that time was completely horrifying. And the level of her superiors' dissociation from the horror and devastation of what she was having to deal with was evidenced by the fact that, at the age of twenty two, she was required to work with large families on her own, with limited and variable supervision, families with histories of extreme violence and dysfunctional, aberrant, and often psychotic, behaviour. Social workers in London in the 1970s knew the trauma of domestic violence and sexual abuse very well, and were up against the terrible effects every single day.

At the same time in the privacy of the psychotherapy room and 'consciousness-raising' groups of the 1970s, slowly women started to try and understand their experiences, to put a name to them, and speak out; but the cost was often high in terms of their financial status, their safety and that of their children. The first widely known women's refuge in the UK opened in 1971 in London, called Chiswick Women's Aid; and in the USA Haven House opened in California in 1964. At the same time as women were dealing with current issues of domestic violence, they also started to speak out about childhood experiences of sexual violence and abuse at the hands of parents or other family members.

Many were not believed, and the emergence of so-called 'false-memory syndrome' (never an actual official designation) was one of the most appalling phases of trauma avoidance when applied to the disclosures that women were making.[27] To be sure, in the confusion of the client – and of the therapist as she or he tried to comprehend and make sense of what it was they were hearing – there may well have been false assumptions, but think for a moment of the potential retraumatisation of the woman who finally gains the courage to share her

---

[27] The designation of 'false memory syndrome', as I said above, has never become a formal categorisation, and is mired in controversy, mainly because its origins as a designation came from several people who had themselves been accused of sexual abuse (*Whitfield, 1995*).

confused and disoriented fragments of memory, then to be accused of purposely falsifying these memories. We are back to the frightening and self-denying origins of psychotherapy. And many therapists, to be sure probably confused and over-whelmed themselves by what they were hearing and having to manage, came under fire as having put these ideas into the heads of their clients. I grew up as a psychotherapist in the late 1980s and early 1990s and I remember clearly the confusion and stomach churning nausea I felt the first time a client told me about the abuse she had experienced as a child. I remember how hard I found it to believe, even at the same time being convinced that it was true, and I remember how much every fibre in my body wanted to avoid it.

Today

During the 1990s there was an increasing interest in trauma, reflected in the proliferation of literature on the topic by writers such as Judith Herman, Babette Rothschild, Peter Levine, Charles Whitfield, Donald Kalsched. Sandra Wieland, Jonathan Shay, Bessel van der Kolk, Leonore Terr and Kaethe Weingarten amongst many others. Broadly the approaches to understanding trauma fall into the following categories: under-standing shock and trauma (Herman and Weingarten), Post Traumatic Stress Disorder (PTSD) and the bio-physiology of trauma (Rothschild, Scaer, Etherington, Levine, Ogden, Siegel, Minton & Pain, Friedman, Kean, Naparstek, Resick, van der Kolk, McFarlane and Wesaeth), childhood sexual abuse (Wieland, Whitfield, Cloitre, Cohen & Koenen), combat trauma (Shay), the neurology of trauma (Stein & Kendall), the transgenerational aspect of trauma (Auerhahn & Laub, Danieli, Fromm), the formation of psychological dissociative structures (van der Hart, Nijelhuisen, and Steele).

There has always been a difficulty in the psychotherapy tradition of evaluating the effectiveness of what we do, and since there has never been a scientific method that could usefully perform this evaluation, psychotherapy has always kept itself somewhat distanced from other sciences. The basis of psychotherapy is personal experience, and it was only by subjective experience reports that we could make any judgement of what was and what was not effective. This is decidedly unscientific. In the 1950s the English psychoanalyst John Bowlby shocked many of his colleagues, and invoked criticism from some, by his interest in other sciences, particularly the science of ethology and the work of Konrad Lorenz.[28] Bowlby regarded many of his contemporary psychoanalysts, particularly the leaders of the movement in the time following Freud's death, Anna Freud (Freud's daughter) and Melanie Klein and their followers, as "hopelessly unscientific" (Holmes, 1993). According to Holmes "Both [Klein and Anna Freud] argued from intuition and authority, rather than subjecting their claims to empirical testing."

The absence of any useful means of assessing the efficacy of psychotherapy later led many in the 1970s and 1980s to focus on Behavioural Therapy, which aimed to change behaviour. Subsequently in the late 1980s and the 1990s Cognitive Behavioural Therapy (CBT) became popular, based on the assumption that "negative feelings are caused by irrational thoughts and beliefs; therapy aims at changing beliefs." (Shedler in Schore, 2012). Both of these methods in their own way were deemed to be scientifically proven effective; however, the results were generally short term (as far as I can ascertain there were no studies of long-term outcomes), and neither disciplines had any particular focus or understanding of the real dynamics of trauma. Alongside this the Humanistic tradition continued to work with emotion and relationship, and increasingly with trauma.

However, the emergence of the neurosciences in the late 1990s also stimulated an intense focus on child development,

---

[28] Lorenz was famous for his study of the attachment behaviour of animals, particularly greylag geese, in relation to bonding, and for film of orphaned greylag goslings that bonded with him. He was jointly awarded a Nobel prize in 1973.

and the potential for trauma of attachment and early childhood, combining this with a focus on PTSD (Post Traumatic Stress Disorder). The prominent writers of the early 21st century coming from a synthesis of neurobiology and psychotherapy include Dan Siegel and Pat Ogden (Sensorimotor Psychotherapy), Bessel van der Kolk et al (Traumatic Stress), Allan Schore (Affect Regulation Therapy), and Ian McGilchrist, whose seminal book, *The Master and his Emissary*, provides an adventurous account of the evolution of our brain structures and function, and the effects on us.

Allan Schore in his latest book, *The Science of the Art of Psychotherapy*, proposes that the neurosciences finally do offer clear evidence of the effectiveness of psychotherapy, and that this will prompt a paradigm shift in the profession's approach from a cognitive, verbal, conscious and behavioural emphasis to an emotional, non-verbal, unconscious and relational emphasis.

As a final word on the topic of this chequered history of trauma studies I will quote Bessel van der Kolk on the history of psychiatry's relationship with trauma:

> "People have always been aware that exposure to overwhelming terror can lead to troubling memories, arousal and avoidance: this has been a central theme in literature from the time of Homer (Alford, 1992; Shay, 1994) to the present (Caruth, 1995). However, psychiatry, as a profession, has had a troubled relationship with the idea that reality can profoundly and permanently alter people's psychology and biology. Psychiatry has periodically suffered from marked amnesias, in which well-established knowledge was abruptly forgotten, and the psychological impact of overwhelming experiences [were] ascribed to constitutional or intrapsychic factors alone. Mirroring the intrusions, confusion, and disbelief of victims whose lives are suddenly shattered by traumatic experiences, the psychiatric profession periodically has been fascinated by trauma, **followed by stubborn disbelief about the relevance of our patients' stories.**" *(van der Kolk, 2007)* (my emphasis)

1.2 What is Trauma?

> "... Certain happenings ... leave indelible and distressing
> memories – memories to which the sufferer continually
> returns, and by which he is tormented by day and by night"
> *(Pierre Janet in van der Kolk, 1994)*

> "Trauma defeats life" *(Levine, 2010)*

Intuitively we know what we mean when we use the word
'trauma', but for the purposes of developing a good theory we
want to have a clear understanding so that we can be sure
we know what we are talking about. One of the many ways we
may attempt to protect ourselves from trauma study is to
deflect from defining clearly what we mean by the term. In the
last twenty or so years we have come to use the word 'trauma'
quite liberally to cover any event that we find difficult or
disturbing. This common usage, without a clear definition of
what we mean, I think reflects our need to acknowledge it, but
at the same time may be a way of diminishing the power of the
issue, making it somehow safer. We have done something
similar with the term 'abuse', whereby the general usage
covers a range of experiences from extreme violence and
sexual exploitation to mild insult or misunderstanding.

> "The 'helping' professions tend to describe trauma in terms of
> the event that caused it, instead of defining it in its own terms."
> *(Levine, 1977)*

In my reading on trauma to date I find that most writers
describe in detail the effects on people *after* a trauma – the
symptomatology of the *post*-trauma state – giving case
examples of sufferers of post trauma stress (again their
symptoms after the trauma), and have many and varied ideas
of how to treat or work with trauma. But it is hard to find defi-
nitions of what exactly a trauma situation *is,* the "reality"
Bessel van der Kolk refers to in the quote at the end of the
previous section. What, for example, defines trauma as trauma

rather than a high stress situation? As Kim Etherington, Professor of Narrative Therapy at Bristol University, writes:

> "Trauma has been explained and defined in terms of neurology, pathology, psychophysiology, psychology and 'events' that cause it." *(Etherington, 2003, referencing Griffith and Griffith, 1994)*

So as a starting place here is a dictionary definition of the word 'trauma':

> A deeply distressing or disturbing experience; emotional shock following a stressful event or a physical injury, which may be associated with physical shock and sometimes leads to long-term neurosis. (From the Greek word for 'wound')

Following are some quotes from prominent psychological writers describing trauma:

- "[trauma is] a breach in the protective barrier against stimulation leading to feelings of overwhelming helplessness." (Freud in Herman, 1992).
- "... extreme trauma has severe biological, psychological, social and existential consequences..." (van der Kolk, 2007a).
- "Trauma is about loss of connection – to ourselves, to our bodies, to our families, to others, and to the world around us." (Levine, 2008).
- "the whole apparatus for concerted, coordinated and purposeful activity is smashed." (Kardiner in Herman, 1992).
- "... a catastrophic loss of innocence that permanently alters one's sense of being-in-the-world" (Stolorow, 2007).
- "The critical element that makes an event traumatic is the subjective assessment by victims of how threatened and helpless they feel." (van der Kolk, 2007).
- "Traumatic reactions occur when action is of no avail... Neither resistance or escape is possible." (Herman, 1992)
- "[traumatic events] violate the victim's faith in a natural or divine order and cast the victim into a state of existential crisis." (Herman, 1992).

- "Traumatic events overwhelm the ordinary human adaptations of life, and they generally involve threats to life or bodily integrity and confront the human beings with extreme terror and helplessness." (Zepinic, 2011).
- "Individuals with this condition [PTSD] become overwhelmed by ... the extraordinary overload of information associated with the traumatic memory, which they are ... unable to integrate." (van der Kolk, 2007).
- "Trauma is stress run amuk." (Glenn, Jaffe and Segal, www.healingresources.info).

We can see from this that there are some common traits in all of these attempts to describe what trauma is. Trauma does indeed have some very specific qualities. Drawing on many writings by those quoted above and others on the topic of trauma I have put together the following experiential qualities of a trauma situation:

- It is an overwhelming experience where one's usual resources fail.
- It is a 'whole person experience', i.e. it has confluent physical and psychological impact.
- The subjective experience is of being in mortal danger, even if to an objective observer this does not seem the case.
- The defining experience is one of helplessness.
- The emotional component is extreme and the most common baseline emotion is terror or extreme fear connected with the experience of mortal threat.
- Second level emotions are rage, shock, grief, fright.
- Third level emotions are shame and guilt.
- The primary instinctual psychological survival strategies are dissociation and psychological splitting.[29]

---

[29] Reference: Rothschild (2000), Etherington (2003), van der Kolk, McFarlane, Weisaeth (2007), Herman (1992), Levine (1997, 2008, 2010), Shay (1994, 2002), Goleman (1995), Siegel (2010), Ogden, Minton & Pain (2006), Schore (2012a), Kardiner & Spiegel (1947), Weingarten (2004).

The common denominator here is that trauma is defined in terms of personal experience rather than objective reality, which in itself has consequences that I will discuss later in the section on Perpetrator-Victim dynamics. Suffice to say here that if we only talk in terms of subjective experience we miss the fact that people do intentionally act in ways that harm others; that in other words traumas are real life events that cannot just be discerned by subjective experience. Some events would traumatise anyone. Just to think in terms of subjective experience may collude with the trauma survival mode that I will discuss in Section 1.5.

Post Traumatic Stress Disorder

The only category in The American Psychiatric Society's Manual, the DSM IV[30], that relates specifically to trauma is category 309:81 – Post Traumatic Stress Disorder. This gives the post trauma symptomatology the status of a 'disorder', meaning that it is experienced to such a degree of seriousness that the person's life has become, or is in danger of becoming, dysfunctional. The person diagnosed with PTSD is finding it very hard or even impossible to hold their life together.

> "PTSD is a condition that severely disrupts individuals' capacity to perceive, represent, integrate and act on internal and external stimuli because of major disruptions in the neural systems associated with attention, working memory, and the processing of affective stimuli." *(van der Kolk)*

The term Post Traumatic Stress (i.e. without the word 'disorder') is not a formal diagnosis and refers to the stress experienced by a person who has suffered a highly stressful event, but not to the extent that their life is seriously disrupted. This is, therefore, not a category in the DSM IV, but accepted terminology for what we could call a pre-'disorder' situation.

---

[30] *Diagnostic and Statistical Manual* published by the American Psychiatric Association, version IV. Also see *ICD 10*, F43.1 category. (The *ICD 10* is the World Health Organisation's manual)

However, both of these designations are founded on the experiences and symptoms suffered *after* a trauma. As van der Kolk states of the DSM IV system of diagnosis, it "is based purely on....surface manifestations" (van der Kolk, 2007), i.e. the symptomatology, not the actual thing (trauma) itself.

The diagnostic category for Post Traumatic Stress Disorder in the DSM IV starts with two criteria for the event that the person must have been "exposed to", described as 'stressors'. This is the closest we get in the DSM IV to a definition of what trauma is. These two criteria are:

> (1) the person experienced, witnessed or was confronted with an event or events that involved actual or threatened death or serious injury, or a threat to the physical integrity of self or others;
>
> (2) the person's response involved intense fear, helplessness, or horror.

For the diagnosis to be made the person must fulfil both criteria. These are followed by descriptions of symptoms and post-trauma experiences that define the diagnosis as PTSD,[31] such as persistent intrusion of experiences of the trauma either consciously or in dreams, intense distress when exposed to "internal or external cues", avoidance of anything that might re-stimulate the trauma experience and so on.

Franz Ruppert's work

Franz Ruppert's work was founded first on a definition of trauma originated in the work of two German psychiatrists, Gottfried Fischer and Peter Riedesser (1999) as follows:

> "[Trauma is] a critical experience of the discrepancy between threatening factors in a situation and the individual's ability to cope, accompanied by feelings of helplessness and of being at the mercy of people and events, which then cause a permanent shock to the perception of the self and of the world." *(Fischer & Riedesser, 1999, in Ruppert, 2008)*

[31] See Appendix for full DSM IV PTSD criteria.

And second on the notion of psychological fragmentation, or splitting, or what van der Hart, Nijenhuis and Steele termed 'structural dissociation' (van der Hart, Nijenhuis & Steele, 2006).[32] Latterly Ruppert has included in his definition of trauma the fact that the person's 'stress programs' (ability and strategies to manage stress) have failed (see next section on stress, high stress and trauma).

Having worked with these ideas for some years, I would propose the following definition of what trauma is, which differs from the above in that it includes specifically the idea of life-threat (which is in fact included in the first criterion of the DSM-IV PTSD diagnostic category above):

1. Trauma is an experience that completely overwhelms the person's psychological and physical being and resources, rendering him or her utterly helpless in the face of unstoppable and consuming forces.
2. The subjective instantaneous experience is as if "I will not survive". It is a life and death situation – 'life-threat'. This is not necessarily an actual thought at the time, but more likely a non-verbalised, non-conceptualised semi-conscious, then rendered unconscious, experience.
3. Psycho-physical freezing and fragmentation (splitting) are the ultimate survival strategies employed.

From this definition we can understand several things:

- Trauma seems, in a sense, subjective, to do with the person's experience rather than what an observer may surmise. However, later I will discuss the contrasting notion that certain events in themselves can be judged to be traumatising of anyone suffering them, for example

---

[32] Van der Hart et al define trauma as not referring to an event but "only to those individuals who have developed ... a degree of structural dissociation' (*van der Hart et al, 2006*). In other words they define trauma in terms of the post trauma phenomena, the primary one of which is psychological splitting.

extreme torture, and in this sense trauma must also in some cases be defined in terms of the event itself.

- Trauma is relative: the relationship between the situation and the person's ability to cope (the 'discrepancy' in the Riedesser and Fischer quote above) is a distinguishing factor of trauma. If the situation outweighs the person's resources to the extent that the person's experience is of life-threat, and causes a psychological split, it would be a trauma.
- Trauma is holistic: it is of the whole person involving emotions, body, psyche and spirit.
- Trauma is a threat to one's integrity: it involves a psychological dis-integration (fragmentation or splitting).
- Trauma involves a dissociative splitting off of the trauma experience.
- Trauma has fundamental, long-lasting and far-reaching effects. While one can recover from worry or high stress, "traumatic experiences never disappear completely." (Ruppert, 2008)

Stress, High Stress and Trauma

"While it is true that all traumatic events are stressful, all stressful events are not traumatic."
(Levine, 2008)

Stress in itself is a normal part of life and is not always due to negative events. A bride or groom may feel stress on their wedding morning; a new employee may feel stress during their first few weeks at work as she learns the ropes. A definition of physical stress is made by Hans Selye as "the nonspecific response of the body to any demand" (in Rothschild, 2000). I would say that this is the same with psychological stress. Generally we think of stress as being a response to negative experiences, whereas we tend to think in terms of excitement when we are talking about a positive experience, but many of the physical and nervous system reactions are the same.

Another way of thinking about stress is that it is a situation that is challenging to our internal and environmental resources, but not overwhelmingly so. After a stress situation we are usually able to return to a state of equilibrium and balance.

A 'high stress' situation is one in which we feel severely under threat, to the extent that our ability to cope involves just two options, expressed as 'fight or flight'. Note the 'or'. We cannot do both at the same time, and in a high stress situation our judgement will be quick and instinctive as to which one is the better option. Initially we may attempt one, to fight, and then the other if the first seems not to give us a resolution, but instead causes the stress levels to increase. The physiological response to a high stress situation is one of hyper-arousal: high energy mobilisation, release of adrenalin and other arousal hormones (such as cortisol, epinephrine and norepinephrine and adrenalin), increase of heart-rate to get blood to the extremities to enable the necessary action, and so on. A high stress situation is one in which we perceive that we can do something, so we are not completely helpless, and the psycho-physical system gears up to act, our action being in relation to the environment, the source of the stress and the possible resources the environment holds (such as a clear escape route). A high stress situation is also one from which we can return to a place of equilibrium, although it is likely to take much longer than a normal stress situation, whereas a trauma situation is one from which we cannot.

Many writers on trauma talk about fight, flight and freeze as three different reactions to 'traumatic stress', whereas here I am making a distinction between a high stress situation and one that we would define as a trauma. I think the term 'traumatic stress' is in itself confusing, merging the two and so obscuring an understanding of what trauma actually is and the distinction between trauma and high stress. To quote Ruppert:

> "The difference between stress and trauma can be expressed thus: in a stressful situation one has the option of either fighting or fleeing ('fight or flight'), while in a trauma situation there is only one possibility – to become frozen and split inwardly

('freeze and fragment'). The stress reaction leads to a mobilisation of the body's energy, while the trauma-emergency mechanism leads to a demobilisation and disconnection of energy... The stress reaction opens the psychological channels, whereas trauma closes them down." *(Ruppert, 2008)*

In the event of long-term persistent stress situations, such as in 'burnout' for example, a person may be unable to return to a state of equilibrium, but this may be compounded and influenced by earlier (symbiotic) trauma. In the situation of a child who is under persistent stress as in severe childhood abuse, neglect or violence, the child is in a potential trauma situation throughout. The child will likely have suffered a prior bonding trauma (trauma of the infant/parent attachment phase which I will discuss in much more detail later) which means that the on-going stress situation is in fact a persistent retraumatisation. The same is the case with adult 'burnout'. The 'burnout' sufferer is likely to be experiencing a persistent retraumatisation of the earlier attachment trauma, which means he is unable to re-establish any equilibrium. Complicating the situation is the fact that due to the prior attachment trauma the adult's ability to leave a re-traumatising situation is compromised. People who are traumatised are less able to act with autonomy and in the service of their well-being than people who are not.

The physical body can only tolerate a high stress mobilised state of such extremes for a short period of time. The flood of hormones, such as adrenaline, for example, massively increases the heart-rate, making the likelihood of a heart attack or cardiac arrest high, and this high energy emergency state can only be maintained for a short time. At some point the body must close down, or die from this excess. This closing down is the shift from the high stress to the trauma reaction; the stress abilities having not achieved resolution of the event/experience must shift into the low energy 'tonic immobility' (Rothschild, 2000).

Freeze and Fragment

The freeze response, unlike the increased energy high stress response, is a flip to the opposite, a closing down and demobilising of energy. It is an emergency reaction that draws blood back from the periphery to the vital organs that are the source of life. In the life and death emergency the potential sacrifice of a limb, for example, in the cause of saving the life is logical, so the body in effect sacrifices whatever is necessary for life, which is why people who have experienced a trauma find that their hands and feet go cold.

As Ruppert says (quoted above), whereas in a high stress situation there are two clear options, in a trauma situation there is only one, which has two components: freezing and fragmentation. The two happen together and are related. The 'freezing and fragmentation' is a physical numbing and limpness, and a psychological and emotional dissociative splitting. In effect both are dissociative strategies that are last ditch survival attempts in the face of the extreme experience of mortal threat.

Freezing, also known as 'tonic immobility' (Rothschild, 2000) or the 'immobility response' (Levine, 1977), is similar to an animal playing dead, which in some instances may save its life, since many predators in the wild will not eat animals that are already dead and may leave it; or they may leave the 'dead' animal to go and get their young for the feed, thereby giving the prey a chance to revive and escape. Peter Levine (1997, 2008, 2010) makes the understanding of how animals deal with traumatic events a central part of his thinking about trauma and his work. What is clear from his writings and research is that when the danger has passed the immobile animal needs to shake itself back to life, and then leap and jump about as a way of expelling the pent up energy from the high stress experience.[33] The state of tonic immobility also serves to numb the prey's experiences of pain and terror, thereby keeping the animal protected from extreme experiences that may in themselves cause death.

[33] What Levine calls 'punking'.

Dissociation and Psychological Splitting

Dissociation

According to many, although we use the word dissociation easily, we do not as yet have a satisfactory explanation of how this phenomenon happens:

> *"... Dissociation has not yet been fully explained but is generally thought to be a mechanism that creates a split in conscious awareness that allows the traumatised person to disconnect from parts of their experience in order to reduce the impact [of trauma] and thereby survive." (Etherington, 2003)*

The term 'dissociation' was originally used by Moreau de Tours in 1845 (van der Hart & Friedman, 1989) and was taken up and developed by the pioneering psychologist and neurologist in the late 19th century, Pierre Janet.

> "Janet proposed that when people experience 'vehement emotions' their minds may become incapable of matching their frightening experiences with existing cognitive schemes. As a result the memories of the experience cannot be integrated into personal awareness; instead, they are split off from consciousness.... Extreme emotional arousal results in **failure to integrate** traumatic memories ..." *(van der Kolk et al, 2007, my emphasis)*

Freud cited Janet's work defining dissociation as a "splitting of consciousness" (Schore, 2012). So we can see that the notion of psychological splitting in relation to overwhelming traumatic experiences is not new. A more contemporary version is given by van der Kolk et al (2007) as follows:

> "'Dissociation' refers to a compartmentalization of experience: Elements of a trauma are not integrated into a unitary whole or an integrated sense of self." *(ibid.)*

As we can see from this last quote, dissociation is conflated with 'compartmentalization', or splitting. Historically the terms 'dissociation' and 'splitting' have often been used interchangeably in this way, but Ruppert makes a distinction between the two, with dissociation being the process by which a splitting happens, and the means by which the splits are kept in place (Ruppert, 2012).

Dissociation is a useful common daily experience that allows us to do more than one thing at once. For example, in driving, the activity may become habitual to the extent that we know our way home without thinking about it, and we know how to manage the clutch and accelerator without conscious attention. In this example it is not unusual for us to arrive home with little recollection of the journey and of the many choices and decisions that we have had to make in order to do so. Dissociation is also an entirely natural response to intolerable experience; it protects us in a trauma situation, as Etherington states in the quote at the start of this section.

If we look at the diagram opposite we can see that dissociation is available to us prior to a trauma as a daily part of normal functioning. After a trauma, dissociation becomes the means by which we manage the psychological splits resulting from the trauma. Broadly speaking dissociation and distraction are the underlying methods of all our survival strategies after a trauma.

Ruppert uses the term splitting to refer to the structural split of the psyche after a trauma, which stays in place until the trauma experience can be integrated: "While dissociation can be temporary, for example enabling a paramedic to carry out an extremely stressful assignment, splitting is permanent." (Ruppert, 2012)

Van der Hart et al seem to agree with Ruppert when they make a distinction between what they call "dissociation of the personality", what we would call splitting, and "dissociation of consciousness", what we would call dissociation (van der Hart and Nijenhuis in Blaney & Millon, 2008, van der Hart, Nijenhuis & Steele, 2006). So to clarify for our purposes: splitting is structural, and dissociation comes and goes, passing when the danger (of retraumatisation) is over.

Ruppert further makes a distinction between "splitting off" the intolerable experience, and the "splitting up" of the

Figure 1. Continuum from healthy dissociation to severe psychological dysfunction.

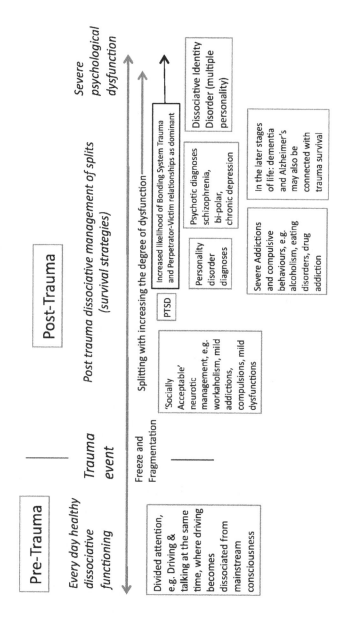

personality, where the splitting off is what happens during a trauma situation by dissociation, and the splitting up is the residual split personality construction which, over time, becomes rigidified and to a great extent permanent. It becomes who we are, and most importantly who we think we are, particularly in the case of very early attachment trauma which occurs during a time when we are developing a 'self'.

Another curiosity is that, as Rothschild muses:

> "Surprisingly, dissociation ... is not mentioned by either the DSM III or DSM IV as a symptom of PTSD ... although it is acknowledged as a symptom of acute stress disorder (APA, 1994) ..." *(Rothschild, 2000)*

... which is interesting, especially since right from the origins of the idea of dissociation it has always been linked with trauma. Rothschild goes on to agree with Etherington (quoted at the beginning of this section) that:

> "No one really knows what dissociation is or how it occurs. It appears to be a set of related forms of split awareness ... [and ranges from] forgetting why you were going into the kitchen [to] dissociative identity disorder". *(ibid.)*

As to what dissociation is and how it occurs, it seems to me that within the topic of trauma it is an entirely natural in-the-moment response to the intolerable. Daniel Siegel, the American 'interpersonal neurobiologist' and professor of psychiatry, sees health as emerging from neural integration: "the linkage of differentiated elements in a system [the brain system]" (Siegel, 2010). He is specifically referring to neural connections in the brain system, and from a neurobiological perspective, it seems that trauma may conversely cause the *disconnection* of the neural pathways in the brain system, which may also be related to dissociation.

Finally, the intersubjective theorist and therapist Robert Stolorow offers a phrase that he uses in the understanding of trauma. He doesn't link it with dissociation, but I think describes it accurately when he talks of 'ontological uncon-sciousness' as he says "to denote a loss of one's sense of being".

Splitting

Despite some confusion of these terms, it seems generally agreed that the psyche will split off intolerable trauma experi-ences from the conscious mind. I think this serves three functions:

- The first is it saves energy: in the emergency moment the emotional and psychological expressions of the trauma are energetic luxuries that the organism cannot afford. The expression and experience of emotions takes energy and all available resources must go to survival, to keeping the vital organs alive, so the psyche splits off the emotional and psychological trauma experience, freezing it in time and relegating it to the unconscious.
- The second is that the primary emotional experience of trauma is terror, which is in itself an intolerable experi-ence. So it is likely that part of the function of splitting off is an attempt not to feel such devastating emotions.
- A third is that, by splitting off the trauma experience, it may also function to preserve a sense of self as much as possible in the face of circumstances that overwhelm any prior sense of self.

So the freezing impulse in the trauma moment also freezes the mind, protecting the organism from the overwhelming experi-ences involved in life-threat. It is a closing down. I will discuss splitting further in the section on The Split Self.

'Metabolisation' of Trauma

In the animal world species that are prey to other species deal with the trauma of predation every day. They have evolved to deal with this daily high stress and potential of traumatisation, and as Peter Levine's work shows, if they survive the predation attack they seem well practised at throwing off the accumulated energy and continuing with their lives, seemingly relatively unaffected. Because the business of being a potential prey is familiar and regular, these animals have evolved to metabolise the trauma of simple predation efficiently.

Some situations, however, do seem to leave the animal traumatised in a way that we would recognise as similar to PTSD in humans. Two particular examples were shown in a television programme recently screened by the BBC in the UK. One dealt with the Elephant Orphanage in Kenya, which takes care of young and baby elephants whose mothers have been killed by poachers for ivory.[34] The other dealt with an orphanage run by the Jane Goodall Institute for young chimpanzees whose parents had been taken by local people as 'bushmeat', to eat.[35] In both these programmes the orphans exhibited clear symptoms of what we would recognise as trauma: fearful and watchful look, easy startle reaction, signs of dissociation, obsessive behaviours, easily agitated and aroused nervous system. It would seem that while animals may have the ability to metabolise predation trauma without negative effects, they are as vulnerable as humans to abandonment and symbiotic (very early attachment) trauma.

Humans have not been prey as food, as a routine, for approximately a million years. Up until two million years ago the predation rates for our human ancestors were approximately the same as other prey species; but about two million years ago there seems to have been a shift, after which the rate of human predation seems to have declined (Hart & Sussman, 2008). So it is likely that any ability we may have had to metabolise and resolve the trauma of predation has diminished. In any event, it is fairly clear that we are as vulnerable to nonpredatory trauma as the orphaned elephants and chimpanzees discussed above, and our ability to 'metabolise' trauma and

---

[34] http://www.bbc.co.uk/news/world-17675816
[35] http://news.bbc.co.uk/1/hi/uk/274464.stm

integrate the split-off experiences on our own is limited.

The primary strategies of survival work against this metabolising and integration as we shall see. Freezing and fragmentation are strategies for survival, employed at the moment of the trauma, but to an extent they remain in place, particularly at any time when we encounter a situation that, for whatever reason, re-stimulates the trauma experience. In effect after the trauma situation we are never the same again, and are always vulnerable to retraumatisation when, to some degree, we will go into a 'freeze and fragment' strategy.

1.3 Types of Trauma

Keeping in mind our trauma definition above involving life-threat, overwhelming experience and helplessness, and splitting, here I am giving an initial categorisation of trauma (Terr, 1991) which distinguishes the following:

1. **One-off events:** Brief, unexpected one-off trauma events, such as accidents, single attacking acts such as mugging, rape; natural disasters.
2. **On-going over time**: persistent, repetitive situations such as ongoing childhood abuse and extreme neglect, ongoing torture, incarceration, persecution.

Ruppert describes four types of trauma in his book, *Trauma, Bonding and Family Constellations* (2008). These are:

1. **Existential Trauma** – where the reality and/or experience is as if I may not survive, for example, in a car accident, attack, rape, persecution, torture, natural disaster, war experience. It doesn't matter if the actual situation is objectively seen as not life-threatening. If the subjective experience is that one's life is threatened this is likely to result in an existential trauma.

2. **Loss Trauma** – for most of us the loss of a closely bonded person is an experience that for a moment we are not sure we will survive. This is to some degree the case in all situations of loss, but is critically so in instances of unusual or unexpected loss, for example the death of a young child for the parents and siblings; the death of a parent for a young child or baby; the death of a son or daughter in unexpected circumstances such as accident, war action or other event. Miscarriages and stillbirths are also likely to fall into this category.

3. **Bonding Trauma** – what Ruppert has called 'symbiotic trauma', where the process of bonding between mother and child (and, somewhat later, father and child) is in itself traumatic for the child. This occurs very early in the development of the child, even in utero, and as such is usually beyond cognitive recall. The existence of this early pre-cognition 'primary' trauma will be discussed in detail later as it underlies and influences all later trauma.

4. **Bonding System Trauma** – a situation where the whole family system over several generations is collectively and similarly traumatised. This begins with some act of perpetration within the family, usually one that transcends common cultural and social values, and so involves extreme feelings of shame and guilt that are also split off. The dynamics of avoidance and repetition get re-played from generation to generation unconsciously until the original act/event is long forgotten. Everyone in the system is entangled with the trauma experiences of those previously traumatised, and relationships within the family system are based on secrecy, avoidance and perpetrator-victim dynamics, which I will discuss later.

I would add two more to this list:

5. **Trauma of Witnessing**: The bystander at a traumatic event, particularly if he feels helpless and at mortal risk himself, as in situations of witnessing torture, extreme

brutality, mass killing, and perhaps even accidents and natural disasters, may suffer a trauma him or herself. This might be the case with a child who has to witness his father beating his mother for example.

6. **Trauma of Perpetration**: We generally think in terms of the victim being the traumatised person, but the act of perpetration can also be a trauma for the perpetrator. This is most commonly understood when combat personnel have to kill, or in the case of people being forced to perpetrate acts against others (as in the case of children being forced to kill as child soldiers, for example in the "Lord's Resistance Army" in Uganda and the Congo). This will be traumatising for them unless they are already highly traumatised from previous conditions, in which case it may be a retraumatisation. In my view a person cannot perpetrate a harmful act on another unless they are dissociated to some degree by trauma themselves, or are forced to. Each act of perpetration is likely to entrench more deeply the splits, causing more dissociated and extreme survival strategies, as the feelings of the person are increasingly denied and deadened.

What is common to all these situations is helplessness, an overwhelming experience, and as part of the survival process, psychological splitting. The primary experiences of trauma are helplessness and life-threat, in the sense that in the trauma moment one is looking over the edge of a precipice, teetering on the edge, and whether one falls or not is completely beyond knowing or our will.

This is obviously the case with existential trauma, but may be less obvious with trauma of loss. The British artist Damien Hirst made an artwork that he called *The Physical Impossibility of Death in the Mind of Someone Living*.[36] This title conveys something, I think, of just how difficult it is for someone living to really come to terms with death, and the loss of a person one is closely bonded to.

[36] The work is a shark in formaldehyde.

If this person is a parent then there is likely for a moment to be some sense of impossibility of one being able to continue to exist without this person. Many people in this kind of situation talk about the experience of having lost some part of themselves, which can feel physical as well as emotional. When we come to look at symbiotic trauma it will become more obvious just how devastating the loss of the mother is to the young child.

1.4 Effects of Different Types of Trauma

Another kind of categorisation of trauma is in terms of how easy or not it is for us to metabolise the trauma effect and integrate the experience. Generally speaking traumas caused by natural disasters, such as earthquakes, or even accidents etc seem easier for people to integrate than those that are perpetrated intentionally by another human. Then there are sub-categories within the human-on-human perpetration depending predominantly on our relationship with the perpetrator. So there follows a form of categorisation based on a continuum of severity:

1. **Trauma caused by natural disasters** (earthquakes, tsunamis etc) is the easiest form of trauma for humans to metabolise and integrate. In some instances accidents may fall into this category, particularly if there seems no particularly guilty person. However natural disaster traumas may always have as part of the trauma the re-stimulation of earlier trauma such as, primarily, early attachment trauma (see below).
2. **Inter-personal, or human-on-human trauma** is a more serious proposition for us to integrate. We could describe this as intra-species traumatisation, and it is far harder for us to comprehend, manage and resolve. Whereas with the natural disaster, or even sometimes the accident, there is no personal intention of harm towards us, in trauma perpetrated by a fellow human there usually is, or we

may certainly perceive it as so. With incidents of ethnic cleansing for example, where for the perpetrator the victim, as an individual, is of little importance, the idea that another human being could so hurt or kill us is deeply shocking and terrifying.

3. **Relational trauma** is more shocking and disturbing still, being the perpetration of trauma by someone we know and have a relationship with. This trauma involves the shock of betrayal and the disorientation and destruction of our sense of the sanctity of relationship.

4. **Parent/child intentional perpetration**: is where the parent's relationship with their child is abusive, highly neglectful and usually continuously so. This includes emotional neglect, violence and sexual abuse. One-off minor incidents within a generally loving and fair relationship may be easier to metabolise than major events and continuing actions over time. Situations where the abuse (whether neglect, violence and/or sexual abuse) is extreme and ongoing may be far more troublesome and pernicious.

5. **Early Attachment Trauma**: what we call symbiotic trauma. This is the first (primary) trauma of our lives, and happens in the pre-verbal (even in utero) phase of life. A symbiotic trauma, unless due to physical separation such as adoption, incubation etc., is usually a complex trauma since it involves a confusion (entanglement) with the mother's own psychological state, particularly if the mother herself is traumatised. I would also propose that within this category there is a distinction between trauma that is actively perpetrated and a trauma that is passive:

- Active: the mother has an active attitude of intentional harm towards the child, for example if the mother doesn't want the child, tries to abort the child, acts intentionally to harm the child in any other way;
- Passive: the mother, herself being traumatised, is dissociated and psychologically and emotionally absent for the child without an active intention of harm.

This last trauma is extremely serious and life-affecting since, because it occurs in the very early, even in utero, symbiosis between mother and child, it will underlie any later trauma thereby increasing its impact.

1.5 The Split Self

"Splitting is a violent affair – like the splitting of an atom."
(Kalsched, 1996)

"... [trauma] fractures one's sense of unitary selfhood."
(Stolorow, 2007)

Splitting as a term has a long usage in psychoanalysis, with I think, some confusion in terms of definition. In order to understand the differences in references to splitting, I am attempting here to define the different ways in which the term has been used historically, and then I will discuss Ruppert's usage. Much of this material has been taken from a paper by J A Brook called 'Freud & Splitting' (1991).

Historically, splitting has been used in three different ways, though according to Brook (ibid) "any such typology will draw clearer lines than we find in the actual clinical material, where mixed types are common".

1. Splitting into psychic groupings. This was the first type of splitting that was discussed by Freud as early as 1894. "This form of splitting is commonly linked to dissociative states." (ibid.) It was this form of splitting that Freud eventually referred to as repression. Much later in his work he said that this type of splitting was primarily found in people who suffered severe trauma as children and was an act of defence (Freud, 1934-38). Freud and others (Breuer, Charcot and Janet) thought that this mainly occurred in cases of 'hysteria', which resulted "when something traumatic which had never been properly integrated into, or synthesised with, the rest of the psyche came to live a mischievous life of its own." (ibid.)

This definition seems to me to be the closest to what we are discussing in Ruppert's trauma theory, in terms of there being a distinct other self, the traumatised self (the "mischievous" element). However, the other two below are also useful in that they are symptomatic of this primary form of traumatic managing.

2. Splitting of representations. This is the most commonly used form of the term 'splitting' in psychotherapy. Melanie Klein and Otto Kernberg made this central to their form of psychoanalysis; Hans Kohut and other 'self-psychologists' termed this as a split in the sense of the self, and it forms the basis of how psychotherapists view Borderline and Narcissistic Personality Disorders. In this case 'representations' mean images and perceptions of 'objects' (other people and things) and events, and of the self. This is most commonly seen as the split of the other person (and more subtly and shamefully, of the self) into either completely good or completely bad, with little sense of the nuances of 'grey' in between. Anyone who has worked as a psychotherapist long-term with someone manifesting either of the above-mentioned personality issues knows very well from experience the kind of splitting discussed here, where the client's perception of the therapist is split into good/understanding/loving/supporting and bad/ignorant/hating/deserting, and where the therapist's experience of themselves is often also split in parallel, causing in both an escalating, and sometimes wild, oscillation of self-experience and other-perception (perception of the other person). The most difficult time I ever had as a psychotherapist was when I worked long-term with someone whose personality process was well within the borderline categorisation. I was not a very experienced psychotherapist at the time and my work with this client sent my whole world into an oscillating spin, outside the therapy room as well as within. My behaviour became quite extreme, my emotions were volatile and I

found it extremely hard to hold a central, grounded place in my own life. My sense of self whirled between myself as I knew myself, and a self that oscillated at times frighteningly towards the edges of sanity. Of course none of this was entirely to do with the client, but her process hooked the potential for instability, the 'borderline' within me, extremely well. I am sure other psychotherapists will have experienced something similar in their practice at some point.

In reference to Ruppert's theory I would suggest that this form of 'splitting' is an extreme form of survival strategy, where the healthy part of the self struggles to hold any place within the chaotic confusion of selves.

3. The third kind that Brooks (ibid) discusses is Splitting of the Ego, which, he says, Freud focussed on primarily for the last decade of his life, almost to the exclusion of the other two. This is the process by which we hold two completely contradictory attitudes and stances on a single topic/event at the same time. Freud mostly saw this process as a 'defence by disavowal', as in: "I know my father is dead, but I act as if he is still alive." Reality is on the one hand acknowledged, and on the other denied. This is also obviously a survival strategy in the theory presented here.

The way we discuss splitting in reference to Franz Ruppert's work (2008, 2011, 2012) combines all of the types given by Brook as noted above but also something more. Whereas all previous references to splitting discuss a split into two, where the trauma experience is split off and the person defends against re-experiencing the trauma, Ruppert sees the split off trauma as a distinct part of the self, the 'traumatised part', separate from the main (healthy) self, the 'healthy part', and the defending function as a third part, an entity in itself, the 'survival part'. Thus:

Figure 2. The Split Self after Trauma.

After a trauma, over the subsequent weeks, months and even years, the splitting-off of the trauma experience from consciousness becomes hardened with a certain rigidity in nature; it then is a *splitting up* of the personality. The strategies of survival (the survival self) become more a part of one's personality and daily existence, and the healthy (original) part of the self becomes less the authority of the self, constantly at odds with the survival self. Each component has its own function that it eternally tries to fulfil, and its own characteristics. The table below sets these out.

Figure 3. Characteristics and Functions of the Split Parts (based on Ruppert, 2008)

Personality Component	Functions	Characteristics
Traumatised Part	Holding the trauma feelings and the memory of the trauma.	• Is always the same age as the time of the trauma • Is constantly engaged with the trauma as if it is still happening • Can unpredictably and suddenly be triggered – retraumatisation
Survival Part	Constructing and guarding the splits by developing survival strategies. Preventing the trauma from breaking through. Denying and suppressing the trauma experience and feelings. Producing new splits if necessary to maintain the suppression.	• Avoidant behaviour* • Inappropriately aggressive behaviour • Controlling behaviour • Compensating behaviour • Dissociation • Somatisation • Fostering illusions and delusions • Inability to make good bonds and relationships
Healthy Part	Being in contact with reality without illusions. Attempting to integrate the trauma experiences – and so is in conflict with the Survival aspect.	• Openness to truth and reality • Capable of expressing and regulating feelings • Capable of genuine empathy** • Is able to make safe bonds • Is able to resolve destructive bonds • Sexual desire and behaviour are appropriate • Has a good memory of their past • Capable of self-reflection • Is able to be self-responsible • Seeks clarity and truth • Desires integration within self • Is confident and makes good contact • Feelings of guilt and shame are situation appropriate

* All or any of these can be seen in any kind of addiction or compulsive behaviour, as well as in the more severe forms of mental illness.
** As opposed to compulsive and merged or entangled empathy.

"... Part of our being can 'die' and while the remaining part of our self may survive the trauma, it awakens with a gap in its memory. Actually it is a gap in the personality, because not only is the memory of the struggle-to-the-death effaced, but all other associatively linked memories disappear ... perhaps forever." *(From the letters of Sándor Ferenczi dated 30 July 1932, in Masson, 2012)*

In Ruppert's model the survival part of the self is that which organises and maintains this gap mentioned by Ferenczi.

Diagrams and graphics are for understanding theory, but in life these aspects of the self are not always so clearly defined. While it is true that the splitting has a structural, reified quality, and we describe these components as 'parts', it is also helpful to see them in terms of process, but a process that is reactive and has a certain rigidity and predictability. The mode of functioning is reverted to without active choice or forethought, as a reaction to re-stimulation. For example, in relationship we may move through all components: the healthy aspect of ourselves desiring relationship and contact with others, seeing clearly the reality of things; then, in a confronting situation, such as increased intimacy (which is highly confronting for the traumatised person because intimacy may trigger suppressed emotion), the traumatised component may surface as anxiety and panic, which immediately stimulates the survival protective strategies, such as withdrawing, deflecting, going blank, talking a lot, obsessiveness, addiction and so on. Our experience of the splits is often as if we are different people in different situations, which often is puzzling to us. It is in this way that the splitting can be experienced as structural.

The Healthy Self

> "The healthy psychological part of ourselves is capable of
> appreciating reality as it actually is, and not as one would like
> it to be." *(Ruppert, 2012)*

After a split we retain a healthy aspect to ourselves, which, when not compromised by survival activities, allows us to think clearly and see things as they are and make good decisions for ourselves. However, after the trauma splitting, this healthy aspect of ourselves is compromised, and always in danger of being overcome by our survival self if our unresolved trauma feelings are stimulated. We can at times be fully in our healthy self, but should something threaten to stimulate our trauma we will immediately go into the split of our trauma and our survival self, at which point the healthy self loses its place and authority. After a trauma the healthy self is always a hostage to the potential re-triggering of the trauma and the resulting supremacy of the survival self. However, in a serious retraumatisation, if the survival strategies fail, the trauma self takes over and overwhelms the personality at least for the time being.

How do we come into contact with another without going into our splits?

To me this is a primary question we are working with. Another way of putting it is: what exactly is entailed in our coming into good clear contact with ourselves and others and how do we maintain that healthy aspect of ourselves in intimate situations without going into our split self? Any situation that connects us with our feelings is also likely to connect us with our unresolved trauma feelings. It is debatable whether we can feel any emotion without to some extent also feeling the split off trauma feelings, even if only as suppressed anxiety or mild panic or discomfort. We may only know by how much we go into our survival mode; and since for the most part this is unconscious (until we start to become more aware of our survival strategies) it is often hard for us to say. In any event, it seems that as soon as any uncomfortable and frightening feelings connected with the trauma start to surface we will automatically move into survival mode and lose our connection with the healthy aspect of ourselves.

In effect when we work with the theory of splits we are working to increase the client's healthy aspect by helping them to become more aware of their survival strategies – the many ways we have developed of disconnecting from ourselves and from the trauma – and increasingly to become able to connect with the split off trauma part of themselves. Integration is the endeavour, and the healthy part of us knows this. Situations of intimacy are often indicators of repressed trauma experiences because the emotions involved are likely to reverberate with and restimulate hidden trauma feelings.

At the more extreme end of the spectrum a person may live almost totally from a survival self, with little ability for real contact or empathy. Coming into any kind of contact with the trauma self and its desire for expression is experienced as extremely dangerous, and any efforts by the healthy self to do so will be thwarted by the survival self. The most extreme form of this would be psychosis where contact with reality is greatly reduced. The psychotic retreats into loss of reality to avoid having to deal with the trauma feelings, and the psychopath retreats into a no feelings state to the same end. To the severely traumatised person the healthy part of the self is seen as a danger and the only safety is seen as in the survival mode.

It is the healthy part of us that takes us into therapy, that persistently desires integration and wholeness, that knows there is another possibility, that fulfilment, love and clarity are possible. It is the healthy aspect of ourselves that yearns for true connection, honest love, real engagement with ourselves and others, but in this yearning it is always in conflict with the survival self. The relationship between the healthy self and the survival self is characterised by mistrust, confusion and conflict, and the therapist rarely encounters the healthy self in the client without aspects of the survival self.

The Traumatised Self

"Experiences of trauma become freeze-framed into an eternal present in which one remains forever trapped."
(Stolorow, 2007)

The trauma self is the part that holds the unresolved trauma, as if suspended in time, frozen at the age of the trauma, and so is often very young, sometimes pre-verbal. The existence of this part of the self is to all intents and purposes blocked from conscious awareness, although the healthy part of the self usually has some idea that something is not right, even if only from the external realities of her life... for example, relationships fail, the person cannot fulfil her potential and knows it. The emotions and experiences of the trauma are held unresolved and fully potent, waiting an opportunity for expression and resolution. The trauma self longs to be seen and recognised, while the survival part ignores and rejects it. Within the constellations process, at the beginning, the traumatised self, if represented or present, cannot bear to look at anyone else and will very often tend to look at the floor, or attempt to hide. It is also often the case that the client ignores it, becoming entranced and held instead by the dynamics revealed by any representation of the family. The split off trauma holds vast reserves of energy frozen within, and the release of this energy is eventually life-enhancing.

In the constellations process we sometimes find that the representative for the client's 'intention' (this will be discussed in detail in part 2) becomes this small traumatised part of the client. However, as a representative they are usually able to put into words what has been, and still is for the traumatised part of the self, wordless. This is immensely helpful to the process of trauma resolution and healing.

Split off trauma is re-stimulated by many things, broadly the following:

- external conditions that unconsciously remind us of the original event through our senses, including smells, sounds, sensations, images, language etc;
- internal conditions that are somatically connected to the trauma event, such as nausea, vomiting, aches and pains, emotions, experiences of disgust, illnesses;
- any event that in itself can be described as potentially highly stressful or traumatic is likely to precipitate a retraumatisation;
- any situation that involves an increase in stress;
- any situation where we begin to feel out of control and helpless;
- any situation that stimulates our emotions, such as situations of intimacy and love, since the arousal of any emotion opens the gate for the expression and experience of unresolved trauma emotions;
- the birth of a child, which may be traumatic in itself, but also may re-stimulate one's own attachment trauma and experiences of the mother's trauma. Post natal depression is likely to be the result of the re-stimulation of the mother's own attachment trauma and her entanglement with her mother's unresolved trauma;
- the death of a loved one.

The Survival Self

The survival self comes into being at the moment of the trauma, doing whatever is necessary to maintain survival:

> "The surviving parts of the self function mainly as the creator and 'guardian' of the splits ... [but] although lifesaving in the short term, and urgently needed in the actual trauma situation, in the middle and long term, especially when the trauma situation no longer exists, surviving parts become a barrier to the development of a person." (Ruppert, 2012)

Primarily this is the dissociative mechanism as we have seen above, that attempts to ensure survival and the avoidance of feelings. Slowly over the weeks and months, and even years after the trauma the strategies become more and more solid, practised and structured, more firmly a part of who we think we are, the self we present to the world, the self that protects us. We don't know this, and we come to believe that this is actually who we are, but it isn't. It is the process by which we come to live through our survival strategies (and our entanglements with earlier system traumas) rather than through our healthy self.

Survival strategies are always in order to avoid the traumatised feelings. Many of our survival strategies, having been dissociative and passive in the beginning, then become translated into activity. It is likely that the feelings of helplessness in the trauma situation are subsequently translated into overactive action in the survival strategies as a way of not having to re-experience the helplessness. The survival self is always under stress since it must by definition be continually watchful. Other survival strategies may serve to dull our senses through inactivity, drugs, alcohol, day-dreaming etc.

The survival self holds the boundary between the trauma and consciousness, between the trauma self and the healthy self, in order to protect the person from unwanted trauma re-stimulation. Most of the time the survival self succeeds, becoming increasingly active if anything occurs that re-stimulates the trauma, so as to maintain control and thicken up the boundary of the split. But at times something happens and the strategies developed are insufficient to maintain the boundary; when this happens a full retraumatisation occurs, and in the wake of this the survival self develops more splits and new, more extreme strategies to keep the trauma at bay. The management of this puts more pressure on the survival self to come up with newer, stronger, more dissociative and distractive strategies to keep the trauma at bay.

> "Because every survival strategy sooner or later ends up exhausted or ... ineffective, with the original problem (the traumatic experience) still unresolved but even more exacerbated, the survival self has to keep coming up with new and increasingly radical methods of suppression." *(Ruppert, 2012)*

Over time, if a person has to deal persistently with trauma and retraumatisation, the survival strategies will increasingly take over more of the person's life, become more extreme, and even in the end life-threatening. For example, addictions are ways of dissociating from, and dulling, difficult feelings, but addictions eventually become life-threatening in themselves. Eating disorders are survival strategies that distract from emotional pain and give an illusion of control over the uncontrollable, but may eventually cause the death of the individual. All self-destructive and self-harming behaviours in this sense have as their function the distraction from and control of emotional pain and suffering and terrifying feelings. Even suicide is a survival strategy, paradoxically protecting the person from the persistent and increasing danger of experiencing the split off trauma.

By their very nature survival strategies exist in the realm of illusion and delusion. They peddle mistruth and confusion, because their sole function is to deny the existence of the truth of the trauma, this denial in itself forming a fundamental myth about the self and one's family. All survival strategies are unreal, in that they are devices to protect the person from the truth about himself, but the tendency is for the person to think of them as being real. They "very often disguise themselves as 'sane', 'rational' and 'normal'" (Ruppert, 2012a), and other people that the person comes into contact with, who are often also functioning from their own survival strategies, will collude with this notion, so that a group of people may make a 'rational' decision that is solely based on survival strategies.

Our survival strategies are always interruptive of real contact with others, with our environment, and most importantly with ourselves. This is not an interruption that we choose, as we might in some instances of clear thinking and perception, but an interruption that comes from the unconscious need to avoid trauma and the feelings involved. The interruption will take the form of reactive behaviour, sometimes quite bizarre behaviour that leaves one feeling puzzled and ashamed, or propels one to accuse another person in order to avoid having to deal with one's own erratic and unexplainable behaviour. Anyone who in a certain situation has behaved in a way that later they feel ashamed of or puzzled by is more than likely to have been functioning through survival strategies.

Couples who find themselves in repetitive destructive patterns of relating are likely to be relating primarily through their survival selves. Because any form of intimacy involves feelings, the threat of unresolved trauma feelings surfacing is always present; the relationship in effect becomes an arena in which both people are always potentially under threat, and much of the relating is a form of defence and defensive attack. It isn't of course so much the other person who constitutes a threat, but intimacy, the urge to love the other, that brings up dangerous, frightening feelings from which the person must defend herself. The place where she should feel safe and comfortable becomes instead the environment where she may feel most under threat. In my view the best form of therapy for a couple is for both people to look at their own early attachment trauma, and it can be very helpful to do so in the presence of each other. In this way each comes to understand better the primary issues underlying the being of the other, and how that relates to their own issues. I will discuss this further in Chapter 10 on working with couples.

The deflection of contact can also be quite subtle, even beguiling and charming, offering a transfixing, charismatic personality behind which to hide. The experienced therapist working every day with trauma can still be beguiled by the subtle and experienced survival self in a client. Many highly successful people are successful precisely because of their refined and practised survival strategies that charm and dominate, while enabling them to avoid terrifying feelings.

Broadly, survival strategies fall into the following categories of symptomatic behaviour:

1. **avoidance**: by distraction, deception and deflection;
2. **denial** of problems, blaming others, refusal to look at self, insisting that everything is fine and that one's childhood was good;
3. **control** of self (obsessive behaviour, compulsive behaviour, eating disorders, self-harm, extreme behaviours); and of others (keeping others at a distance, dominating others, manipulation of others);
4. **submissive behaviour**: adopting a 'victim attitude' – perpetuating one's victim status by helpless and powerless behaviour as a means of avoiding the real trauma;
5. **perpetrator behaviour**: adopting a 'perpetrator attitude' as a defence against feeling the trauma feelings of having been a victim;
6. **compensation**: for the lack of liveliness and joy and good feelings experienced, and compensating for the lack of real love during the early symbiosis, through addictions to alcohol, drugs, sex, medication, television, food, work;
7. **dissociation**: going blank, vague, dull, in a trance; fugue state, amnesia;
8. **somatisation:** developing physical symptoms and

illnesses that distract from the real problem and confirm one's helplessness;

9. **delusional behaviour**: creating illusions that propose that there is no problem; or if a problem is acknowledged it is seen as the person's fault, or everyone else's fault, or just how things are;

11. **depression and depressive symptoms** such as clinical and chronic depression, pre- and post-natal depression;

12. **severe psychological disorders** that all attempt to avoid, deny, compensate for and control the reality of trauma.

Perpetrator-Victim Dynamics

Ruppert's later work has been an exploration of the difficult and entangled issues of the perpetrator and the victim, and the oscillation that occurs between them, where victim turns perpetrator and perpetrator victim. The word 'perpetrator' means anyone who intentionally causes harm to another, and the word 'victim' covers a person harmed, injured or killed as a result of a crime, accident or other event or action.

The reality of the victim

In section 1.2 above, trauma is characterised as subjective. However it is important not to over-emphasise this. There is a danger, if we stick too closely to this definition, that we collude with the client's denial of the actuality of real acts of perpetration. To put it simply, an intentional act to harm another is an actual encroachment; people do intentionally hurt and harm others; the sexual exploitation of a child is a real objective trauma. To say that trauma is entirely to do with subjective experience implies that a child could be abused and not be traumatised by it. I do not think this is helpful. Often it is hard enough for someone to fully admit to their victimisation to the extent of experiencing the feelings of their trauma, and in this sense it is easy for others to collude with their denial by only considering the stated experiential effect rather than the external reality of the event.

Both perpetrator and victim can be understood in terms of survival strategies that protect the person from experiencing the devastating feelings hidden away. The perpetrator experiences power over another, thereby obliterates their own powerlessness and helplessness, their own trauma. The victim experience may allow the person to live from a place of helplessness as a means of avoiding the real feelings connected to their real trauma, thereby avoiding change. Ruppert calls these two surviving strategies the 'perpetrator attitude' and the 'victim attitude' to distinguish them from the actual situation of being a perpetrator and that of being a victim. Splitting off the real trauma experience creates a perpetrator attitude as a survival strategy, or a victim attitude as a survival strategy, and sometimes both in oscillation.

Victim attitude

The person with the victim attitude as a survival mode tends to deny the reality of his[37] victimisation, of his trauma, behind an attitude of victimisation. His survival self utilises the attitude of being a victim to suppress the memories, permanently feeling guilty and justifiably punishable, along with a disgust at his own weakness. He often will not recognise perpetrators as dangerous to him and will instead cling emotionally to the original perpetrator (e.g. the mother or father), and others later in life who perceive him as a victim. The victim attitude protects the person (and the perpetrator) from the truth and he will identify with and try to fulfil the needs of, and take care of, the perpetrator. He will often indulge in self-destructive behaviour (the internalisation of the perpetrator turned against the self) and may suffer from chronic depression and illnesses, and will be constantly involved in his victimhood, at the same time as denying it

---

[37] Our ideas of victims usually veer towards the female, and so I have used the male generic here to remind us that men too may be victims.

and avoiding feeling the original feelings involved in his trauma.

In this way the victim attitude becomes in effect a perpetrator to others and to himself, constantly displaying his victimhood and persistently relating through these dynamics, provoking the perpetrator ability in others. The self-destructive tendencies are the internalised victim-perpetrator dynamics acted out against the self.

Perpetrator attitude

The act of perpetration can be traumatic in itself to the perpetrator (See section 1.3 item 6.). If not already traumatised they will suffer massive feelings of guilt and shame, and a panic of being socially ostracised and despised. If the perpetrator is already severely traumatised these experiences will be diminished and split off. In the situation of the psychopath, these feelings are virtually obliterated, having been split off in the process of defending against feeling anything that might be distressing.

The 'perpetrator attitude' is another form of survival strategy: the harm done to others, the facts of what happened, and the guilt are all denied. Instead the perpetrator feels righteous and justified in her[38] actions. She will blame the victim as having provoked the situation and as such will experience herself as being victimised. She may claim an ideology as a justification for her acts and secretly feel satisfaction and pleasure in destruction and aggression. The feelings of power replace the more hidden feelings of powerlessness and helplessness of her trauma. In effect she is permanently splitting off and making unconscious her own victimisation and feelings connected with her trauma.

Where victim-perpetrator dynamics are involved the person will usually embody both, but will primarily display one more

---

[38] Most diagnosed psychopaths are male, but I decided to use the female generic here to alert us to this possibility. Too often we assume perpetration to be the domain of men.

than the other, and will always re-create these dynamics externally in relationships with others as well as internally in relation to themselves.

The traumatised bonding system

The consequences of the victim-perpetrator splitting are an oscillating, vicious cycle that tends to draw in all those who come into contact with these dynamics. It is extremely hard in relationship to avoid becoming part of these oscillating dynamics. As the dynamics escalate, more and more violent and extreme acts become part of the process, and are increasingly regarded as normal behaviour by those involved, which typifies the traumatised bonding system first mentioned in Section 1.3 above, item 4.

This category of traumatisation delineates an entire system over several generations where the only possible kind of relationship is based on victim-perpetrator acts and dynamics. The origins of this are usually lost in time but will have begun with some act of perpetration that is socially and culturally unacceptable, even criminal, involving extreme feelings of guilt and shame that are split off within the perpetrator-victim survival attitudes. What everyone avoids is their own trauma feelings. They adopt and develop the survival strategies of the system, which are those of the perpetrator-victim. Increasingly the actions within the family become more extreme, bizarre and harmful, dislocated and crazy, and often extremely dangerous. Such behaviours are denied to be harmful, even being regarded as normal and for the good of other family members. For example, violence, incest and sexual abuse become 'normal' behaviour within such a family, where the children grow up to expect such behaviour from others, and to behave towards others in similar ways. Traumatised bonding systems always harbour secrets, extreme illusions and delusions, and cannot tolerate the truth of reality. The pressure on family members to keep silent and persist in self and other destructive behaviours is massive; parent/child bonding requires it, life depends on it.

Those from a traumatised bonding system, both as children and adults, are drawn to others who come from similarly traumatised systems. There are strong feelings of guilt and shame, and a reluctance to mix with people who are not similarly entangled, and so those who marry will tend to marry others similarly entangled, and perpetuate the trauma and perpetrator-victim dynamics in their new family. It is extremely hard for those from such a family to make a different choice. It isn't impossible, and some people do find a way of breaking away, but usually through long therapy and many crises. At some point they will need to address the many traumas and the underlying attachment trauma that they are holding in order to integrate their splits.

The consequences
The consequences of victim-perpetrator splitting over several generations (via the symbiosis between mother and child, to be discussed in the next section) are the more severe personality disorders, psychoses, schizophrenia, dissociative identity disorder, any conditions with delusions, self-destructive behaviours (the internalising of the victim-perpetrator dynamics within the one person) even to the extent of suicide; chronic diseases; criminal behaviour, even murder; extreme behaviours towards others.

What are the solutions to this?
The illusionary attempts to resolve such dynamics usually involve revenge and rebellion, and 'forgiveness' and quasi-compassion. Forgiveness as such is not real, in that it is an attempt to take away the guilt and shame of (and so take care of) the perpetrator, which is impossible, and denies the perpetrator his need to acknowledge responsibility for his acts. The solution is in seeing and acknowledging the truth, not confusing reality by acts of 'forgiveness' and 'compassion'. The person must acknowledge the truth of their victimisation, not just by enacting the victim in a victim attitude, but by confronting their trauma and feeling the feel-

ings. The acts of perpetration need to be acknowledged by the victim. The feelings of guilt and shame need to be felt by the perpetrator, along with the acknowledgement of their own trauma. Ultimately the desire for revenge must be relinquished, since it only serves to perpetuate the dynamics, not resolve them.

1.6 Potential for Resolving Trauma

> "Is it possible, then, to free ourselves altogether from illusions?" *(Miller, 2012)*

The work of healing the split 'disintegrated' structure must be towards integration, and while this sounds simple in theory, in practice it is complex, and takes time and patience. In terms of the potential for integration there are two things to hold in view: one is that the whole process of splitting and the subsequent processes of living from one or other split is essentially unconscious, and so under most conditions is inaccessible to the person cognitively. The second is that the relationship between the self parts is complex and conflictual in itself:

- The healthy component seeks liberation and integration of the splits.
- The traumatised self seeks recognition, resolution and expression, an endeavour that is in tune with the healthy self, and in conflict with the survival self.
- The survival self's only function is the prevention of both these desires, by controlling and dominating the healthy self and the traumatised self, and keeping them apart. The survival self is always on the precipice and unconscious of anything else, always involved in surviving.

This fixed internal conflict is what used to be called 'resistance' and 'repression' in psychoanalytic theory (and still is by some therapists). Many a therapist has been caught in a clash of wills with their client, becoming entangled with the client's internal conflict, thence interpreting their client as 'resistant', an unfortunate, accusatory interpretation that risks a breakdown in the therapy relationship that is sometimes not recoverable.[39]

If the therapist understands the terrifying nature of trauma feelings, and the function of the survival self as a natural instinctual reaction to trauma, to a great extent he will be able to avoid such a situation. As a result I have developed a simple rule for myself: Never, ever, argue with the client. The argument posed by the client is usually energised by their survival needs, and if the client's survival self is active then the therapist knows that the client's anxiety is heightened, their trauma is re-triggered. The message from the client is clear: whatever it is, it is too much for the client for now. For the therapist to engage with such argument is likely to entangle him in the client's inner confused and conflicted process. This is particularly the case when victim-perpetrator dynamics are at play; it is incredibly easy for the therapist to be drawn into these dynamics and become entangled with the client's process, acting in a persecutory manner towards the client, and at the same time feeling victimised by the client. Of course it isn't easy to avoid such a situation because the forces at play are at times strong, but the therapist can remember: If the survival strategies of the client are activated, the client's trauma is re-stimulated, her trust in the therapist and the situation in that moment is diminished, and to try to go further is unlikely to be useful or possible.

---

[39] This is a primary psychotherapeutic process in relational therapies called 'rupture and repair', where the work of repairing the rupture in the relationship between therapist and client is seen as a fundamental part of the work of strengthening the relationship, and offering the client something that didn't exist in their childhood. A colleague did a doctoral research paper looking at clients' experiences of such ruptures, with a particular focus on those incidents that were not repaired, not dealt with and in some cases caused the person to leave the therapy. For some of those interviewed the incident still held painful memories some twenty years later (*Schmidt, 2012*, unpublished)

There is a repetitive nature to the stuck dynamics of the split self, what Freud called the "repetition compulsion" (Freud, 1922). The person is compulsively drawn to repeat the original trauma as a complex of the desire to heal and the desire to avoid; the confusion of safety in the familiar (what is actually the trauma situation), and the frightening risk of change. This can be explained as the tussle of the survival self's desire for safety within the familiar, which, when faced with the re-enacted terror, rebounds into a flurry of survival strategies, and the healthy self's desire for healing by re-visiting the trauma, its longing for re-connection and integration. Every psychotherapist with some experience knows that all clients come into therapy in an ambivalent state: part of them wants healing and resolution, and part is reluctant and reserved. This is exactly the healthy self/survival self conflict.

The survival strategies, as potentially destructive and life-limiting as they are, provide a thin protection between the person and these terrifying forces of trauma, and will only dissolve when the person feels safe enough with the therapist and with themselves. The experienced practitioner becomes efficient at distinguishing between when the client is relating from the healthy part of themselves and when from their survival self:

> "Without a willingness on the part of the survival self for the trauma to be processed, no real inner change can be possible."
> (*Ruppert, 2011*)

I am of the opinion that it is not to do with the "willingness" of the survival part so much as the strengthening and increase in influence of the healthy aspect of the client. Through understanding his trauma and the strategies involved in surviving it, by increased awareness as to which of his actions and feelings come from his healthy self and which from his survival self, the client becomes emboldened and encouraged, thereby diminishing the *need* for the survival self's services. In my view the survival self doesn't have the kind of rationality necessary, it is a reactive entity; but the healthy part does. The nature of trauma is that it confuses reality and truth for the victim, which makes it hard for him to trust himself and from here he has little basis for knowing if he can trust anyone else, including the therapist. As he becomes clearer, his trust in the therapist and the therapy increases, and correspondingly he is increasingly able to distinguish what he can trust in himself; he recognises and becomes familiar with those actions, thoughts and impulses that come from his healthy self and those that come from his survival mechanisms.

So the aims of healing trauma, exceedingly simplified, are as follows:

1. The disintegration of the fixed and hardened split structure of healthy, traumatised and survival parts, allowing for movement and better connection between the parts of the self; followed by
2. the integration of the split off trauma components through increased good contact between the self-parts.

This is a making conscious of the unconscious, and a re-structuring of the psyche of the client.

The ongoing process by which this happens involves the client in the following:

1. The strengthening and enlarging of the healthy structures of the client by . . .
2. an increased awareness of his survival strategies, how he dissociates, which in time allows . . .
3. the client increasingly to be more trusting of himself, and safely to get in touch with his trauma, and
4. increasingly to integrate his splits, thereby becoming more truly himself.

However, before we go further into the practice of this work, we need to consider attachment theory and the particular issues of symbiosis, symbiotic trauma and symbiotic entanglement.

2

Attachment

Introduction

> "In retrospect it seems obvious that species have evolved by
> natural selection, that people are attached to one another and
> suffer when they separate." *(Holmes, 1993)*

It is hard for us to understand what it must have been like for
Freud back in the final years of the 19th century and the early
20th century trying to understand the human psyche. It is easy
for us today to feel incredulous at some of the assumptions and
omissions. But even so it is important to understand that, as
much as some of our ideas today seem so completely obvious
and evident to us now, they have become obvious only because
of the accumulated knowledge developed through psychotherapeutic understandings. As the English psychoanalyst John
Bowlby, famed for his work on infant attachment, said in his
seminal paper 'The Nature of the Child's Tie to his Mother'
(1958):

> "... we cannot understand Freud's evolving views without
> tracing them historically. In reading his works we are at once
> struck by the fact that it was not until comparatively late that he
> appreciated the reality of the infant's close tie to his mother,
> and that it was only in his last ten years that he gave it the
> significance we should all give it today." *(Bowlby, 1958)*.

Bowlby believed that Freud's failure to recognise this early tie to the mother until very late in his life had "far-reaching effects on psychoanalytic theorizing" (ibid.). He quotes Freud (from *The Interpretation of Dreams*) as saying "When people are absent, children do not miss them with any great intensity, [which] many mothers have learnt to their sorrow",[40] expressing surprise that this passage remained unamended or qualified throughout later editions of the book.

Freud's thinking at the time was more oriented towards our sexuality as defining and motivating us. To think of a baby as being primarily influenced by sexual feelings is alien to current thinking. Freud did, in his later years, observe babies' dislike of being left alone, and later he discussed why children desire the presence of their mother and fear losing her (*Inhibitions, Symptoms and Anxiety*); and yet he seems never to have been able to move to understanding this connection as anything other than the child's fear of not having his needs gratified, even though he did see the separation as a cause of great tension "against which it [the baby] is helpless" (ibid.).[41] The child's fear of losing his mother is seen as a "displacement"; it isn't the mother herself that is lost, it is the gratifier of his (the child's) needs (ibid.).

Freud's final words about this relationship of the child with his mother have more in common with current thinking. They come within, as Bowlby puts it, a "pregnant but highly condensed paragraph", where he described it as "unique, without parallel, laid down unalterably for a whole lifetime, as the first and strongest love-object and as the prototype of all later love relations – for both sexes" (*An Outline of Psycho-Analysis, 1938*). I would absolutely agree with this, as we shall see.

---

[40] The actual quote is: "The fact that the child does not very intensely miss those who are absent has been realised, to her [the mother's] sorrow, by many a mother, when she has returned home from an absence of several weeks ..." (*Freud, 1931*)

[41] Within our working hypothesis when the word "helpless" appears, we can remember that helplessness is a defining feature of the potential for traumatisation.

Most followers of Freud continued to adhere to his Secondary Drive libidinal theory, seeing the mother/child relationship, as Anna Freud put it (1954), as no more than a 'convenience': "... the libidinal cathexis [of the child] ... is shown to be attached, not to the image of the object [mother], but to the blissful experience of satisfaction and relief [at having his needs met]" (Freud, A. 1954) However, it is in Anna Freud's writings that Bowlby detects the first instances of infant observation, and the understanding that the child's need "for early attachment to the mother [is]... an important instinctual need" (Freud, A. 1949)[42]

Other analysts of the time, such as Melanie Klein, seem to have been the conduit through which attachment theory could metamorphose into Bowlby's work. In his paper quoted above, Bowlby describes the inconsistency between the expressed theories of Klein at the time, for example, and her experiences from infant observations, where she witnessed young babies lying awake after feeding in their mothers' lap, looking at her, listening to her voice and responding to her with facial expressions – Anna Freud writes: "it was like a loving conversation between mother and baby". And then she writes: "Such behaviour implies that gratification is as much related to the object [mother] which gives the food as to the food itself." (Bowlby, 1958).

John Bowlby is generally considered the father of attachment theory. He trained as a psychologist and subsequently as a medical doctor. He studied psychoanalysis at the Institute for Psychoanalysis and at the same time trained in adult psychiatry. For a time he worked with maladapted and delinquent children, and became increasingly interested in the developing

[42] The Freudian focus on needs gratification seems to me to be the basis of the therapeutic notion of getting one's needs met as the primary focus and desirable outcome of therapy. The question then always being: by whom? Such a view continues to put the onus on 'out there' as the source of healing and wholeness, keeping the person a hostage to fortune so to speak, as we shall see when we look at symbiotic entanglement. The healing consists in the integration of the splits: a process of coming into contact with oneself, which is quite beyond 'need gratification'.

child. By the late 1950s he had accumulated a considerable body of research and observation that indicated to him the fundamental importance of the child's early attachment to his mother as influencing development. Bowlby was in analysis with the British psychoanalyst Joan Riviere, who was very close to and influenced by Melanie Klein, Bowlby's supervisor. As Bowlby developed his ideas about infant attachment and the relationship between the child and the mother, he came into considerable conflict with both Riviere and Klein, who considered his ideas irrelevant, and when he presented his groundbreaking paper, 'The Nature of the Child's tie to his Mother' (1958) in effect he was ostracised by his colleagues[43] (Holmes, 1993).

Attachment Theory

> "... unless there are powerful in-built responses which ensure that the infant evokes maternal care and remains in close proximity to his mother throughout the years of childhood he will die." *(Bowlby, 1958)*

Attachment theory as developed by Bowlby and others[44] is based on the understanding that there are powerful emotional forces at play between a child and his parents, particularly the mother. Attachment is crucial for the survival of the child. For Bowlby attachment was rooted in the biological programming of the child to seek proximity with the parent (Bowlby, 1969, 1973, 1980).

Bowlby understood that the human child is more helpless than its nearest relatives, the primates, which are born with an active clinging response enabling them to clutch onto their mother's skin and fur immediately. The more extreme help-

---

[43] Shades of Freud's fate on presenting his paper on childhood sexual abuse in the late nineteenth century.

[44] Notably Mary Ainsworth who amongst much other invaluable work developed the 'strange situation' experiment of mother and child observation, and Mary Main who introduced the fourth crucial form of attachment disorder: 'disorganised attachment'.

lessness in the human child makes the likelihood of symbiotic trauma for the child much more acute. The human child is completely and utterly helpless in those first few weeks... all he can do is cry and suck, and he can only suck if given something to suck. He cannot hold onto his mother and cannot, as many animals can, follow the mother.

Attachment behaviour, which is the diagnostic means in attachment theory, is seen as triggered by any physical separation of the child from the mother. What is observed in the behaviour of the child during and after a brief separation from his mother is then initially categorised as 'secure' or 'insecure' attachment. Typically a child with a generally 'secure' attachment can tolerate short separation from the mother and re-connect with her joyfully and happily when she reappears. A child with an 'insecure' attachment when separated from his mother, even briefly, will exhibit behaviours that range from distress and/or anger to disinterest or wariness. He may also show behaviour that we would consider distinctly trauma-like, such as high stress, freezing and dissociation. On reunion with the mother the child may ignore her, be watchfully on edge, seek contact but then resist, sometimes with violence, oscillating between anger and clinging.

Eventually the 'secure'-'insecure' categorisations were further distinguished as follows:[45]

- **Secure attachment** – a child with a secure sense of attachment may or may not be distressed when separated from his mother. When reunited with her, however, he will go to her, receive comfort if necessary and then return to his play.
- **Insecure-Avoidant** – this child will often not show many signs of distress on separation, but may ignore the mother on reunion, particularly if the separation occurs a few times. He is likely to be watchful and less spontaneously playful.

---

[45] There are different versions of the insecure categorisations, for example Anxious-Resistant, Anxious-Avoidant.

- **Insecure-Ambivalent** – this child will be very distressed when separated and is not easily comforted on reunion. He wants contact with his mother, but then may resist, sometimes with violence. He will move between anger and clinging behaviour, and often will not play.
- **Insecure-Disorganised** – This categorisation was added subsequently by Mary Main (Main & Solomon, 1990), and is a typical double-bind oscillating situation, where the parent is seen by the child as both a source of safety and a source of harm or anxiety. Main described this as "fear without solution" (ibid.).

It is impossible to overstate the contribution made by Bowlby and his followers in helping us towards an understanding today of these early stages of life. However, it is also important to realise that, as the neuro-psychologist Allan Schore states "Bowlby's original descriptions occurred during a period of behaviorism and included an emphasis on . . . secure base behaviors, which [subsequently] gave way to the dominance of cognition . . ." (Schore, 2012). In other words early attachment theory was based on behavioural observations and the interpretations made, and developed into a dominance of the cognitive and behavioural therapies as the means of treatment. Schore goes on to state that with our current advances in neurobiology "we now have a deeper understanding of how and why the early social environment [the home and family] influences all later adaptive functions." And further: "the individual['s] development arises out of the relationship between the brain, mind and body of both infant and caregiver held within a culture and environment that either supports, inhibits, or even threatens it" (ibid.).

Additionally it is important to include the fact that the behavioural observations were of the physical separation of the child from the mother. This does not take into consideration, or make any assessment of, the impact of the implicit separation from the child of a psychologically distracted or dissociated mother, which, while not a physical absence, is, for the child, a psychological and emotional absence.

Most mainstream psychotherapy disciplines today include a theory of child development in their general thinking and curriculum, primarily based on the original work of Bowlby and others, but also increasingly including more recent neurobiological developments of what is coming to be known as modern attachment theory.

3

Symbiotic Trauma and Symbiotic Entanglement

Introduction

> "Many souls in their young nudity are tumbled out among
> incongruities and left to 'find their feet' among them,
> while their elders go about their business."
> *George Eliot, Middlemarch, 1874*

Symbiotic trauma is the trauma of the early symbiosis between child and mother. It is the personal trauma the child experiences when the attachment process between mother and child is severely interrupted. Although the attachment theorists understood the potentially devastating longterm effects of early attachment as a *disorder*, which they would at times describe as having traumatic effects, I think they underestimated the potential for the attachment itself to be traumatic.[46] As we explore symbiosis and symbiotic trauma further perhaps this notion will become clearer.

With the emergence through the neurosciences of evidence of detailed brain system activity in utero, and a more in depth understanding of the nature/nurture, genetic/environmental relationship, this is changing, and the notion of attachment as

---

[46] I quite frequently work with clients who would be designated as having secure attachment under attachment theory, but even so appear to have an attachment trauma.

potentially a trauma is becoming much more of a focus (Schore, 2012).[47]

The question here is: what is the nature of a trauma that occurs in the earliest moments of life, in the womb or in the first months after birth, and what is its impact as we grow and develop? First we need to look at what we mean by symbiosis and its relationship with autonomy.

3.1 Symbiosis and Autonomy

"... Over and over again a violent struggle rages between these two basic aspirations ... the very fabric of the drama of human existence." *(Ruppert, 2012)*

The term symbiosis originated within the field of biology and covered the ways in which organisms relate and live together to some advantage. Ruppert's latest book in English, *Symbiosis and Autonomy* (Ruppert, 2012), gives a detailed account of the symbiotic nature of everything in life and on the planet, including humans; symbiosis as "an evolutionary principle" (ibid.).

The word 'symbiosis' comes from the Greek word meaning 'living together' and there are different types of biological symbiosis which broadly speaking cover:

- Mutualism – where both organisms benefit
- Commensalism – where one organism benefits and the other, while not benefitting, is not harmed
- Parasitism – where one organism benefits, and harms, or even kills, the other.

---

[47] Schore talks interchangeably of 'disorganised attachment' and 'attachment trauma'. However within attachment theory 'disorganised attachment' is the most serious designation and in my view does not allow for the possibility that even those with 'secure attachment' may have a symbiotic trauma. (See previous footnote.)

While symbiosis seems to have received less attention from evolutionary theorists than other interactions such as predation or competition, it is becoming increasingly recognised as an important selective force behind evolution, with many species having a long history of a symbiotic interdependent co-evolution.

The notion of 'interdependent co-evolution' involves several or many species existing within the same ecosystem, in some way contributing to and/or benefitting from the overall dynamic symbiosis, at the same time affecting, and changing the environment in which they live. In some studies of large ecosystems there are many, sometimes thousands of intricate ultimately beneficial relationships that work consistently towards a dynamic equilibrium. And we human beings are as much a part of this as anything else: we simply cannot *not* live in symbiosis; there is no life-form that is not in some kind of symbiosis.

Ruppert looks at the transfer of the term 'symbiosis' from the field of biology to the field of psychology, and discusses the different perspectives taken by several people[48] in adopting this term. However, Ruppert criticizes these perspectives as not "measuring up to the far-reaching meaning of 'symbiosis' as an evolutionary principle, which has a fundamental meaning for the existence of us humans and our co-existence" (Ruppert, 2012).

The main reason for this is that most discussions of symbiosis within the psychological field refer either to the symbiotic relationship between mother and the newborn child only, or to the kind of merged adult relationship between two people where the autonomy of one or both is severely restricted: both people talk and think of themselves as 'we' rather than upholding their individuality. Ruppert, however, is looking at symbiosis as "a permanent challenge of how we get along with other humans and other creatures and all life on the planet, and how these intertwined life-concerns are reflected emotionally in each one of us" (ibid.).

---

[48] Erich Fromm, Margaret Mahler and Martin Dornes.

So symbiosis as Ruppert uses it, and I am using it here, covers two interrelated meanings:

1. The first is that period of our lives when we are not physically, emotionally or psychologically separate from another being, our mother, and to a lesser extent, our father. This, for the baby, is a state of dependence on the life and living of another, where we have no choice as to the nature and psycho-physiological state of that other living being.

2. The second is a more general understanding of the state of existence as being always in dynamic tension between our symbiotic interdependence – our need for relationship with others, with the world and our environment – and our autonomy, our separateness, individuality and uniqueness. These two poles of existence, symbiosis and autonomy, are always in a dynamic interplay, with one or other being more figural while its partner is more in the background. In fact our autonomic and our symbiotic existence may at times oscillate from figure to ground and back quite rapidly. We can see this dynamic interplay represented well in the yin yang symbol (below), where the black (let's say autonomy) begins small and then moves to take the major space, but always with the seed of its opposite (symbiosis) within, which in turn will also then grow and take the major space and so on.

Figure 4. Yin Yang symbol

Another way of seeing this is in this infinity diagram:

Figure 5. Relationship between Autonomy and Symbiosis

"The paradox between separateness and union can [only] be temporarily bridged where and when the walls of individuality remain strong enough to hold the sense of self together, yet permeable enough to allow the sense of what is other to be experienced." *(Stevenson, 2004)*

Our whole life is played out between these two poles of existence and their constant interchange. Autonomy is our ability to make independent choices, to be 'self-governing', self-responsible and self-authoring of our lives, and yet this must always take place within the context of our symbiotic existence and need for relationship and interdependent co-evolution, just as all of our relating and interdependence can never be a perfect merging since we are also always separate, and as such, alone. So our autonomy and independence are always functioning within a context of interdependent symbiosis. We are never completely separate and we are never completely merged. We can never be fully autonomous because we are also interdependent, and we can never be fully interdependent because we are also autonomous beings. We can only ever make autonomous decisions within an interdependent framework, and we can only ever be part of collective decisions within an autonomous reality.

In a healthy dynamic interplay between symbiosis and autonomy there is a feeling of freedom and flowing between and within each, a clarity of purpose and ethics. This last is very important, because the danger in group situations is that we lose connection with our autonomy and agree to group decisions that may go against our autonomous beliefs and ethics. This idea is in common with Hellinger's ideas about belonging and conscience, as I described in my previous book (Broughton, 2010 Chapter 1). The force of our need to belong will at times invoke compromise with our autonomy. This is particularly so if we have experienced an early trauma in our symbiotic relationship with our mother, because then our need to belong, to attempt to gain what we never had, dominates our life at the expense of our autonomy.

Extremes of Symbiosis and Autonomy

While in reality we can see that there can be no such thing as absolute autonomy or absolute symbiosis it is worth looking at such polarities in order to complete our understanding of these concepts. Both involve a high degree of dissociation and delusion. Extreme (psychopathological) 'autonomy' would be psychopathic tyranny, where others are not permitted any kind of meaningful autonomous existence and the reality of life is denied. This extreme existence is psychopathic and sadistic, and is only possible in a highly traumatised person for whom empathy with others is impossible, because all access to meaningful emotions and feelings has been split off. Of course, this is not real autonomy, because real autonomy must always include and acknowledge symbiosis.

Extreme symbiosis, apart from our initial state after

conception, would be the total giving up of one's individuality, a kind of complete slavery to another, and is also delusional and a denial of reality. The two exist in a sadomasochistic complementarity.

Trauma and Autonomy

If we hold that 'life-threat' is a defining feature of relational trauma, then in the trauma event another person holds my life in his or her hands, and I am helpless and without choice. The balance and oscillation of autonomy and interdependence then is likely to be destroyed, and as an early life event it has devastating implications for one's ability to mature into an autonomous adult. Trauma seriously affects our ability to be truly autonomous, as is evident in the case of very early attachment trauma.

Healthy Symbiosis

"Constructive symbiosis is beneficial to all involved. It promotes the development of everyone as far as is necessary and possible for the particular stage of . . . development [of each person]." *(Ruppert, 2012)*.

A good and healthy symbiosis between two people is first and foremost natural and supportive of evolutionary growth and creativity. It is rooted in a healthy and wholesome attachment process between mother and child, where the child does not experience the symbiosis with the mother as traumatic: any separation from the mother is tolerable because sufficient experience of her 'thereness' is established during the pregnancy and in the first moments, days and weeks of life. However, it is important to state that we do not know the point at which sufficient 'thereness' can be established for a separation not to invoke terror of death for the infant.

There is mutuality in the adult symbiosis, when it is creative and healthy, that does not require an unequal or burdening degree of compromise. All parties benefit and are able to fulfil their own creative and productive needs. Both can be fully present to each other without the shadow of past entangled relationships; they see each other clearly as they are, and without illusion, and are able and willing to be open about themselves. Both people are able to express their feelings authentically as appropriate to the present situation, and both are able to value their own and the other's separate autonomous existence. Any disputes or difficulties between people in a healthy symbiosis are open to discussion in an environment where both people feel heard, valued and understood, and take place fully in the present with a minimal shadow of past entanglements. Both people see each other as they are, not confused with people and situations from the past, and in this way disputes can find resolution.

Entangled Symbiosis

The word 'entangled' here means a confused and unclear connection as opposed to an autonomous clarity of one's relationship to another. Entangled symbiosis originates from the symbiotic trauma of the child, confused by entanglement[49] with the mother's and/or father's unresolved traumas, and even those traumas of the family with which the mother or father are themselves entangled from previous generations. The result is an inability to develop autonomously, and a persistent legacy of unresolved trauma and entangled, confused and confusing relationships that never satisfy the primal need for good, healthy loving connection. Since the original attachment process was traumatic, the child does not have the support and framework to develop independently, and stays helplessly entangled with the mother and/or father, constantly yearning for the satisfying relationship that he never could have, and projecting this early entangled relationship onto all later relationships.

---

[49] The New Oxford American Dictionary defines 'entanglement' as 'A complicated or compromising relationship or situation' (*New Oxford American Dictionary*).

As discussed above in the section on splitting in the face of trauma, the psychological structure after a symbiotic trauma is reified: stuck and resistant to real change. Since unresolved trauma underlies the whole sense of being, relationships are confused by survival strategies and illusions ("this time I will get the right relationship, this time it will be different"). Entangled symbiotic relationships are dogged by projections, with the other person rarely seen for who he or she actually is, but confused with important figures from the early bonding process. Intimacy is terrifying because it always re-stimulates the trauma feelings, which sets in train the defensive survival strategies. We shall discuss this more later.

True Autonomy

> "True autonomy ... means saying an unconditional 'yes' to oneself and to the reality of one's own life... taking full responsibility for living it, whatever may have happened in the past." *(Ruppert, 2012)*

The word 'autonomy' is from the Greek, meaning 'self government', in other words the capacity of a rational individual to make informed and un-coerced decisions and choices for him or herself.

> "In relationships based on dependence and subjugation, it is difficult to develop this form of autonomy and assert 'one's own law' against the demands and pressures of others." *(Ruppert, 2012)*

True autonomy requires clarity of thought, an ability to be in touch with reality as it is, including the fact that everything in one's life is not always as one would wish it to be. It is in effect within the domain of the healthy aspect of the self, rather than the survival aspect. The survival self cannot act autonomously, since its nature is reactive and unthinking, and it comes into being in the original trauma situation and re-emerges at any later time of re-stimulation. Any reactive action is by definition not an autonomous act, even if life-saving.

The healthy aspect of the self is likely to be able to act with autonomy, but only insofar as it is able to be independent of the survival component at any particular time.

"Saying an unconditional 'yes' to oneself" (above) means seeing clearly and accepting the things about oneself that one cannot change, but also not hiding behind certain things about oneself by saying "I can't change this or that", when that is not true. Something similar goes for our partner. It is a very common occurrence that when two people come together and decide to live together, to make a permanent life together, that once they do so they begin to see the things that are less acceptable about the other, and often set about subtly to change him or her. This takes the place of being able to see the person clearly for who they are, and often involves whatever is unresolved in our own background influencing our ability to be in relationship in the present.

Pseudo Autonomy

Everything we are and do in life can be in the service of health or in the service of survival, and so we can develop a survival self that looks autonomous but is not. Even autonomy can be distorted into a survival strategy. For example, a high-ranking corporate figure may appear autonomous, and will be insofar as his autonomous behaviour is not operating to protect him from his trauma. But his position and authority may operate as a primary means of keeping him from connection and intimacy, as those situations are more likely to take him close to his unresolved trauma. Many a successful business person or politician may have become successful precisely as a means of unconscious protection from trauma, just as much as the person addicted to drugs or alcohol may take drugs or drink to dull the senses and keep the trauma unconscious.

3.2 Symbiosis of the Infant Child

The symbiosis of the human child (as with all mammals) starts at conception – or maybe even before. Often the constellations I have been a part of in my work go to foetal trauma, and over recent months I have facilitated a few constellations that have spontaneously introduced the concept of the damaged or traumatised pre-fertilised egg. Since all female babies are born with the full complement of eggs for their life, all of which develop within the foetus fairly early on in gestation, we have an intriguing situation: the potential for the next generation is already within the pre-fertilised egg. The question I am left with after such a constellation is: when exactly then does consciousness start? I don't have an answer, but I remain open to see what happens next.

Within the womb the symbiosis between child and mother is at its most intense and merged. The child grows within the body of the mother in a symbiotic relationship. Certainly the survival of the foetus depends entirely on the survival of the mother, although the survival of the mother does not depend on the survival of the child. However, there are usually benefits for the mother, particularly if she wants the baby; and in terms of evolution and survival of the species, there are definite advantages to the symbiotic relationship.

It is possible (and I think likely) that we are affected to an extent by everything that goes on around us from the moment we are conceived. The first nine months of our life are spent inside the body of another person, our mother. We do not yet know exactly what this means for the child. During this time the child is not separate from the mother; the child eats what the mother eats and drinks what she drinks. If she smokes, the child is affected. If she exercises, the child exercises. If she is stressed, the child is stressed. If she feels love, it is likely the child feels love, and just as much if she feels anxiety or suppressed terror then the child is also likely to feel these feelings. The baby's whole nervous system is not separate from her nervous system; and his metabolism is not separate from her metabolism. These are the basic conditions for what we call 'symbiotic entanglement', which in effect means entanglement with the psychological and emotional state of the mother, including her own psychological splits and any unresolved traumas from others with whom she is entangled.

It has always intrigued me how easily we accept that we may have the same physical structure and features as a grandmother; that we may even have a tendency to the same illnesses and physical vulnerabilities as our grandmother, and yet we seem reluctant to accept the idea that we may also inherit psychological and emotional similarities, and may have the same tendency to grief or despair, loneliness or sadness. The notion that something like schizophrenia or depression may be inheritable is generally accepted within the thinking of genetics, but that such an inheritance might be due to an emotional and psychological entanglement is not considered. The less severe and more subtle emotional and psychological characteristics of others in our family are not generally considered inheritable. If the foetus is not separate from the mother as outlined above, how can we possibly say that it is not affected by the mother's emotional state, both conscious and unconscious?

So if the mother has suffered trauma herself, perhaps a symbiotic trauma in relation to her own attachment with her mother, according to our theory, she is likely to be psychologically split, with the trauma feelings split off into her unconscious. What, we have to ask, might the effect of this be on the unborn child?

> "A mother's tangible fears and grief are reproduced in the sensitive structures of the child's body during pregnancy, which is why some children are born fearful, clinging to their mother and not wanting to be alone." *(Ruppert, 2012)*

Within the field of interpersonal neurobiology[50] it is now well established that the right, more emotionally oriented, brain of

---

[50] The term generally used to cover the field of interdisciplinary study of human relationships using clinical evidence from the neurosciences and other sciences, eg anthropology, physics, psychiatry, developmental psychology.

the infant develops earlier than the left, more rational, literal, calculating and categorising brain, and that the main communication between mothers and babies is known as a "right-brain-to-right-brain" communication. It is thought that this is why mothers are much more likely to hold their baby with the baby's head to the left, in her left arm, thereby giving the baby closer access to the mother's left face side which accesses the right brain (Schore, 2012a). It is also reasonably understood that those children who are held by their mothers to the right (giving child access to the mother's right face side – left brain) are more likely to have developed an attachment disorder. "The role of the right [brain] hemisphere is crucial in relation to the most precious needs of mothers and infants" (Sieratzki & Woll, 1996 in Schore, 2012).

Since the baby's right brain develops earlier and faster than the left (Schore, 2012, Schutz, 2005, Price, 2005), the initial communication between mother and child is pure emotional and physical resonance, devoid of literalism, thought and explicit (recallable) memory. So we could say that this early communication held on the emotional level cannot resist or avoid the emotional splits in the mother. In fact the child's survival depends on this connection, even if it is a connection with the mother's unconscious terror and split psyche.

So the child's symbiosis with the mother works in two ways: on the one hand the child passively absorbs, we could even say copies as a psychological imprint, the mother's psychological state, and on the other the child actively tries to adapt to and support the mother. For the child's survival he needs his mother to survive, and as helplessly as he absorbs her psyche, he is as active as he can be in trying to ensure his mother's survival by adapting to her needs, compromising himself and his needs as much as he can. Infant observation has drawn attention to the newborn infant's active attempts to interact with his mother, but, as Ruppert points out, this does not take into consideration "how the psychological development of the child is dependent on the psychological state of his parent" (Ruppert, 2012, p.27).

While an understanding of the emotional effect of the mother's state on the child is included in modern attachment theory, it is usually only discussed in cases of severe neglect or abuse of the child, as an explanation of the mother's behaviour towards her child. The mother's effect on the child is seen more at the level of her behaviour – neglect and abuse – and the mother's psychological state and history are seen as the explanation: it is understood that a mother will only behave in a neglectful and abusive manner if she is somewhat disturbed herself. But we may have a mother who manages to behave reasonably well under observation with her child, but who even so, under the surface is struggling with her own trauma splits. Here is a case example that demonstrates some of the complexity at play:

> Sarah was having a difficult time with her relationship with her twenty-one year old daughter, who alternately moved warmly towards her mother and then would do or say something spiteful that hurt Sarah and increased the separation between them. In the constellations session Sarah started to talk about how, when her daughter was born, she had an experience of leaving herself, as if she had lost a part of herself in that moment. Subsequent to this she had no feelings for her daughter, and felt no connection with her. For ten days her daughter was quiet and Sarah did the necessary things, but without feelings for her daughter. On the tenth day her daughter started to cry, and according to Sarah she cried virtually non-stop for 6 months, after which she developed many behaviours to keep her mother's attention. Over the subsequent years they developed an intense and absorbed relationship, that also became increasingly problematic and destructive.
>
> It also emerged that Sarah's own early attachment to her mother was disastrous; her mother was completely psychologically absent and quite disturbed, and Sarah said she had felt as though she lived in a constant state of stress and trauma where fight, flight and freezing were her main survival strategies. It then became clear to her that the birth of her daughter had re-stimulated her earlier attachment trauma, causing her to split again,

losing part of herself. The entanglement was a question of who was she looking for when she looked into the eyes of her daughter: the lost part of herself, or her own absent mother, or a combination of both? The outcome of the constellation was an understanding that in order to have a better relationship with her daughter she had to look at her own internal splits through subsequent constellations, and that her daughter was also split as a result of her attachment trauma with Sarah.

I agree with Ruppert's view that *all* disruptions of the connection between mother and child, in utero or postpartum, particularly in the case of a child born of a traumatised mother, are likely to be traumatic for the infant, since they initiate experiences of life-under-threat, a severe disruption to his sense of safety. The attachment theorists talked of the attachment process for the child with the mother or 'other important caregiver', as if someone could easily stand in for the mother without that having severe consequences for the child. This seems to me to fall short of an appreciation of the potential trauma for the child of any separation from his mother.

Even people diagnosed as having 'secure attachment', what is generally termed as healthy, 'good-enough' mothering (Winnicott, 1977, 2000), people who to the outside observer are managing their lives reasonably well, in my experience are usually harbouring some kind of attachment trauma that to a degree inhibits and disrupts their ability to be fully present in relationships and effective in their lives. It is true that for many, the compromises incurred are manageable, often unconscious and not fully seen by the person themselves; and even if seen, often the compromise is perceived by the person as preferable to the business of resolving their difficulties. There is a sense in many of us that there is a dark area of ourselves that we think best not to disturb, where fear and shame and guilt may reside, and so it is usual to steer clear of this unless our situation becomes such that we can no longer avoid it. However, my experience generally of working with these issues is that for most people the journey to resolve these deeper issues is far less frightening than the anticipation of it.

In the constellations that I have participated in that have gone back to in utero dynamics, it is common that the person involved has had a persistent feeling of danger in their lives, often combined with a sense of not being fully alive, or of continually feeling on a knife edge between life and death, sometimes accompanied by suicidal fantasies. If we consider what it might be like for a foetus, growing in the body of another human being who is living with unresolved feelings of terror from some trauma of her own, perhaps even her own attachment trauma from her early bonding with her mother, we may understand the sense of threat to the unborn child. This may help us understand better the many psychological challenges our clients have.

Another phenomenon that sometimes occurs in constellations that venture to the foetal stage is that death, as an option in the face of intolerable psychological and emotional entanglement with the mother, is often not experienced as frightening, but simply as an option. Living is what becomes a trauma and requires splitting.

Many pregnancies start out as twin pregnancies, but end up as single births. This is known as 'vanishing twin' syndrome (Landy and Keith, 1998). The dead twin is usually reabsorbed in these cases unless it reaches the second or third trimester in which case it can become a danger to the surviving twin due to the risk of infection, premature labour and haemorrhaging. These deaths are explained as due to competition for space and nutrition, placental deficiencies and other unknown factors (Sulak & Dodson, 1986). My question is whether one of the 'unknown factors' might have some connection to the psychological state of the mother as being experienced as intolerable.

An additional issue I have seen is where the client's twin did not survive, and the client feels a form of survivor's guilt. In one case the person felt that his survival was dependent on the death of his twin, that he absorbed the twin and became stronger and more sure of survival as a result. The medical evidence is that early foetal death does result in reabsorption of the foetus, whereas later foetal death is more likely to result in miscarriage.

3.3 Birth

Birth is a particular issue that often involves a trauma of its own. When we are born we take a gigantic step towards individuation and separation. In a natural birth, so far as I can ascertain, it is still unclear as to how the birth process is triggered. Of course there is a release of hormones (most prominently oxytocin, known as the "bonding hormone"), but what initiates this process? In my view it is likely to be a symbiotic 'decision' between the baby and his mother, perhaps even more the baby's than the mother's. In any event since this is perhaps the child's first act that we could consider a step of autonomy, it seems to me that it would be crucial to leave it in the hands of the baby as much as we can. It is interesting to speculate on how much a caesarean birth, that robs us of this first momentous decision, may affect our later ability to be autonomous and make good decisions for ourselves.

Due to the size of our highly developed brain, which is larger in relation to our size than any other animal's, our skull is also larger in relation to our body than in any other mammal. "Women know from experience that pushing a baby through the birth canal is not an easy task. It's the price we pay for our large brains and intelligence; humans have exceptionally big heads relative to the size of their bodies. . . for humans this tight squeeze is complicated by the birth canal's not being a constant shape" (Rosenberg & Trevathean, 2006). The shape of the human birth canal is not as direct as it is in apes, and is thought to have evolved in this way due to our ability to stand upright. Human birth is a precarious business since the baby's head needs to be fairly exactly aligned to get through the mother's pelvic girdle, and then the baby has to twist in order to follow the birth canal. Even though the baby's skull is soft and malleable to a degree, it is also easily damaged, and still has to pass through the pelvic opening at just the right time.

The human mother apparently suffers more in childbirth than any other animal because of this, and is much more likely to need assistance (ibid.).[51] The human baby is born prematurely by comparison with all other mammals, and so is much more vulnerable. This was understood by John Bowlby from his knowledge of contemporary ethology:

> "Perhaps largely as an adaptation required by his large head, in comparison to other Primates the human infant is born in a relatively immature state. Neither his clinging response nor his following response are yet effective. Indeed, apart from sucking, the only effective mother-related response available to the newborn human infant appears to be crying." *(Bowlby, 1958)*

The human baby can do less after birth for longer than any other mammals, which are able to move about, walk and find their mother's teat fairly soon after birth. They need to do so for their survival; fragile and wobbly young mammals and birds are easy food for predators, and so must develop as quickly as possible to be able to keep up with the herd, stay close to the protection of the mother and learn how to survive quickly. The human child is more vulnerable and helpless than any other mammal, and apart from the possibility of trauma having occurred in utero, the critical time between birth and roughly two years old is the time when symbiotic trauma is most likely.

Apart from these issues, it is not unusual for the birth process to have been traumatic for the child for different reasons: the cord around the baby's neck; being the wrong way round; the mother having a very long and painful labour; the child having to be delivered with forceps; drugs and medication given to the mother; the mother's panic or anxiety; and the near death of the child for other reasons. Often the birth is a traumatic experience for the mother, and may re-trigger her own birth experience and trauma of attachment with her mother. As much as during the pregnancy, the emotional state of the child must to some degree resonate with, and be

---

[51] It is possible that the more we have caesarean births to avoid this difficulty, the less the female pelvis will evolve in tandem with the human skull growth, and we may in future be stuck with caesarean sections in order to give birth.

impacted by, the emotional state of the mother during birth. If the child has to be put into an incubator or separated from the mother for any reason at all, this is likely to incur a trauma of attachment for the child, even though the action taken keeps him alive.

Some constellations that I facilitate go spontaneously back to birth trauma, sometimes clearly indicating difficulties with the birth that the client did not consciously know about but is sometimes able to corroborate later. I have experiences of many constellations where the representative for the client's 'intention'[52] goes into a state of tonic immobility, or listless disinterest, lying on the ground and reporting experiences of feeling held in suspension, of there being a fog or mist between them and the client. Often these constellations revolve around the experience of near death. It is as though a part of the client 'died' and has remained in a deathlike catatonia ever since. The resurrection of this part of the self involves a process of the client finding in themselves the part of them that holds the will to live, often a process that brings them sharply into contact with how much they have actually wished to die, perhaps having had suicidal fantasies. It is interesting to speculate on what the general effects may be of our customs surrounding childbirth from the 1940s to the 1960s and even to some extent in the 1970s, when it was common for children, once born, to be taken from the mother and put in a crib in a children's ward. This was done with perfectly healthy children as well as those who needed special care.

---

[52] This refers to the form of constellation we use to work with the intra-psychic splits resulting from trauma. (See Chapter 7.)

3.4 The Needs of the Newborn Child

The needs of the new born child are simple but crucial for his survival. They are:

- Nourishment: preferably the mother's milk as the perfect bonding activity and sustenance;
- Physical contact: warmth and metabolic regulation through limbic resonance[53] with the mother;
- Emotional contact: love and emotional regulation through limbic resonance with the mother;
- Safety and protection.

Without any one of these needs being met the experience for the baby may be of his life being under threat; all are inter-linked and equally crucial to the wellbeing of the child, and without one the child may fear for his survival, and perhaps even actually die. Rene Spitz (a psychoanalyst of the 1940s), describing the fate of orphaned children reared in foundling homes and institutions, as well as babies separated from their mothers in prison, found that even though fed, clothed and kept warm "they inevitably became withdrawn and sickly, and lost weight. A great many died." (Lewis, Amini & Lannon, 2001) "Spitz had rediscovered that a lack of human interaction – handling, cooing, stroking, baby talk, and play – is fatal to infants" (ibid.).

---

[53] It is now established knowledge within the field of neuroscience that, quite apart from the emotional benefit of bonding, at the beginning of life the child is unable to regulate his internal metabolic processes and relies on the mother's regulatory processes through the resonance and regulation provided by the limbic brain system. This means that without sufficient connection with an adult (whose regulatory system is established) the child literally will die. (*Lewis, Amini and Lannon, 2001*, and *McGilchrist, 2010*)

3.5 The Traumatised Mother

"But mother is our first love affair. Her arms. Her eyes. Her
  breast. Her body." *(Winterson, 2010)*

The commonest cause of symbiotic trauma for the child is
when the mother herself is traumatised, and here we move into
the transgenerational aspect of traumatisation and the understanding of symbiotic entanglement. If the mother has suffered
a trauma herself in her life, particularly if related to her own
early attachment with her mother, she may be psychologically
split and there are likely consequences for both child and
mother:

- The first emotional and psychological imprint on the
  child's psyche from within the womb will be the psyche
  of the mother, which to some degree is likely to be replicated in the child. He cannot *not* connect with his mother
  in this way just as, because the mother's trauma is unconscious, she cannot protect her child from her own split
  traumatised psychological state.
- When the mother feels love for her child, her split off
  trauma feelings of terror/grief/rage are likely to surface
  in her as well, usually in a suppressed form experienced
  by the mother as anxiety or panic. When we feel one
  emotion, for example love, the gateway is opened for any
  other feelings that are pressing for expression and resolution to arise. In this moment she may helplessly
  dissociate, suppress all feelings, experiencing instead
  anxiety or panic, and withdraw from the child. Over time
  intimacy with her child increasingly becomes a potential
  retraumatisation for the mother, stimulating her dissociative survival strategies, which interrupt good connection
  between child and mother.
- When the mother withdraws or dissociates the child experiences the mother's panic as his own and experiences her
  dissociation as abandonment. As a client expressed to me,
  this experience is like "flailing about for a life jacket that

turns out not to be there", and the child is likely to experience despair and desolation, and fear for his life.
- Eventually the child paradoxically may become the source of terror for the mother, and the mother the source of anxiety for the child, thus creating confusion and increased entanglement with the mother's own confused and unresolved split psyche.

This situation then is likely to set up an existential paradox for the child. He experiences:

- fear *for* his mother, because he feels love and need of her love and protection;
- fear *of* his mother, because she rejects him and is a source of anxious feelings;
- desire to *take care* of his mother, to protect her in order to help him feel safe;
- desire to *stay away* from his mother, to protect himself because he doesn't feel safe with her. (Ruppert, lecture 2010)

This results in what I call 'the child's dilemma':

> "I want to get close to my mother and yet when I try and do that I see/sense this terrifies her, and so in order to protect her I must stay away. But when I stay away from her this is very painful and frightening for me and I fear I might die."

Already here we can see the potential for the onset of an oscillating relationship style for the child. The connection with his mother is vital under any circumstances, and he will do whatever is necessary to maintain contact and connection with the mother. For the child the deep bond of connection may actually be a bond with terror, panic and anxiety, and as he grows he may actually seek situations and connections that involve terror and anxiety, because it feels safer than real love. Paradoxically love feels terrifying and terror feels to a degree 'safe'. The cost of survival is sometimes massive, and may have unavoidable implications for the child's development and maturation.

The result of these dynamics is very confusing for the child, and for the mother, and because the situation is unconscious and essentially unresolvable (without trauma psychotherapy, which the person must find for themselves as an adult), it leaves the child and mother helplessly entangled symbiotically, sometimes for the rest of their lives. The child is confused as to what his feelings really are, and what feelings he experiences really belong to his mother (or father or grandparents).

In order to stay in some kind of relationship with his mother the child may develop the following survival patterns:

1. He struggles all his life to be loved by his mother, not knowing what real love actually is.
2. He idealises his mother (he may oscillate between idealisation and demonisation).
3. He replicates her survival strategies, being confused in his survival with her survival.
4. He continually tries to save his mother from her suffering, which of course he cannot.
5. He ignores his own suffering and pain in favour of trying to relieve his mother and others of their pain.
6. He continually entangles with his mother's trauma and feels her trauma feelings as his own. (Ruppert 2012a)

In this way the child remains in an entangled symbiosis with his mother and cannot really distinguish who he is separate from her. His feelings are confused with hers (and others in the family through her); his permanent focus is on his mother's suffering at the expense of his own; his idea of who his mother is is confused, idealised and/or demonised; his idea of himself and all others in his adult life are also confused, sometimes also idealised and/or demonised. He replicates in himself his mother's psyche, all her survival strategies and her traumatised feelings, and cannot distinguish himself and his feelings from hers and others', and this influences all his later relationships.

3.6 Traumatised Fathers

The situation is different for fathers, in that the father's contact with the child comes later. In a sense it is the father's tragedy that the first contact of the child is always with the mother, beginning in the womb. The first contact with the father is not until the child is born at the earliest, and even then the bond between mother and child is so crucial for the survival of the child that the connection with the father is usually secondary. If circumstances require the father to take on the major parenting role, perhaps because the mother is ill or dies, this will entail a loss of connection with the mother for the child and so it would seem must result in a symbiotic trauma.

In some situations the child will turn to the father to find some kind of safety and acknowledgement, but this turning can only happen when the child is able to have that kind of contact with the father, must involve opportunity and is always founded on an early attachment trauma with the mother. Many people as children do find solace with the father in the face of a traumatised mother, but there is also the potential for danger here. We have to consider the fact that this man chose to be with the mother and ask questions such as: what do these two people find in each other that arises from their own attachment trauma? How do these two parents live out their own symbiosis issues with each other? In the situation where a child can find solace with the father the danger is that the father also finds solace with the child, that they become a unit in defence against a traumatised mother/wife, which has its own potential confusions and consequences. The relationship between father and child itself becomes a survival strategy for both father and child and may involve a confused intimacy, sometimes having sexual undertones or even overt sexual activity, particularly but not exclusively if the child is female.

The psychological state of the father does impact on the child, but if the child has had to turn to the father because of a severely traumatised mother, this will be a major impact on the child, entangling the child with the father's own unresolved traumas and entanglements from his family past.

3.7 Symbiotic Trauma and Symbiotic Entanglement

Symbiotic trauma then is the trauma of the early symbiosis between child and mother; it is the personal trauma that the child experiences when the attachment process between mother and child is severely interrupted either by the mother's death, or by adoption or the child having been given away, but primarily because the mother herself is traumatised and therefore emotionally unavailable for her child. Symbiotic trauma resulting from the mother being traumatised can never be separated from symbiotic entanglement, since the symbiotic trauma is caused by the mother having a split psyche herself, having suffered her own trauma, and thus the child's symbiotic trauma involves entanglement with the mother's split psyche.

Symbiotic Entanglement

Through the child's helpless confusion with his mother's traumatised split psyche, he is then entangled with whatever traumas the mother is confused with. One aspect of the mother's trauma, in addition to her own attachment trauma with her mother, may be her own confusion with other traumas that happened in her own mother's or father's life. For example, if the client's grandmother was raped or suffered violence at the hands of her husband, or suffered incest as a child with her father, the client's mother in her attachment process is likely to be entangled with these traumas of her mother. Our current client then, as part of her resolution of her own trauma, may have to look at some point at her own confusion with her grandmother's traumas. The continuing process of trauma resolution is a process of gaining clarity as to what feelings and traumas are really to do with the person, i.e. happened to him or her, and what feelings may in fact be the feelings of others with which he has become confused through the symbiosis.

Ruppert has proposed that the more serious mental diagnoses such as schizophrenia, psychosis, bi-polar disorder and chronic depression occur in people who are really suffering the after effects of traumas that didn't actually happen to them, but originated two, three, or even more, generations back, and have been exacerbated down the line over time, to a point where the connection is obscured but the dysfunction is serious (Ruppert, 2008). In other words, serious psychological problems have their roots in symbiotic entanglement. He has made tentative correlations between serious psychological disorders and the particular kind of trauma involved. For example, his view is that an existential trauma results in panic attacks and chronic anxiety; an unresolved loss trauma is likely to result in chronic depression over the generations; and a severe bonding or symbiotic trauma is likely to result in full-scale personality disorders. Schizophrenia he sees as coming from bonding system trauma where the confusion and secrecy, combined with unresolved guilt and shame prevalent in the family, and the perpetuation of perpetrator-victim dynamics as the accepted form of relational behaviour, make for an environment that is highly confused with survival tactics that at times have been so divorced from reality as to become psychotic and crazy.

If we see these ideas combined with a current professional approach that rarely considers asking questions about the client's family several generations back, doesn't hold a multi-generational perspective, and to a large extent has avoided the proper study of trauma, it is easy to understand why the cause of some of these conditions is still thought of as mysterious. We can also understand our fixation on chemical imbalances, DNA and genetic disorders and neurological disorders as causal explanations. This may be preferred, for many reasons, to seeing the connection between these conditions and unresolved trauma.[54]

3.8 Severe Childhood Abuse

> "Recurrent exposure to major stressors over time, such as
> child abuse, appears to have the most pernicious effects on
> survivors." *(van der Hart, Nijenhuis, Steele, 2006)*

In the section above (1.4 Effects of Different Types of Trauma) I put the symbiotic trauma as the most serious, since it is the earliest. Situations of ongoing and persistent child abuse, violence, neglect and sexual exploitation, have a devastating effect on the person, but will always also encompass a prior attachment trauma. Any family that contains any kind of such abusive behaviour and tendencies is likely to be a family of traumatised people, a traumatised bonding system, in which case the attachment process of the child must have been in itself traumatic.

Even if only one family member is obvious as the 'abuser', one has to question the psychological state of the whole family. Abuse in families is a systemic issue that it would seem must follow perpetrator-victim dynamics (see Chapter 1.5). Whether on the surface a family member can be identified as perpetrator or victim is not so much the issue; systemically everyone is a victim of trauma of some kind, even the overt perpetrator. The dynamics of such a family absorb everyone, even if there seems only one obvious perpetrator and one obvious victim, and the enactment is kept secret. In truth everyone is affected.

Working with clients who have suffered such severe and persistent traumatising abuse will follow the same course as I will describe in Part 2, in that the client is the authority for what trauma is addressed, when and how. In this way the therapist trusts and follows the natural healing course that the

---

[54] There is now scientific credence given to the fact that trauma alters the DNA expression which over a few generations can actually alter the DNA structure.

client exhibits, even though the client is unlikely to be able to say it directly. To the alerted therapist the symbiotic trauma and symbiotic entanglement will be evident throughout, and will show in therapeutic work that is apparently oriented towards the childhood abuse. Within all traumas one can see the seed of the symbiotic trauma.

4

Trauma, Attachment and The Brain System

"There is no real independent self, aloof from other human beings, inspecting the world, inspecting other people. You are, in fact, connected not just via Facebook and Internet, you're actually quite literally connected by your neurons." *V S Ramachandran*

I think it is helpful to our understanding of emotional bonding and of trauma, to look briefly at the human brain system. Additionally I will refer back to this chapter in the section on understanding how the constellations process works, and when we look at the formulation of the client's 'intention' as the preliminary necessity for setting up the constellation.

One of the most important discoveries within neuroscience in the past 12 or so years is the discovery of mirror neurones, which seem to show, amongst many other things, how we are able to understand and experience to some degree the experience of another. Sometimes called 'empathy neurones', the most exciting aspect of mirror neurones is exactly that: it plays an important role in our ability to be empathic, to know how another feels. Alongside this is a developing understanding of our ability to resonate with another through the limbic part of our brain. While the relationship between mirror neurones and limbic brain resonance is, as far as I can ascertain, unclear at this time, it would seem that there must be some relationship.

In addition there is also the discovery of the hormone oxytocin, also known as the 'bonding hormone'.

4.1 Mirror Neurones

> "We have all experienced moments in which we find
> ourselves moved – not because of what happened to us,
> but because of what happened to someone else."
> *(Keysers, 2011)*

Mirror neurones were first discovered and written about by the Italian neurophysiologists Giacomo Rizzolatti and Laila Craighero and their research group at Parma University in Italy (Rizzolatti, Fadiga, Fogassi and Gallese, 2002). They observed that neurones positioned in the frontal and parietal cortex of the brain of the macaque monkeys they were studying fired when a monkey performed an action, and that neurones in the same areas in an observing monkey's brain also fired (Rizzolatti & Craighero, 2004).

> "Mirror neurones are a means of understanding another's intentions, amongst other things, ... they form part of our capacity to understand others and empathise with them." *(McGilchrist, 2010)*

> "The mirror system builds a bridge between the minds of two people and shows us that our brains are deeply social." *(Keysers, 2011)*

Further research was carried out scanning human brains during the performance of certain tasks, and during the observation of others performing the same tasks with the same results. This allowed for speculation that mirror neurones are implicit in our ability to be empathic, to be emotionally touched by and understand others' experiences (Blakeslee, 2006). This is not only true of observing another act, but also of listening to another, hearing about actions, feelings and thoughts:

> "By attending to someone else performing an action, and even by thinking about them doing so – even, in fact, by thinking

about certain sorts of people at all – we become objectively, measurably, more like them in how we behave, think and feel. Through the direction and nature of our attention we prove ourselves to be partners in creation, both of the world and of ourselves." *(McGilchrist, 2010)*

For example, if we see someone hurt themselves, perhaps by stepping on a thumbtack, we are likely to experience the pain as if it were our own. This phenomenon is even more subtle than that: if we hear of another's distress or illness or fear we can become distressed or fearful ourselves.

In addition, it is now known that mirror neurones no longer function properly under highly stressed conditions such as a trauma. This means that a traumatised mother's ability to be empathic and resonate with her child will likely be severely compromised, perhaps completely absent, since her mirror neurones will not be firing properly. If the mother's mirror neurones are malfunctioning she "...is incapable of correctly interpreting her child's needs." (Brisch, 1999 in Ruppert, 2011)

> "The mother's survival self ignores, fails to appreciate or misinterprets her child's emotional needs. Instead [she] focuses more on [her] own needs and moods rather than those of the child. To the survival self of a traumatised mother, the child represents a permanent threat, which she needs to keep under control." (ibid.)

The inability of mirror neurones to function properly when highly stressed also supports the assertion that highly traumatised people are less likely to be able to be empathic, the 'psychopathic' diagnosis being based on a complete lack of empathy (ibid.).

4.2 Limbic Resonance

"It is limbic resonance that makes looking into the face of
another emotionally responsive creature a multi-layered experience ... our vision goes deep ... as two mirrors placed in
opposition create a shimmering ricochet of reflections whose
depths recede into infinity." (Lewis et al, 2000)

The limbic brain, also known as the mammalian brain, sits
above the brain stem at the top of the spinal cord, and the
cortex and neocortex cover and enclose the limbic brain. This
gives us the evolutionary model of the brain known as the
'triune brain', conceived of and developed by the American
physician and neuroscientist Paul MacLean (MacLean, 1990).

Figure 6. The Triune Brain

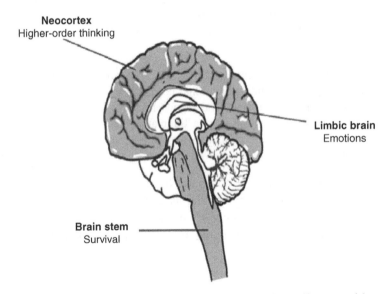

Neocortex
Higher-order thinking

Limbic brain
Emotions

Brain stem
Survival

The brain stem, or reptilian brain, is evolutionarily our oldest
brain, and deals with our more primitive abilities to do with
survival, including our primary trauma reaction, the startle
response. If we think of a typical reptile such as a lizard or

crocodile, and how quickly they move when startled, that is an example of a primitive reaction to sudden danger. The reptilian area of our brain also gives us other abilities that enable us to survive and protect territory, abilities such as aggression (employed to seem bigger and more dangerous to another threatening being), rage and anger for the same purpose; fear and anxiety as our primary indicators of danger; revenge and retaliation, again as a means of keeping oneself and one's territory safe. The primitive brain also deals with primary physiological functions such as breathing, digestion and the reproductive instinct.

The limbic brain system is a collection of brain structures[55] that sit on top of, and evolved from, the reptilian brain, and collectively constitute the seat of our emotionality. It is also known as the mammalian brain since it evolved as the mammal evolved from the reptile, when reproduction of young changed from external egg laying and hatching, to the development of young within the mother. Whereas the reptile relies on laying hundreds or thousands of eggs in order to ensure that some young survive the predatory threats that are manifold, the mammal keeps her young with her, inside her, until older, larger and more developed, and so more able to survive. This allows the mammal to produce fewer offspring as they are not in such danger of predation. This evolutionary development from reptile to mammal gave rise to the development of more refined emotions than the fear/aggression of the older brain. This was to ensure that the mother care for her young. Such instincts as the desire for connection, emotional warmth and to care for another, to love and to be loved, come from the limbic brain system.

> "Within the effulgence of their new brain, mammals developed a capacity we call 'limbic resonance' – a symphony of mutual exchange and internal adaptation whereby two mammals become attuned to each other's inner states." *(Lewis et al, 2001)*

---

[55] Also known as the paleomammalian brain, it consists of the septum, amygdalae, hypothalamus, hippocampal complex, and cingulate cortex.

'Limbic resonance' is seen as the ability for two people to resonate, understand and communicate subliminally with each other. We are, it seems, at all times in resonance via our limbic brain with those around us; not just by our ability to detect the subtle messages of facial and bodily changes and muscular shifts, but much more unconsciously and profoundly. This limbic resonance is likely to be increased and more active between closely bonded people, such as family members, and particularly between parents and children.

The function of limbic resonance, as with the evolution of the limbic brain structure, was and is to support survival. It ensures that the mother will be emotionally tied to her offspring to the extent that she will care for, love and protect her child, sometimes even with her own life. The evolution of emotionality ensured that the child is not isolated and alone, but is protected, fed and nurtured as needed until he or she can protect and provide for him or herself. Limbic resonance endures and forms the basis of our ability to be emotionally close to others, to find a mate and produce children of our own. (For an extended account see Lewis, Amini and Lannon, 2000.)

It is interesting to speculate about the fact that the basic reproductive instinct comes from the area of the brain concerned with survival (what we might see as the primary sexual compulsive instinct), and our ability to love and feel emotionally towards another comes from a different part of the brain, the limbic brain. Might this contribution by the emotionality of the limbic brain mediate and moderate and civilise the primal mating, and support the couple to bond well and remain together long enough for the children to grow, separate and become adult?

There are studies that look at the relationship between mirror neurones and limbic resonance, and so far the current thinking seems to be that "mirror neurone areas ... monitor this interdependence, this intimacy, this sense of collective agency [limbic resonance] ... that is tightly linked to the ability to form empathic resonance" (Farrow and Woodruff, 2007).

And what about oxytocin?

Oxytocin is a hormone that primarily acts on the brain. It is best known for its role in sexual reproduction, birth, bonding and mothering. It is released in very large amounts in the mother on the dilation of the cervix during labour and birth, and also during breast feeding, and is also in the child. It is sometimes referred to as the 'love hormone' since its primary function seems to be to do with bonding and trust, creating loving and affinity feelings and social activity. Experiments involving people sniffing oxytocin seem to demonstrate that it enhances people's trust and ability to make eye contact. It is therefore associated with empathy, and is also thought to activate the mirror neurone system.

The existence of mirror neurones, oxytocin and limbic resonance presents us with intriguing additional possibilities for understanding our relationships, our interconnectedness and interdependence, our empathic and social ability. It also gives insight from a neurological perspective as to why some people lack empathy. However, we must always consider the question as to what, then, triggers such chemical and neurological differences, and is it sufficient to say that a person lacks empathy and is able to commit psychopathic crimes merely because of such chemical and neurological differences? Traumatic experiences unquestionably impact us neurologically, and trigger the release of vast amounts of some hormones and chemicals, and in the aftermath may, through the persistent stress of survival mode, continue the flood of these stress-associated chemicals into the system.

These phenomena also throw light on the process of the constellation, which I will discuss later. There are other ideas relating to our interconnectedness that emerge in a range of thinking from quantum physics, systems theories, complexity theory, the morphic resonance work of Rupert Sheldrake, and the 'informational field' work of Irvin Lazlo. The interested reader can find more about these topics in my previous book (Broughton, 2010).

Conclusion

At this stage it may seem that we have an enormous, over-whelming and even hopeless task ahead of us; that the world is full of traumatised people, and that for many of us there is no escape. We may all be traumatised from our attachment to our mother, and entangled with the many traumas in the history of our family. Where in all of this can we find hope?

As much as this is true, it is also true that people do develop creative survival strategies. People do manage to leave destructive situations and relationships, even though they may repeatedly find themselves gravitating towards similar situations. People do go into therapy, and they do find ways of improving and managing their lives. Most of these ways may only be providing better, and safer, survival modes, but never-theless they can keep people alive and surviving, sometimes reasonably well. The healthy aspect for many does have some authority, and may manage by avoiding situations that are sensitive and stimulating, a degree of compromise that the person may find acceptable. Much current 'trauma therapy' is oriented towards helping people manage their underlying anxieties in just this way.

Any activity, if its purpose is one of distraction, deflection and dissociation, can be considered a survival strategy, but many such activities have a dual purpose. An artist, for example, may produce some of his most profound work from a combination of survival, trauma and healthy components. His work may at times be more from his survival self, but at others more an expression of his healthy self.

Some survival modes spiral down into self-destruction as the person increasingly struggles to manage the repeated destructive and terrifying retraumatisations, whereas other survival modes may provide a person with a point to his life that, at the same time as protecting him from his trauma, also may make some contribution to his life and his community, and satisfy his own aspirations to some extent. None of this heals the splits resulting from trauma, or changes the fundamental compromises of his life, but may provide purpose and a degree of stability as a way of compensating for and managing his internal despair and devastation.

For the person wishing to resolve her underlying problems, however, the model presented here provides an explanation that may help and encourage, and when we have a coherent explanation we are more able to consider what is necessary in order to address the issue.

There is a simplicity to Ruppert's model that comes from an ability to look beyond the constraints of established perception. Ruppert is an academic, but his language is simple and his books are reasonably easy to read and understand. Above all the model he presents is logical, and sits comfortably on its own, and proves itself again and again through the methodology we are about to explore. His model doesn't deny many of the basics of other theories, although some of his concepts do call some seasoned assumptions into question, but I think it asks deeper questions. It looks over the top of PTSD to the distant origins in the family over several generations, sees all traumatic events in a much larger context, and looks into the situation of the child attempting to bond with a traumatised parent at a time in his life when he is, without doubt, at his most vulnerable.

Part 2

Trauma Constellations

"The stability of an individual mind, what we know as identity, exists only because some neural pathways endure ...

And the plasticity of the mind, its capacity to adapt and learn, is possible only because neuronal connections can change ...

[This] lies at the heart of who we are and who we can become." *(Lewis et al, 2000, p. 100)*

A good theory needs a complementary practice, a means of working that fulfils the potential of the theory, and in this section I will be looking at the methodology of the constellation as the foundation of this practice of working with symbiotic and transgenerational trauma. For those readers who have never experienced a constellation, I would strongly encourage you to explore this, since what follows may be better understood when you have done at least one constellation.

5

Introducing Practice and Method

The constellations process that we call the Constellation of the Intention (also known as the trauma constellation) was devised by Franz Ruppert. It grew out of what is known as Family Constellations – the process developed and originated by the German psychotherapist Bert Hellinger in the late 1980s – in response to Ruppert's theoretical developments as outlined in Part 1. While in Family Constellations there was always a loose connection between the client's 'issue', what she described in the opening interview, and what was set up as the starting constellation, this constellation was always framed out of the facilitator's thinking after hearing information from the client. The representations then included in the constellation were decided by the facilitator. This already introduces the potential for a bias on the part of the facilitator as to what the constellation is going to be about. In addition, in Family Constellations the client usually chooses a representative for himself, so in the beginning stages the client sits outside the constellation and observes.

Ruppert's experiment, which resulted in the development of the 'Constellation of the Intention', consisted of having a representative for the client's presented issue in the constellation from the start, together with the client herself. This concept of the 'issue', being essentially in answer to the question "what do you want from this constellation?", he then re-termed the client's 'intention'. This word 'intention' assumes that the client wants something from the constellation that isn't oriented towards a problem, but is oriented towards something better, an improvement of his situation.

The client, having clarified what her intention is for the constellation, then chooses a person from the group to represent this 'intention', and places this representative and herself in the room according to her intuitive sense. Including a representative for this 'intention' revealed several interesting, and some unexpected, advantages:

1. The facilitator/therapist is no longer the determinant of what the constellation becomes, since all constellations start in the same way: the client and a representative for her stated intention.

2. The representative for the 'intention', apart from knowing what the client's intention is, has no other pre-disposing information of how to be in the constellation, and so is forced to focus on her experience as the only source of information. Even though ideas related to the client's intention are possible, they rarely seem to be the defining influence of the representative's reported experience. For example, the representative for an intention "to be more confident and grounded" might report her experience as feeling frozen to the spot, rigid in her legs, with a trance-like gaze and a sense of impending doom. This is the distinction between a role-play and a representation. In a role-play the person is given characteristics to enact; in the representation the person just focuses on her experience from where she is placed and in response to what occurs in the constellation. 'Representation' as such is *not* an enactment.

3. The experiences reported by the 'intention' usually seem to point directly to the underlying issue related to the stated intention. In effect the representative seems to hold both the intention and an indication towards what obstructs the achievement of the intention.

4. The beginning constellation of the client and her intention already represents the potential of a split psyche: the client and her intention. The intention reflects something

the client does not have but would like to, thence is, so to speak, outside of and separate from her – 'other' to her.

5. The potential for a relationship between the client and another part of herself immediately addresses the task of integration, as the potential for a coming together of fragmented parts of the self.

6. The client and her 'intention' hold the framework for what develops in the constellation; they might support each other, or show the lack of support, thereby demonstrating something of the level of intra-psychic disconnection. They are free to move, talk, share experiences and appeal to the therapist for help if necessary, and in this way they direct the process of the constellation out of their own experience.

From this we can state simply the tasks of the therapist:

1. To observe the developments of the constellation.

2. To comment on what he sees of the dynamics, preferably without interpretation but perhaps with a tentative hypothesis.

3. Focus on what supports improved contact between the client and her 'intention'.

When working with trauma, which always poses issues of power and authority, this situation is highly desirable.[56] The less the therapist's hypotheses influence the work, and the more the client feels in charge, the safer the situation will be and the more it is likely to stay close to the client's stated intention rather than stray into territory that the client is not ready for yet, thereby risking an unhelpful retraumatisation. In this work the assumption is that on some level the client does indeed know what can be addressed at this time, and provided

---

[56] There is a precedent for this inclusion of the intention in the constellation in the coaching and organisational work of Insa Sparrer and Matthias Varga von Kibéd (*Sparrer, 2007*) and others, which uses the constellations process. The client's 'goal' is usually included in the constellation, which is an obvious parallel, but misses the topic of trauma and the word 'goal' has a different feel and orientation than 'intention'.

the therapist stays in tune with the client, the work will remain within the client's range of safety.

The trauma constellation is essentially an intra-psychic constellation, a constellation of different aspects of the self. Apart from the client and her intention, other aspects of the self may be represented as deemed necessary, such as a younger part that had a particular experience, or more abstract elements such as the client's own grief (as distinct, say, from her mother's). Representatives for family members may be included, but only in order to understand the 'traumatised field' of the family system that informs the client's present situation. The primary focus remains always with the relationship and potential for connection between the client and her 'intention' and any other aspects of the self represented.

The approach is always experimental. Each constellation is best allowed to develop itself as far as possible before any therapist intervention. Ruppert's approach is always one of "does this constellation support my theories or does it show me something new?", which is an exploratory approach. Any intervention made is always in the form of a question or proposal to the constellation, with an openness to the answer that comes. The therapist never knows where the constellation will go or what the end result will be, and ideally should not think in specific end-result terms (other than the broad idea of integration). To do so endangers the potential of the open process of the constellation. The therapist who sits with an idea of what the result should be will communicate this closed frame subtly to the constellation, which will lose trust in itself and the therapist. Any loss of trust in the self and/or the therapist immediately limits the potential success of the constellation.

In the following section I will look in detail at the procedures of the constellation of the intention. I do not propose to cover Family Constellations; those wishing to understand Family Constellations better can refer to my previous book (Broughton, 2010) and other literature. However, as we proceed I may point out some marked differences between Family Constellations and the approach focussed on here that seem important.

6

Basics of Practice

6.1 Can we Heal Trauma?

"The core issue in trauma is reality." *(van der Kolk, 2007)*

Perhaps the first thing we need to address is the question: Can we heal our trauma, particularly such early trauma as the trauma of symbiosis?

In truth I do not have an absolute answer to this question. Partly this is because the theoretical work explained herein is still relatively new and we do not have the long term evidence available as yet; and since the business of coming out of the trauma splits of the psyche can only be achieved in time and with patience, we are in effect in the middle of our research and understanding of this work. There is a need for much more study and detailed research.

But it is also because the notion of being healed from something is, in itself, subjective and comparative, and cannot ever be an absolute. In the practical sense of thinking about a split psyche, healing would be a united and integrated psyche, and while the purpose of our work *is* the integration of the split off parts, to what extent this can happen we do not, and I think cannot, know in absolute terms. However, we can think creatively in terms of increasing the healthy self, becoming increasingly aware of the survival strategies, and coming safely into contact with the trauma.

Many people will tolerate an awful life because to think of doing anything about it is terrifying. We tend to think in 'all or nothing' terms, in absolutisms, rather than understanding that improvement is everything; healing is a process, a journey of improvement. The idea of feeling better, less distressed, more functional, more at peace, more able to be in good relationship, to think and perceive more clearly, to be able to sleep well at night, to feel in control of one's life rather than a victim of one's life, to be able to deal with the vicissitudes of life without becoming confused and disoriented, is what I am talking about. These are statements of improvement.

From my own experience, and from the feedback of many of my clients, this improvement does happen, and while the healing journey is probably lifelong, it is also true that people who address their own trauma do increasingly come to find that they can live their lives from a more peaceful integrated place, with greater autonomy and less emotional disturbance. In fact in the early phases of working, I often see that the changes and insights are big, and come quite rapidly, most often related within the terms of "I just feel better", or "I feel more myself", or "I don't feel so panicky". These are subjective statements and are the kind of thing clients say.

Over time the sensitivity of the person to herself increases, and the subtleties of her issues and increased awarenesses become sharper. In a way it's like living with a beautiful painting, where the longer you live with it the more you see it, and the deeper your appreciation and understanding become of the subtle nuances and changes of colour and texture. For a while one brush stroke can form a complete focus, then to remerge with the whole. In a similar way the constellation can encompass such a single stroke, represented by the 'intention', within the context of the whole as represented in the constellation, and the person's life.

6.2 What is Integration?

Integration means the combining of two or more things into one where they become a whole in themselves. In the constellations process when the client and the representative for another part of herself are able to look at each other, see each other, relate to each other, talk about their differences, their trust and mistrust of each other, there comes a point at which they move towards each other, and the conditions for the client to integrate a part of herself are there. Often in the constellations process this comes quite spontaneously, in a great variety of ways.

A constellation where the client is able to see the situation of psychological fragmentation and the degree of traumatisation of the family field is often the very best starting point, even if she doesn't really find any way of relating to her 'intention' in the constellation at that time, and integration as such seemingly does not occur. In effect the process of integration must ride on such prior accumulated awarenesses and understandings; such are the steps towards integration. As a client at this stage once said to me:

> "I saw in the constellation the degree to which my mother was traumatised and not there for me ... I had always known it of course, but to see it enacted in front of me and to see the representative for my mother just being exactly how she is ... and seeing her mother, my grandmother, completely caught up with her own trauma ... well I feel quite different about myself now. My mother couldn't do it, she couldn't connect with me, and she couldn't help it. It was how it was."

A statement people frequently make who are dealing with the confusion of symbiotic entanglement is "I realise I don't know who I am"; or, as a client said to me the other day:

> "I went home and looked at my mother, and saw her and how she is and I realised that I am her ... I am so her that there is no division ... and I realised that I am so much my mother I truly don't know who I am if not her. This was a great shock, but also in some way a great relief, because now I can get on with finding out really who I actually am."

This process happens over several, or even many, constellations. The psychological splitting in reality is not just the simple three-way split of Ruppert's basic diagram (see page 69), but more often involves a reinforcement of the original split with any retraumatisation, further development of the survival strategies, and sometimes further splits. Each constellation will be a step towards strengthening the healthy self, understanding more clearly the survival strategies and integrating one or more splits.

The process of integration of the splits in our psyche is entirely natural and unavoidable once the necessary inhibitors become conscious and lose their purpose and power. Becoming aware of our survival strategies, the ways in which we obscure our relationship to our trauma, disempowers these strategies. The more we see clearly how we hold ourselves in survival mode, the less we find we need to do it, and the easier becomes the natural process of integration as the survival self eases its grip on the increasingly conscious trauma. The more we see and understand, the less frightened of exploring ourselves in a deeper way we will be.

Psychological splitting in the face of trauma is in itself a paradox: on the one hand it is a very real means of survival of life-threat, and on the other it is a profound betrayal of the self, an abandonment by one part of the self by another. And this paradox means that there are often complex intra-psychic issues of trust and betrayal to be dealt with at some point in the person's journey towards integration. The betrayal of the self that splitting is, means that trauma not only harms and betrays one's trust in life, but also one's trust in oneself. Many people find a deep and consistent truth in statements such as "I don't trust myself" or "I don't know what aspects of my self I can trust and what I can't", or "I've never felt able to trust myself". To understand this and be able to voice it is a major step towards healthy integration.

Our entanglement with the traumas of others in our family is the complicating factor in this process. The split parts of the self cannot simply come together if they are entangled with unresolved family traumas, and so, much of the process of the work is taken up with understanding and disentangling from our unconscious absorption with these other traumas. In fact, it seems from much of the work that I have done, that we cannot really approach our own trauma fully until we understand and experience just how entangled we have been in the family's unresolved trauma. So in a sense, often the first step for the client is to see the confusion; then she knows more what she is dealing with, and she gains a wider and deeper context for her problems.

The process of healing from trauma and symbiotic entanglement can prompt, for a while, intense feelings of loneliness and aloneness. There is the seeing and experiencing just how alone and frightened the original child was, how lonely the split parts of the self have been, separated from each other without any good connection. And then there is the aloneness of the disentanglement, of the moment of stepping away from the entanglements of the family and towards autonomy. True autonomy means I am responsible for myself, and in the first instance this can feel like an awful aloneness, where the illusion that others were there – or could be if I could just figure out how to help them, heal them, take away their suffering – is gone. The reality in this sense is that I was always, to an extent, alone and helpless, but my survival strategies hid this truth from me. A client once described this moment as follows:

> "It feels like setting off on a journey on a rough sea in a small boat, with a hole in the bottom and no oars... but it also feels real ... frightening but also a bit exciting."

With healing and integration, I am alone in a sense, but more whole, more complete, more separate, more integral, and from there I can come into relationship with another with clarity, real love and affection, in a true and clear adult symbiosis.

6.3 The Therapist and the Therapy

Understanding the subtle and hidden dynamics of trauma requires us as therapists to reassess our approach to our client, and highlights once more the importance of understanding and working with our own trauma in order to resolve it, so that we can understand and work effectively with that of others. So long as the therapist is under the control of her own survival self, and unaware of this, she is likely at some point to collude with the survival strategies of her client, and as such will be of limited usefulness. We need to understand the ubiquity and nature of trauma, particularly symbiotic trauma, so that we diminish or eliminate the likelihood of our collusion with the client's survival strategies. This requires a shift in perception. In my view, many a psychotherapist and counsellor of good training and much experience even so may not have addressed their underlying trauma, simply because the topic, the understanding and a good methodology have not been present in the therapy. To focus on the symptomatology of the client, for example an eating disorder, alcoholism, obsessiveness, even suicide attempts, without understanding that these are all likely to be deflective strategies, as extreme forms of terror and despair management, misses the point.

Most therapy today is based on the relationship between the client and his or her therapist as the focus for increased awareness, and thereby change. I think this has limits: if the relationship itself is the primary focus, then both people are likely to be vulnerable to their propensity to split and resort to survival strategies. If the therapist is not fully aware of the dynamics and ubiquity of trauma, then the topic and its importance and relevance are likely to be missed. The shift in perception has not been achieved, and a lack of understanding of symbiotic trauma entanglement may render the therapist liable to be caught up unconsciously in that of the client.

A therapy that relies on the client's relationship with another, has limits in terms of her coming into relationship with herself: the focus is the client's relationship with the therapist, not her relationship with herself.

"Relationship therapy can seem like a kind of ersatz friendship, but 'it doesn't make you better friends with yourself.'" *(Sykes Wylie, quoting van der Kolk, in Sykes Wylie, 2004)*

In Ruppert's thinking, the client can only come into good clear relationship with another when she has found and come into good relationship with herself, which entails the integration of her splits. In a sense, therapy that relies on relationship puts the situation the other way around: the client is thought, by coming into relationship with another, to find a good relationship with herself. But the therapist can only reflect the client's self to the client through her own, the therapist's (flawed) self, as was the situation with the original mother. This perspective may encourage a reliance on the other, on the relationship with the therapist, in order to find the self, to find one's autonomy, and becomes, essentially, a kind of re-parenting process. As an infant it was a sine qua non that this should be so ... as an adult it isn't.[57]

To step back from the relationship between therapist and client as the primary focus and 'workplace' of the therapy, giving both client and therapist the space to look elsewhere (the constellation) offers a different possibility. Within the construction and process of the constellation in the group, both therapist and client can allow the process to unfold and inform in ways that the relational field of therapist/client alone cannot. In this way the therapist can be free to observe, and comment if necessary, without the observation being in part a self-observation and reflection of a relationship in which the therapist is a primary player.

---

[57] I realise that to say this is likely to be experienced as contentious, and it brings us back to the nature of the relationship between symbiosis (in-relationship) and autonomy (self-relationship). I am sure there is further thinking to be done here as we all develop a greater understanding of trauma and its impact. I offer this thinking for on-going debate and consideration.

This is not to deny that there *is* a relationship between the therapist and the client. Of course there is, but it isn't the primary object for appraisal and comment. The crux of the therapist/client relationship in constellations work is that the client will only venture where she needs to go in the work to the extent that she feels able to trust the therapist; and this cannot be talked about, because trust cannot be contrived, it can only arise naturally and spontaneously. Even to discuss it with the client falsifies it. We feel trust in the body, in our emotions, not our intellect. To gain this trust requires three things on the part of the therapist:

1. An adherence to reality and fact as it is currently known by the client and understood by the therapist, over speculation and hypotheses;
2. A trust in the healthy autonomy of the client, even though the client, herself, may feel confused, and functions more from survival mode than healthy mode. The therapist relates to the healthy part of the client rather than the survival part; and
3. A trust in the process of the constellation itself: in the autonomy of the representatives and the mysterious process of the constellation.

Trust

My experience is that the more I can trust the healthy aspect of the client and behave towards her as an autonomous person, the more the client will trust me; the more the client can experience the therapist's trust in her, the more she is likely to increase her own trust of herself; and the more I trust the process of the constellation, the more the client, too, will trust what happens in the constellation (and the representatives will trust themselves, which is always helpful). Trust breeds trust, and mistrust breeds mistrust. The nature of the survival self of the client – and of the therapist – is seductive and alluring, and is based on mis-truth and illusions, promising relief from pain and frightening emotions that cannot be fulfilled. It is easy to succumb to its allure and end up on an increasing spiral of mistrust. The therapist holds the key to creating an increasing spiral of trust.[58]

This issue of trust is also particularly crucial in the private one-to-one session, where we just have the client and the therapist, since the therapist will be a representative in the constellation along with the client, and so is managing two distinct roles at once: that of therapist and that of representative. However, because the individual method is best understood as an adaptation of the work in a group, it makes sense to acquaint ourselves first with the work in the group, and I will discuss the private session more fully later.

---

[58] It is interesting, when thinking back to the History of the Study of Trauma section (1.1 above), to see how much psychotherapy's beginnings were in fact founded on a mistrust of the client.

7

The Constellation of
the Intention

"A constellation is an open process with many degrees of
freedom and individual decisions that limit the number of
options available. These limitations must arise from the
internal logic of the constellation ... system itself."
(Ruppert, 2011)

Introduction

The constellation is a construction, a method and a process. It
is constructed by the client as a representation of his intuitive
internal picture of his presented issue, and is the means by
which he can learn something about this internal picture. It is
also the method that allows for this beginning construction to
move, change, evolve and transcend the original situation; it
allows for the client to intervene, or the therapist if necessary;
and for the free interaction between the represented elements,
and between the client and these elements. And through the
puzzling phenomenon that allows the representatives to experience fairly accurate portrayals of the person or intra-psychic
part of the client that they represent, it offers deeper insights
than are possible by just talking. I know of no other means that
allows such direct access to the very essence of the person's
current situation, to his unconscious knowing about himself
and the family system from which he comes.

Advantages of the constellation as a method for resolving trauma

There are some distinct advantages to the constellations method when working with trauma, and particularly when exploring very early, pre-verbal trauma:

- It allows access to the client's unconscious and pre-verbal memories, information and constituent parts.
- It is an embodied experience, and so reaches a more whole sense of truth than just talking.
- It enables the split-off aspects of the self to be embodied separately, allowing for movement and the disintegration of the reified split structure.
- It shows graphically the nature of the relationship between the split-self components, and the dynamics involved.
- The 'representative experiences' give valuable information about the needed processes for the split components to come into good contact (integration).
- At times it is a representative for a part of the client that may be able to hold and even express some of the unresolved trauma feelings, which can be helpful to the client in her overall journey. So the unresolved trauma impact can be shared in the constellation if necessary, which may increase the sense of safety for the client.
- The collaborative nature of the constellation offers an increased safety to the client: the client's issue is spread between the client and the representative for her intention, any other self-parts and family members that may be represented, the 'holding group' and the therapist.

7.1 Basic Procedure

The working group may vary in number and, if possible will sit in a circle. Larger groups may be structured in a lecture format with the participants seated in rows. The therapist usually sits in the group circle with a vacant chair beside her.

This is the chair that the client will sit in while he clarifies his intention. It is not necessary to strictly follow this format, and it is quite possible for the client to stay in his own chair and discuss his intention with the therapist from there.

Generally there is an agreed condition of confidentiality. In my view this is best oriented towards respecting the information people share about themselves and not discussing with others outside of the group anything that may identify someone from within the group. We usually need to discuss our own experiences as part of our process of learning and integrating, but this should be within the above confines.

I usually open the group by saying a bit about myself, and perhaps a bit about trauma. And then I will usually make four things clear:

1. Coming out of our trauma is a step by step process, and a constellation will constitute a step on this journey.
2. The client is the person who knows what needs to happen even if not fully consciously. She or he is in charge of the constellation.
3. I believe that the constellation will not go beyond what the client is ready for, and that this offers a safety net that supports the client.
4. No one who is invited to be a representative is obliged to accept. Everyone can make their own decisions about whether to agree to represent or not.

Beyond this the only rule I have is that participants do not hurt themselves or each other or damage the environment. There are often violent impulses in families, and in the constellation it is important that this can be seen and understood. The representatives can say any such violent feelings they have, but must not act on them. Those representing someone else are also always themselves, and so will take responsibility for their own safety.

The simple starting process of the constellation is as follows:

1. The client clarifies her intention for this current constellation in conversation with the therapist.
2. The client then chooses a group member to represent her intention.
3. The client places this 'intention' representative standing somewhere within the space provided, and then places herself in relation to this representative.
4. This forms the starting constellation: two people, the client and a representative for her intention.

The subsequent constellations process evolves from this starting point. The initial experiences of the client (which may be completely different from when she was sitting down before the constellation) and the representative for her intention are given time to emerge, clarify and strengthen. During this phase the therapist usually waits to see what develops in this relationship.

From here several things may happen:

- The client and her 'intention' may find their own way to resolution of the issue through dialogue and connection with each other without any intervention from the therapist at all.
- The client and her 'intention' may get stuck and start to repeat movements or statements of experience. This is a situation where they are unable to move on or find a connection with each other that provides a shift. At this point one or other may appeal to the therapist for help. This is an indication that something is missing, and other representatives may be required. This broadens the context of the client's intention.
- The client and/or her 'intention' may get a strong feeling of what is missing and suggest in some way that this missing element be included. This is a request to the

therapist that may be specific; for example, the client or the representative for the 'intention' says clearly "I think the mother (father/grandmother etc) should be here." Or it may not be so specific.

• The client understands something from the developing process and gives further information that seems to be relevant, gaining access to her less conscious awareness.

• If the process seems to get stuck the therapist may ask the client for more information, and then make a suggestion.

• Needed extra representatives are added in order to fill out the relevant 'trauma field', the context of the client's intention.

The 'trauma field' is that part of the family field that may show the traumas that impact on the client and her current issue, the traumas that she may be entangled with. The primary element of this trauma field is usually the mother, but may also require the father and grandparents or great grandparents, and sometimes siblings. Even if the focus of the work is a later trauma, parental support from the earlier time of life is what will determine the person's ability to manage the later trauma, and to include the mother or both parents will show clearly how available this support was/is.

If the client's intention relates to an event later in his life, for example when he is a young teenager, or even later, it might be useful to represent this event in some way. However, it should always be borne in mind that later traumas are always influenced by earlier traumas. The client's intention and the constellation itself will show what can be addressed at this particular time.

The end of the constellation often occurs naturally, and is usually the point at which the client has got what he wanted for now. This may be more or less obvious: it may be that he has seen something that he hadn't seen before, understood something new, experienced his situation in a different way, expressed some of the unresolved trauma emotions, come into better contact with his intention or some other part of himself represented in the constellation. Any or all of these constitute progress, remembering that coming out of trauma is a step-by-step process that cannot be rushed and has its own pace. To reiterate from Chapter 1.6, the basic healing process of the split psyche is:

1. The disintegration of the fixed and hardened split structure of healthy, traumatised and survival parts, allowing for movement and better connection between the parts of the self; followed by
2. the integration of the split off trauma components through increased good contact between the self-parts (e.g. The client and her 'intention')

And the ongoing process by which this happens involves the following:

1. The strengthening and enlarging of the healthy structures of the client by
2. an increased awareness of his survival strategies, how he dissociates, which in time allows
3. the client increasingly to be more trusting of himself, and safely to get in touch with his trauma, and
4. increasingly to integrate his splits.

Now I will go into more detail of this process of the constellation.

7.2 Clarifying the Intention

Just where and how the early glimmers of intentions coalesce,
like glittering dust motes into the whirling jinni of action,
remains beyond the ken of today's science.
(Lewis et al, 2001)

"The first step has to be empathetic listening, with no
searching questions and definitely no well-meaning pieces of
advice." *(Ruppert, 2012)*

" We are all convinced of our ability to listen. But we can't
listen!" *(Pallasch & Kölln, 2009 in Ruppert, 2012)*

The first phase of the constellations process involves the client
clarifying her intention for this particular constellation. People
don't just turn up at a workshop or private session, having
taken the trouble to make the arrangements, pay the fee, travel,
arrange childcare, or whatever other effort they have put into
getting there, for no reason. They want something. But in my
experience it is not always the case that someone clearly knows
what she wants from the constellation, *what* her actual
intention is in being there, beyond a generalised desire to feel
better, to have the pain or discomfort go away.

Generally, the culture in counselling is that a client arrives
and has the space and attention of the counsellor to herself to
talk about her problems. Somewhere along the way, it is
hoped, she gets something useful out of it. Both therapist and
client are agreed that it might take some sessions (perhaps
many months) to see what is usefully coming out of the
therapy, and proceed accordingly. The therapeutic devices are
usually oriented around respecting the person, offering her the
space to tell her story and elucidate her problems and
suffering, while the therapist attends to what she says, perhaps
making some interpretations or observations that may, or may
not, be helpful. While at the beginning of the therapy the
therapist may try to establish what the person wants overall
from her therapy, it may be rarer for the therapist to ask the
client what she wants from each particular session, and to stay
attentive as to whether this is actually achieved in the session.

It isn't so in, for example, Solutions Focused Brief Therapy, originated by Steve de Shazer and Insoo Kim Berg (Sparrer, 2007). Solutions focused therapy makes the primary focus of the work what the client wants to achieve from the overall therapy (which is usually only a few sessions), and from each session. De Shazer and Berg and their colleagues developed what is known as the 'miracle question', a device that sets up a clear image/idea of what the person's preferred life will look and feel like once the goal is achieved. The 'miracle question' tries to keep the focus of the work on the desired goal rather than the problem. Each session maintains a strict focus on the desired outcome of that particular session.

What we do with the constellation of the intention is somewhere between these two approaches. We accept that most people do not know clearly what they want, and the therapist is willing to sit with the client patiently while she explores this, which may involve talking about her problems for a while. At the same time the trauma constellations therapist knows that the constellation cannot start usefully until the client has developed an intention. We also know that any intention will to a greater or lesser extent be influenced by both the healthy part and the survival part of the client. The tension between these two is always present in this clarification process. Everyone approaches healing in this ambivalent state, between wanting something different, and the restraining influence of the survival self. For this reason there is no such thing as an intention that comes wholly from the healthy part of the person.

In addition, in understanding the nature of trauma, it is clear that the original trauma situation is one in which 'wanting' is not an option. The 'wanting self', so to speak, in the trauma event is severely harmed, maybe even destroyed. In a relational trauma (as opposed to a natural event such as an earthquake or sometimes an accident) the person's wants are non-existent, over-ruled and dominated by the wants of the perpetrator. The person may then grow up not daring to want anything, because wanting something for herself tends to take her dangerously close to that original situation, and the emotions therein. To want something and then have that want crushed is, in a sense, the same as having her identity crushed and destroyed; and so it seems safer not to want. I have sat with many a client for whom the notion that she can want something for herself is completely alien... and confusing, even terrifying. Such a person, when confronted with this question, may simply go back to the problem, perhaps repeating in another way the story of the disasters of her life. Thus the survival self shows itself: the question was too much.

> I had a client recently for whom it was so painful to think about wanting anything that he persisted in coming up with more and more stories from his history that confirmed how awful his childhood had been. Even though I attended very carefully to what he said, he was so used to the experience of not feeling heard, and so attached to the stories as defences against the pain, that it seemed nothing would induce him to come up with an intention for the session. Eventually I stopped him. I said that I was quite sure he could fill the entire time with further stories of how awful his childhood was, and how dysfunctional his parents were, but I also thought he wanted to do something about it. I made it clear that a constellation would constitute a step, just that, a step amongst many. I reiterated that coming out of trauma takes time, and perhaps within that framework he could find what this constellation, right now, could be for him. After another short while he found an intention that crystallised what he thought possible, for that particular moment, and went on to do a constellation that was, in the end, very productive.

I may not ask the person outright "What do you want?" I may couch it in terms that perhaps allow the person to take a step towards defining an intention without getting too stimulated by their trauma.

As Ruppert says in the quote above, our task is to "listen, with no searching questions", and no clever interventions or even 'reflective listening' words. If you are really paying attention the client knows it, and you do not need to demonstrate it by using such techniques as reflecting what he has said back to him. I think this is more often a means of helping the therapist feel helpful, and not so much really in the service of the client. A client can feel rushed and pressurised by vigorous therapist intervention. Be patient and sit quietly with your client, only asking a question if there is something you really do need to know. You might want to ask if the client knows of any traumas in the background of his parents, but it is better to find this out when the client's intention is pretty well established, because then you have a framework within which such information may have relevance, or not. However it is also as well to realise that once he has related any information from his parents' backgrounds, his intention may have changed. This happens; and then again, when he chooses the representative for his intention and tells the representative what his intention is, it may have subtly changed again. Keep listening to make sure you hear these slight changes. The client's intention must always be in her own words; the therapist cannot provide any influence on what the client's intention will be; if he does he is likely to have become entangled with the client and usurped authority.

To ask a person what their intention is implies a deeper sense of purpose:

> "Intentionality refers to a state of being, and involves to a greater or lesser degree the totality of the person's orientation to the world at that time." *(May, 1965)*

Our intentions are luminous, and their beginnings are a strange coalescence of "glimmering" parts.[59] The intention that the client finally admits to is what it is. It is always found within the tension of the healthy aspiration and the survival self's caution, and in this sense it provides the therapist with information as to what may be possible, this time.

The nature of the intention that clients state varies enormously in content, from the existential as in, for example, "I want to see really who I am, and love all of me"; or "I know

---

[59] See the quote at the beginning of this section.

that my life is limited (from someone who is terminally sick) but just for once I want to see clearly who I am, disentangled from my mother"; and the seemingly every day such as "I want to get on better with my children" or "I want to decide about my job". All issues, whether seemingly profound or mundane, will likely have at their roots some connection with symbiotic trauma and symbiotic entanglement:

> Recently a client was preoccupied with several interrelated decisions: buying a house, moving to another part of the country for a good job, and whether to be in a particular relationship with a man who was already living in this new part of the country. The decisions were paralysing her and making her feel helpless, lonely and vulnerable, to the point where as they loomed closer she felt more incapable of acting. The resulting constellation eventually showed a connection with her mother's parents and grandparents, who had been refugees from a major international conflict, all of whom had been killed on a transport train by the enemy. At this level the client saw her entanglement with the reality in that situation, when decisions had been about life and death, and the wrong decision, the wrong train, being in the wrong place at the wrong time had resulted in death for all her mother's family except her mother, who had been left behind with an aunt. For this client the context of her decision-making was a much larger one than she had thought, where decisions did mean potential death.

There is a lot happening in this initial phase of the constellations process and it is a mistake, and a common one when learning to work in this way, to rush this process or consider it a less important phase than the constellation itself. It isn't: it is just as important as the constellation and requires just as much attention, and may also in some cases need as much time, particularly if the person is not known to the therapist. Not only is the client having to face defining what she wants, she is having the opportunity to sit with the therapist, and thereby subtly develop a relationship with him. Understanding that the effectiveness of the subsequent constellation will be directly related to the degree that the client feels able to trust the therapist, gives an idea of the importance of this phase. Often in the workshop, and the individual session, I am meeting the person for the first time. Trust is not something that can be taken for granted; it cannot be contrived. It has to develop, and allowing this time is not a sideshow; it is crucially important and productive. The client is laying the groundwork for the possibility of very deep and emotionally laden work. The therapist needs to allow that time.

What is possible right now?

Beyond all of the above, when the client states his intention, I accept it as it is, for now. I find it useful to think in terms of the question: what is possible right now? I apply it to the process of clarifying the intention as much as to the general process of the constellation. The question, "What is possible right now?" relates to the ongoing and ever-changing tension between the healthy self and the survival self, and is mediated by the level of trust that the client can have of herself, the therapist and the constellation moment by moment.

Always the therapist is working up against the tangible, moveable, changeable boundary that is defined by this idea: what is possible right now? Every experiment, question, suggestion, proposal, quiet waiting moment that the therapist provides is, in a sense, asking this question. What is possible in this moment may be completely different to what was possible a moment ago, and the therapist does well if she is constantly working as if asking this question of the client, the representatives and herself. The question applies as much to the current session in relation to what was possible in the last session as it does to the present moment in relation to the previous moment.

In this sense nothing is fixed and potentially everything is possible. It is a mistake to think that because something was not possible before, it is not possible now. This is the nature of process, change and life.

7.3 Opening Phase of the Constellation

Having established her intention for now, the client chooses someone from the group to represent this intention. She may repeat her intention to this person, which may offer a moment of contact between the two that may develop, or she may move on to placing the representative for her intention somewhere in the available space. She then stays in the constellations space with the representative.

If there are just the two people at the beginning phase of the constellation, the client and a representative for her intention, the therapist can focus on increasing his understanding of the client and her issue as the relationship of these two parts of the self develops. That isn't to say that one can only begin with just the two, but generally this seems the best starting point because it is simple. It gives the initial focus where it belongs, with the client and her 'intention'. The therapist may not assume, at this point, that any other representatives are necessary.

Sometimes it takes a little time for the two people's experiences to develop, and the therapist will wait to see what happens next. As the two interact (or not) gradually the therapist can come to understand what is being expressed. The self-components of the healthy self, survival self and trauma self will all be present in some way between the two people, sometimes more visible, and sometimes less, and will move between the two of them. They are rarely fixed in either. Usually what the therapist sees is mainly healthy and survival modes, often with survival dominant, and the trauma self much less visible. The 'intention' representative may become helpful and supportive of the client, or they may not talk to each other, or even look at each other at all. There are many different variations of how this initial dynamic will be and develop. It is very useful for the therapist, particularly the learning therapist, to give this phase of the constellation time. Part of the growing skill of the therapist is being able to recognise the different aspects of the self as they show.

The therapist can wait until the two get stuck, ask for help, or the energy seems to dissipate. With practice the therapist will be able to understand what is going on with more assurance, and then will know better when to intervene and how.

Presence

The presence of the therapist is important throughout; by presence I mean being fully present, listening and attending. Presence is the opposite of absence; in the sense of mindfulness: an attentive awareness of the reality of things. It is an ability to sit quietly, internally still, with minimum thinking. You don't have to have the answers, you can just watch and see what you see. It isn't something done forcefully, and the more effort you make to be present the less present you will be.

Presence doesn't mean you have to reassure the client or prove your presence. People recognise presence when they experience it with you, and it helps them trust you, and trust themselves. In fact they may trust you less if you try to reassure them of your presence. It doesn't mean that you necessarily look at the two people with intensity... you might be looking at the floor, but even so you are present to the minutest shift in energy or body of either person. Coming to be able to be present in this way takes time and practice, and is enhanced, of course, by increased self-clarity, by working with your own trauma.

7.4 The Phenomenon of the Constellations Process

> "a poem begins as a lump in the throat ... it is never a thought to begin with" *Robert Frost*

Once the constellation is set up, the 'representatives' (including the client as a representative of himself) attend to their physical and emotional experience as it evolves, and differs from what their experience was before they were chosen. It is also the case that the client, once in the constellation, may have different experiences from when he was seated with the therapist. A central phenomenon of this process is that the experiences of the representatives usually are significantly relevant to the person that they are representing in the constellation. This is to such an extent that representatives will often experience things that they could not possibly have known about the person they are representing, and yet often these can be corroborated by the client.

For example, I was once representing a grandfather, and kept having the odd experience of being unable to stand on both feet, only being able to fully stand on the left foot, and constantly feeling as if I was about to fall over unless I had something to lean on. It turned out that the client's grandfather had lost his right leg in the first world war, but this had not been mentioned by the client in the initial clarification process, and the client was someone I had never met before.

Another example is an experience I had of being a great grandmother to the client, about whom nothing had been said. Slowly as I stood there I began to feel very strange, and increasingly disoriented and out of touch with reality... after a while I began to feel quite crazy and started to turn persistently in circles until I became dizzy and eventually had to sit down. The client at that time knew nothing about her great grandmother, but subsequent to the workshop she learned that her great grandmother had lost two children very early in her life, and that there was a secretive rumour in her family that she had killed them and subsequently gone crazy. In any event the client was told that her great grandmother had lived her life out locked in an attic at the top of the house and was never talked of.

This kind of thing is more the norm in constellations work than not. It is true that at times things emerge from the representatives' experiences that cannot be corroborated, particularly information that concerns two or three generations back, and in this case the therapist has a responsibility not to take any such information as absolute, and not treat it as such with the client. However, it may well have some explanatory value that can be usefully supported by other evidence that *can* be corroborated. I would emphasise here that, since essentially when working with trauma the work is focused on the intra-psychic situation (the internal split self), the degree to which it is necessary to delve back into the person's ancestral history, and confirm factual information, must be limited to what is required in order to facilitate the internal integration of the split self. The point of the constellation is not to unearth information about the ancestors for its own sake, but only insofar as it helps expedite the internal integration process. Usually this is in the sense of the client seeing something of the systemic trauma that impacted one or other of his parents, and subsequently him.

The Basic Assumption of the Constellations Process

This, then, is the constellations phenomenon, and gives the basic assumption of the constellations process:

> **the representatives' experiences in a constellation will have relevance to, and provide useful information about, the presented issue of the client.**

This assumption enables the therapist to work fruitfully with the constellation, but she can only develop a confidence in this by working with the process over time, and increasing her experience.

Access to the Unconscious

The constellation seems to provide an access to the client's unconscious or less conscious self. In this sense very often the described experiences of a representative may suggest something, rather than categorically state anything, and the client may then be able to recall an event or piece of information of importance or an experience that had not been consciously available to her before. The constellation is, in a sense, a journey into the less conscious processes of the client, which she does in collaboration with the representatives in the constellation.

Meaning of the Constellation

The meaning of the constellation must ultimately be left to the client, with the therapist only commenting on the constellation and offering an interpretation if necessary, but always deferring to the client's current meaning-making ability. Keeping in mind the difficult journey to autonomy after trauma, the therapeutic approach must always respect the client's autonomous ability at this moment, even if the client's survival mode has developed by handing over authority, decision-making and meaning construction to others. It is often tempting to try to impose one's view, especially if in the end one is in fact right. But it offends the client's autonomy and undermines it in the present situation. Thinking again of the notion of "what is possible right now": if the client sees the constellation differently it is better to leave it there. The meaning that emerges from the constellation is part of the process, and does not end when the constellation ends, which is one of the reasons I do not see clients on a weekly basis. It is illuminating to see, after several weeks, where the client has come to in her process of meaning-making from the last session.

But how does it work?

This is the most intriguing topic. Having worked with the constellations process now for close on fifteen years, and having developed a trust and confidence in it as being benefi-cially productive, I still cannot fully explain what it actually is or how it works. As yet there is no comprehensive scientific explanation, but there are various proposals, the most useful of which in my view are what are known as 'mirror neurones', and the concept of limbic resonance (See Part I, Chapter 4). However, this is not to discount other explanations from the world of quantum physics, chaos theory and systems theory. All of these add information and support notions of our inter-dependence and non-separateness. Understanding symbiosis, the need for relationship and interdependence, and how influenced we are by others' moods and state is helpful:

> "Like other beings who live in groups, we humans are easily infected by the behaviour and moods of others. You only have to go to a football stadium to see how tens of thousands of people behave like a single organism, shout when the others shout, cheer when the others cheer or are all devastated together when their team loses. Following an emotionally disturbing football game, it is difficult to disengage from the state of this collective 'contagious emotion'." *(Ruppert, 2012)*

Under normal circumstances it seems that it simply is not possible for us *not* to be affected in some way by others' experiences and emotions, whether by 'contagious emotion' or by empathy. The conditions that moderate and compromise this ability are of course those of trauma. It is the very traumatised person who has developed their survival strategies to such a high degree that empathy is severely compromised, or even eliminated, who cannot relate to others' experiences in an empathic way. This has a bearing on the origins of the psychiatric definition of the sociopath, and the legal definition of the psychopath, and may even have some relevance in diagnoses such as autism and Aspergers syndrome, although as yet we have no relevant research in this area.

If we intentionally create a space in which the focus is working with psychological and emotional dilemmas, and the person designated as the client offers his story with the attention and willing state-of-being of the therapist and the rest of the group, this space becomes imbued and resonant with the client, his intention and his story. In the moment of stating his intention for the constellation and choosing someone to represent this intention, the client sets the tone and possibility of what can follow. The constellations process has a different and particular feel to it, and even though I cannot more fully explain what happens, neither can I dismiss it. I like that there is this mystery to us and our interrelationship, and as tantalising and fascinating as it is to attempt to explain, I find the challenge of working with something that retains its mystery exciting.

7.5 The Representatives

The therapist's relationship to the representatives in the constellation is best based on a trust that whatever happens and whoever is chosen to represent whom is somehow right. A straightforward way to work with the constellation is always to assume that whatever the representative says or does is in some way to do with the constellation, and so include it; the therapist thereby is absolved from making judgements (which may be wrong), and becoming critical (which is definitely wrong). The therapist needs representatives who feel respected and validated. They are the working tools of the constellation, and they work best when they feel that the therapist trusts them and has confidence in them. Over time people become more familiar with being a representative, less concerned about what to do, and more efficient as a working tool. Being a representative helps people become more trusting of themselves, which is a personal gain and a side benefit.

Let's say that a client chooses someone to be her 'intention' who has never represented in a constellation before. This person may feel rather self-conscious and uncertain about what to do and how to be ... what might the rules be. The therapist may choose to help by suggesting the representative attend to her experience, trust it and just report whatever it is. Or he may decide to leave the person to find out for herself. Left to her own devices she may appeal to the therapist, at which point the therapist may help: she may say "Can I speak?" to which the therapist may answer " Yes, of course" ... and in this way she discovers that she can ask if she needs to, that her instincts are okay, and she can say something about her experience, which may include her difficulties.

The therapist then can understand several things: the client has chosen someone who is new to representation. Why? Someone who may be uncertain and self-conscious. Might this also reflect something of the client in relation to her stated intention? If the therapist assumes so and includes the representative's uncertainty as part of the client's constellation she benefits in three ways:

1. She shows respect and validation towards the representative for her contribution, which in turn increases her confidence and assurance in her experience.
2. The therapist does not end up fighting with anyone. By 'fighting' I mean getting into protracted and entangled conflict with anyone. This doesn't mean denying the reality the therapist may see, but 'entangled conflict' is a conflict of survival selves.
3. She is able to include information as possibly relevant which can be corroborated or not by the client.

This both helps new people become confident as representatives and contributes to the overall success of the work.

> Recently at a workshop a client chose someone to be her intention who had already been a representative in several constellations (even though this was her first workshop), and who had proved to be a person not frightened of saying things as she saw them. As the client chose her to represent her intention she said to her "I know you will speak out!". The group laughed, but I knew how important that was: this client wanted to have someone as her intention who was going to be forthright and outspoken; in other words she wanted strength and honest results from her constellation. And she got it.

The people who are the representatives in the constellations work very hard; I have never met anyone who didn't want to be the very best she could be as a representative for another. It is an extraordinary act of service, since some of the representations are difficult and emotionally demanding, but people rarely baulk at it; on the contrary they usually agree readily. It is quite something to step into the shoes of someone we do not know and feel feelings and experiences that are not ours. These may be those of a person with an alcohol problem, or one who has perpetrated harmful acts, or has schizophrenia, a very young pre-verbal child, or even a foetus. And all the time, as a representative, we are also always ourselves. Over time one gets more and more experienced at knowing what is me, and what is definitely not me.

7.6 The 'Intention'

The representative for the client's intention is like a wildcard in the sense that it has no definition other than the stated intention. The person to represent the client's intention has little to draw on for enactment, and so has to draw on her present experience. To represent, for example, an intention to see more clearly, or to understand why the person behaves in a certain way in some circumstances, or to feel more confident/at peace/whole/integrated/calm or any other myriad of notions people come up with as their intention, is never definable really in terms of enactment or behaviour. To think how to enact any of these isn't easy, and it rarely happens. The 'intention' representative then has to fall back on her experience.

These experiences are often quite specific, differentiated and often multiple, even conflicting. So a person may describe his experience in this way: "I feel timid, a bit small. . . . maybe young, I'm not sure yet. My legs are shaky . . . yes in fact they are very shaky, I'm not even sure I can hold myself up much longer. At the same time my arms feel different . . . particularly my lower arms. Yes, my lower arms feel quite strong, and full of energy . . . buzzing with energy. And yet in a funny sort of way I feel different on my left side from how I feel on my right . . . even my eyes, I can see more clearly with my left eye than with my right . . ." and so on. Many different things may be represented in such a description, some of which may develop and others may disappear.

Another person may not describe her experience, but may show it with her body: she may slowly start to bend to one side, her legs may perceivably shake and her eyes may close. Her hands may start to try and reach out, or touch the air in front of her. At some point she may say: "I feel like I will fall over, and I am scared if I do that that I may not ever be able to get up again, it's like looking into an abyss." This version is both metaphoric and descriptive.

And yet another may not speak at all, but stand fixed as if frozen to the spot. If asked she may confirm this, but perhaps not much more. Another may refuse to speak, feeling the insufficiency of words or, perhaps, the existence of things that cannot, or should not, be spoken, indicative of secrets within the system.

The way in which people represent will have to do with the actual person he or she is as much as to do with the representation itself. Some people are comfortable to be in their body and let it contort or move. Others prefer to describe, sometimes in minute detail, their experience, as if with a kind of fascination and absorption. And yet others may stay at a purely cognitive and conceptual level.

An inexperienced representative may find any of these more difficult, and instead talk to the client (remember always that the client chose the person... for a reason), perhaps try and help the client, even become a 'therapist' to the client. Or the client may question the 'intention', trying to understand who or what she is, even believing that if she keeps asking, the 'intention' will come up with the magic answer.

These are just a few of the beginning dynamics you will see. The wildcard nature of the 'intention' gives it a freedom to develop, and it usually seems to develop in a way that leads somewhere useful. The representative for the intention holds the stated intention, "the more or less conscious goal" (Ruppert, 2012), of course, but also then, as if underneath that, portrays through her experiences the underlying obstruction to the achievement of the intention, along with the tension between the healthy, survival and traumatised selves. By using such a means the therapist avoids having to hypothesise too early in the constellation as to the nature of the constellation.

It is uncanny how often the initial experiences of the 'intention' are experiences and emotions that the client knows very well, that are hers, often never stated, on the edge of her awareness, and yet nevertheless familiar. Many a person, doing her first constellation, is stunned by another person telling her some of her own scarcely verbalised inner experiences. This in itself is often a very powerful and validating experience for the new client: someone isn't just telling her that he understands her feelings, but is telling her that he is feeling and experiencing these feelings as if they were his own.

Two specific forms of experience that the 'intention' often seems to have are of being split, and/or embodying confusing and often contradictory experiences. This 'split' experience usually suggests that the intention is holding either two parts of the self (often a survival or 'protecting' part and the traumatised part), or a confusion with another person, for example the mother. Here are examples of both:

1. The 'intention' as part of her experience feels a sense of anxiety, behind which she can discern a strong discomfort, maybe fear or fright, but her main experience is a desire to help, to support the client. She may also feel protective of the fright experience. In this case the therapist might deduce that the 'intention' holds a healthy aspect (desire to help/support) and a sense of the underlying trauma (the discomfort and fright), and survival self (desire to protect and keep the trauma part separate). It is not unusual for part of the 'intention' to be interested in the client, and available to the client, but also cautious about allowing the client to see the other more traumatised part. It is helpful to remember here that splitting is in a sense a betrayal of the self (see chapter 6.2), and part of the healing process is an increasing trust of the self . . .

exhibited here by the 'helpful intention' wanting contact with the client, but protecting the younger traumatised self from the client at this stage. After all, in the beginning split, one part of the self abandoned another in order to survive the trauma ... these two parts cannot come together until trust is established. In a situation such as this, the function of the 'intention' could be said to be increasing the healthy aspect of the client, by forging a creative and supportive relationship between two parts of the self (as represented by the 'intention' and the client), in order to take the next step (in a subsequent constellation) of engaging with the more traumatised part.

2. The client as she looks at the 'intention' is unsure from the experiences described by the 'intention' representative whether the 'intention' is really part of herself or in fact is her mother (or grandmother etc). In other words, the 'intention's' experiences may describe the symbiotic entanglement with the mother (or grandmother etc). The experiences are merged and confused, showing that the client, in a sense, does not recognise herself as separate from her mother's traumatic experiences (or grandmother's etc). Sometimes the 'intention' may feel confused about whether the client herself is the 'mother', or not. Any such 'confusion' is likely to indicate symbiotic entanglement with others' traumas. One example of this is if the client chooses someone of the opposite sex for her 'intention'. While the therapist should not automatically jump to the conclusion in such a case that the client is confused with, for example, her father, it certainly indicates something and the therapist should hold it as a question: why would someone choose someone of the opposite sex to be her intention, to be another part of the self?

In short, throughout the duration of the constellation, the 'intention' may have many different experiences; may at one moment feel weak, listless and ineffectual, and in another moment, feel strong, clear and effective. These changes are always due to what happens in the process of the constellation. It is interesting to ask the 'intention' at what point she began to feel stronger. This can often give the client useful information about what strengthens her healthy self.

The 'intention' covers many roles in different constellations: a helper and supporter, a stubborn uncommunicative child, a helpless and traumatised child, a mediator between the client and her traumatised child; the person who says "we have to get out of here... it's no good for us here", the person who shows just how entangled the client is by her obsessive attachment to the mother or other person in the constellation. As the therapist you can never presume what the 'intention' will be or will show. Don't try. Wait and see, and trust your representatives.

7.7 Resolution in the Opening Phase

If the client and her intention find a good resolution on their own, this may be several things. At some point in the person's journey this kind of resolution will represent an integration of the symbiotic trauma... however, there are many steps towards this, and even many steps *within* such an integration.

A resolution of a kind at this early stage of the constellation may constitute the healthy part strengthening and enlarging itself. For example, two parts of the self that until now have seemingly been out of contact, perhaps even unaware of the other (as may be shown in the constellations process), may come together and be in contact. This can be a good step towards preparing to address the underlying symbiotic entanglement, a working alliance so to speak. Working with symbiotic entanglement is often complex, confusing and emotional, and strengthening the healthy part is a prerequisite to venturing to experiencing the tangled web of the 'trauma field'.

Another instance of what one often sees in the beginning phase is a collusion of survival selves; both the client and her 'intention' are predominately working from survival mode. In this instance one can interpret this as a step towards becoming increasingly aware of her survival strategies. Additionally, a client who does not feel sufficiently safe or trusting of the therapist and/or the group/environment will unconsciously control what happens and how far the constellation will go. It is at times hard to watch an interaction between the client and her 'intention' that seems to address only surface issues and relates in a disconnected and seemingly superficial way. It is helpful to remember that generally people do not in the first instance understand trauma in the way that a practitioner of trauma constellations does, or even someone who has read a book on the topic such as this. It requires a shift in perception, and that shift happens in its own time. This may be a step in that direction. At the least it can be a useful heightening of awareness of the person's survival strategies.

On occasion the client and her 'intention' seem to re-enact a very early, even in-utero, version of the primal splitting, and from there find a way of coming together in an intensely moving and satisfying way. They may even spontaneously re-enact the birth process, if it was traumatic and a split occurred. This has frequently happened in my work.

It is impossible to relate here all the possibilities of this first phase, but as the therapist, be prepared to wait and see if the client and her 'intention' can work out something useful for themselves. If, however, the interaction between them seems to run into the sand, the energy goes, or they reach an impasse where nothing more seems possible, it may be the moment to consider bringing in further representatives. If the client and her 'intention' cannot find a way to come together, to improve their relationship and find some resolution, then the assumption is that symbiotic entanglement confuses and inhibits them.

7.8 Including the 'Trauma Field'

"There is a saying in Germany: 'Detours increase your local knowledge'." *(Ruppert, 2012)*

It is best to approach the inclusion of further representatives as an experiment. You do not know what will happen, and to hold onto an idea of what you think should happen is likely to inhibit the open process of the constellation. Get used to working with the constellation as an ongoing experiment, where everything provides information; even if something included makes no difference to anything . . . that is also important information.

Including other elements requires the therapist to at least consider **who or what** to include, **why** a particular representative, and for what purpose, the **what for**.

'Who or what' are included falls broadly into the following categories:

- **The mother**: the mother will always be an important potential first inclusion in the constellation, and sometimes her mother (the grandmother) as well.
- **People**: father, other family members or other important person mentioned.
- **Other parts of the client**, such as younger parts, split off emotional parts etc.
- **Emotions**: such as the unexpressed grief/rage/sorrow/guilt/shame. These may be general free-floating elements to see where they end up, or they may be more specific as in "the mother's unexpressed grief", or "the client's feeling of guilt", as a means of clarifying what feelings belong to whom.
- **Abstracts**: such as "whatever happened in the past that traumatised the mother". This can be helpful in the absence of sufficient facts and information. If it is clear from the client's account and the constellation that the mother was indeed traumatised, but by what isn't clear, in order to proceed it may be helpfully included.

The 'why'

Inclusion by guessing what is needed is not helpful, and puts too much responsibility and focus on the facilitator's guesses. So the **'why'** keeps us focused. It is best if all inclusions have some basis from what has happened so far in the constellation. Following are some examples of what may prompt a particular inclusion. I have roughly ranked them in an order according to which I think has a stronger rationale for inclusion:

1. Since symbiotic trauma is thought to lie at the heart of all later traumatisations and life difficulties, it makes sense to think first of including a representative for the **mother**. Even in situations where the focus of the work is a later trauma, when troubled most people think first of their mother as the potential source of love and solace... and if the mother was not able to be present for her child due to her own traumatisation, this is a serious situation for the child, and for the later adult. In my view, in all situations of childhood abuse and trauma, an important consideration is whether the mother was a source of good and loving connection and solace for the child or not, whether instead the child felt she had to protect her mother from her, the child's, experiences.

2. If the client, while in the constellation, suddenly starts to talk about something that happened in her life when she was a certain age, you could consider including a representative for the **client at that age**. For example, the 'young child who felt frightened at night'. I tend to stick as closely as I can to the client's words rather than interpret her words with my own. For example, if she says: "When I was four I felt very frightened because I thought my father was hitting my mother in the next room," I might suggest including a representative for "the four-year-old who felt frightened".

3. If either the client or her 'intention' tells you directly that someone is missing, certainly you can include a represen-

tative for this person. For example, the client says "I think my **mother/father/sister/the unborn child** should be here." This could be a deflection away from some tension that is building with what is already there, so you might decide to wait for a bit to see... but if it is a distraction and you do include it, it is likely to become obvious quite quickly that it isn't really relevant. That is the experimental nature of the constellation. If it is relevant, and useful, it will show by what happens next.

4. If the client starts to tell you about a particular **incident** in her or her mother/father/grandmother's (etc) life that seems relevant, or to have been sparked by something that happened in the constellation, then you could consider including some element of that incident, or the person involved.

5. If either the client or her 'intention' mention someone several times, for example the mother's mother, always consider including this person at some point. For example, the 'intention' says "I miss my mother/sister/ father," or "I'm not sure if you [the client] are my mother/sister/grandmother or not."

6. During the intention-clarifying conversation, if the client gives information about things that happened in her family that she knows about which could have had a traumatic impact on her mother, you might consider including representatives for the **relevant people**. For example, the client says openly "my mother was very traumatised... I know that her mother was very hard and cold, and already had six children and didn't really want my mother... my mother never felt wanted...". You could then think of including the client's mother and grandmother, and even the great grandmother. This last might be included in answer to the question: what then happened that resulted in the grandmother being "hard and cold"? Including the great grandmother may show something that illuminates this.

7. It might seem useful to include **split-off parts of the mother or father**. For example, if the client's perception

of her mother is that she was very jolly and enjoyed life and everyone loved her, and the representative is mostly showing this mother, but the client has also mentioned a severe trauma in the mother's background, such as death of a sibling, or abuse, you could propose including a representative for "the mother aged 6 when her brother died", or the "abused mother as a child". The thinking here is that the traumatised mother is also split, and it may be helpful for the client to see this. I have at times simply included "another part for the mother", which makes no assumptions as to how this representative will behave, with useful results.

8. If, during the intention-clarifying conversation, the client shows **strong feelings** while talking about someone else or the suffering of someone else, this could indicate an entanglement with the other person's trauma emotions. In which case you might suggest including a representative for this person. For example, while talking about her mother she mentions that her mother's mother lost a child just before the mother was conceived, and becomes very tearful while telling the story. In such a case you would consider including the client's mother and grandmother, and perhaps also the 'lost child'.

I have a personal guideline that goes like this: anyone – or anything – the client mentions during the interview and the constellation may at some point be important, just because she/he/it has been mentioned. The more times the client mentions a particular person, the more it may be important to represent this person at some point.

The 'what for'

It is also important to understand the purpose for including further representatives, the **what for**. Considering that the focus of the work is always the relationship between the client and her 'intention', the underlying question is: what can be included that may support better contact between the client and her 'intention'? A shift in perception may be needed. A client may know very well the story of her mother's trauma, but this does not necessarily mean she realises the degree to which this has impacted her. If a representative for the mother is included she may actually see this. So, again roughly, here are some answers to the **'what for'** question:

1. **To see the degree and nature of the systemic trauma.** For example, to *see* the traumatised relationship between the client's mother and grandmother portrayed in the constellation. To *see* how unavailable to the client his mother was.

2. **To attempt to understand the origins of the traumatisation.** This may not in the end, be possible, since the facts may be mired in contradictory stories, in the distant past, or never mentioned. However, the attempt often shows just how confused and entangled family members were, which then highlights the psychic state of the client's mother when the client was an infant, hence the symbiotic trauma. The constellation may imply specific traumas, but the therapist, rather than ratify and solidify such information, is better advised to stay with the general atmosphere of confusion. It is a situation where, in my view, we must not assume that the constellation portrays facts. It may well show the general malaise of the system, but that is all. 'Facts' are only useful if they make sense to the client from what she actually knows. Much of what we 'know' is not conscious, and in this sense the constellation often triggers such less conscious or unconscious knowing.

3. **For the client to *experience* just how transfixed and entangled she is** with the system's suffering and confusion, even craziness, to the point where she gives it far more attention in the process of the constellation than she gives her 'intention', persistently trying to fix it, change it, feel feelings that aren't hers and so on.

In my view, extra representatives are best brought into the constellation as a collaborative process between the client, the therapist and the client's 'intention'. This keeps the authority for the constellation more with the client than the therapist. During the subsequent process other representatives may feel the need for further inclusions, in which case the therapist and client can follow this if it seems useful.

It is also important to understand that just because a representative for, say, the client at the age of four when something particular happened is placed, it doesn't mean that the representative will necessarily experience what is expected.

In contrast with the common practice in Family Constellations, in the trauma constellation the therapist does not address any interventions or observations to representatives of the client's family, or even to the client's 'intention'; only to the client. For the therapist to 'work' with the family members undermines the client's move towards autonomy. To think that "I can only be healed if others in my system are healed" leaves the client dependent on others and looking outside of herself for her intra-psychic healing. This is likely to increase the client's entanglement with her traumatised family rather than resolve it, and interrupts her contact with herself and her journey to autonomy through improved relationship with her 'intention'.

The general purpose of this phase is to illuminate and clarify what, exactly, from the family field is underlying the client's current situation as represented by her stated intention. The experiences of the 'intention' point to what needs to be looked at, to the underlying issue. This isn't often discernible in the beginning, but if followed and allowed to develop, in my experience is always so. Whether this leads to a satisfying conclusion and increased relationship with her 'intention' or not is, in a sense, not relevant. It is useful if it does, but actually what is more important is that the client sees something that broadens her understanding of herself. To urge the constellation on towards a satisfying ending is not in service of the client herself, and may even send her into an overload of information, potentially retraumatising her. It is helpful for the therapist to watch his client carefully, to stay scrupulously in touch with her, in order to know when she has actually seen enough, for the moment. If the work continues beyond this point it is likely that the client will adopt a glazed and even dissociated demeanour (the signals of feeling over-whelmed and close to retraumatisation). A good strategy is just to ask: "Is this enough, for now?" In my experience, when asked, most people can relate to the question, often with relief. It is enough.

The Function of the Therapist

During this phase the therapist may choose to describe and comment on what she sees, and even offer, with a sensitivity towards the client, an interpretation of what she sees.

To comment is merely stating the facts of what has happened, for example, to say: "What I see is that your mother doesn't look at you and seems to take no interest in you, but rather seems absorbed with her mother, who also seems to take no interest in her child." Or: "I notice that you look more at what happens in your 'mother's' background, and her mother and father's background than you do at your 'intention', who has moved right away from you and out of the circle."

These comments merely state what is actually evident, and although you may think it unnecessary because it seems obvious and the client should also have seen this, often this is not the case. We see what we have been conditioned to see, and stepping aside from this is not always easy and cannot be taken for granted. It is helpful for the client to have someone make such observations.

The issue of interpretation is a complex one. An interpre-tation takes what one sees and ascribes some meaning to it. For example to take the last comment above, an interpretation might be: "My hypothesis is that as a child it was safer for you to stay in contact with your traumatised mother than to move away and stay in contact with yourself, that part of you [the 'intention] had to split off and stay away." This will either make sense to the client or not.

It is not beyond the therapist's brief to offer such an interpretation in an exploratory manner; it *is* beyond the therapist's brief in my view to state it categorically and with an authority that overrides whatever the client may say in response. It does not serve the establishment of autonomy for the client if she has to take on another's perspective. She should be allowed to decide for herself what, at this moment, is useful and can be integrated and what cannot. This is a demanding stance for the therapist, but is worth aspiring to, even if at times he succumbs to the temptation to interpret authoritively. The therapist may be right, but does not contribute to supporting another to trust herself and her autonomy. To attempt to convince an unconvinced person potentially entangles the therapist with the client's issues, and may damage her trust in the therapist. This is what I mean by 'fighting' with the client; it serves no useful purpose, and rather tends to re-play the original perpetration and traumatisation.

7.9 Ending Phase

In my experience the constellation usually ends in one of the following ways:

Client and her intention come together

This is where the client and her intention come together, often fairly oblivious of the rest of the group, talk to each other, perhaps hug each other, maybe cry together, but eventually come to a peaceful togetherness in which, in the end, both people spontaneously come back to themselves as participants in the group. Often the client (without prompting) thanks the representative for her 'intention', and you can tell that she recognises the representative as the person she is, apart from the constellation. Sometimes this requires the therapist and group to wait as patient witnesses while the client and representative do what they need to do. In the individual session, if I am representing the 'intention', my own experience of the ending is of not feeling like I am representing the 'intention' any more: I am back to being fully myself. This may occur without any outside intervention, with no inclusion of representatives for the trauma field, or it may occur after some considerable journey, with other representatives included.

Something new is seen

This is where the client has seen something that he has not really ever seen before, and it has such an impact that it is obvious there is unlikely to be any point in continuing the constellation at this time. For example, a person has a certain image of his mother, perhaps as having been suffocating with her 'love' for him. He then sees in the constellation that his mother's mother, having lost a child, tries to get consolation by focusing obsessively on her other child (the client's mother); his mother then attempts to escape the predatory advances of her mother by focusing obsessively on him, the client. When he really sees this he has to reconfigure his mother's suffocating 'love', as not being love, having as its origins nothing to do with him, but her survival strategy in relation to her own symbiotic trauma with her mother. This reconfiguring, seeing in effect his whole existence in a different light, is a major event and may need time to settle in him. In this instance there may be little point in continuing the constellation.

A situation such as this, even though the client and his 'intention' may not be together in the constellation, can nevertheless be seen as an important step on the way to the client having sufficient attention for his 'intention' rather than remaining transfixed by the trauma field. A considerable step in such a case is if the client moves away from the trauma field and towards his 'intention', even if he remains looking at the trauma field more than he looks at his 'intention'. However I would not even suggest this. I think such a move has to come from the client himself.

What is enough?

In the past I sometimes asked a client after the constellation had ended what had been the most memorable and important thing he got from the constellation. Often it was something that happened halfway through the constellation, and I realised that the rest of the constellation at that time may not have been so useful to the client. In fact I realised that it was often more for my benefit than the client's! It made me feel effective and useful.

Over time I learned to watch the client carefully, and if he looked overloaded or distracted, to slow down and stay with him, sometimes even suggesting that maybe what he had done so far was enough. Some people know the truth of this, and may even say so themselves. Some ignore this and try to continue, but it soon becomes even more obvious that this is not possible... because in a sense it isn't. The psyche can only accommodate and metabolise so much in one go; it is like eating too much at a meal, the metabolising system goes into overload which is not of any benefit to the person.[60]

The 'unsatisfying' constellation

At times the ending of the constellation seems unsatisfying or 'unfinished'. In my view this is usually for one of two reasons:

1. because what is evidenced by the constellation is so contrary to the client's traditional perspective she cannot find a way to allow it at this moment; or
2. there are some secrets held within the system that the client, at this moment, cannot allow to come to the surface, to her consciousness or to the consciousness of the constellation.

---

[60] Interestingly in Chinese medicine the stomach is regarded as the organ of digestion not just of food, but also of information, thoughts and ideas, and just as we can feel physically full and over indulged after a meal, so we can feel the same after a big shift in perception in a constellation.

To integrate a perspective that may be almost entirely the opposite of what one has always believed requires time, and will likely instigate resistance, and a resort to survival mode. In this instance it does not serve to try and convince. The constellation is better seen as perhaps offering something the client could take and sit with for a while, and see if there does come a point at which it makes some sense. I do not think that at any time the therapist should consider such a constellation as a failure. It may not immediately be perceived as useful or 'successful', but many a time I have had a client come back to me at a later date having found something beneficial from such a constellation.

In the second case one is usually working with a trauma- tised bonding system, where the secretive nature of the family at the present moment overrides the possibility of revelation and integration. Bonding system situations are often the most confusing constellations because of the embargo on informa- tion, shame and guilt being strong prohibitors. The work will require patience and acquiescence in what is possible at this time.

Another situation is where the client sees something in the constellation that he has always known but never really allowed himself to know. This is like the psyche having hauled something from the depths of consciousness up to the surface to the full light of day for the first time; something that, until he really looked at it, he didn't actually know that he knew. It's like a semi-conscious knowing that, perhaps because it feels unbearable, he has kept in the dark, away from conscious light. This has an added rawness in that the person may feel ashamed and exposed. One client said she felt like a criminal who had been found out, and felt ashamed in front of the group, not so much for knowing this information, but for having hidden it from herself and 'pretended' to the group that she didn't know it.

In all these instances it is helpful for the therapist to know just how disorienting such moments can be.

The ending in relation to the original intention

If one reflects back at the end of the constellation on what the client's original intention was, it is uncanny how often the whole journey of the constellation has exactly addressed the intention. Even an intention such as "I want to understand what this is all about" often will do exactly this, and no more. The client may understand what is going on behind her intention better, but since she has not said anything further that she wants instead, the process stops at this point. What "it is all about" is clearly perceivable, but does *not* include the resolution. Take the client's stated intention literally! If the client was ready for resolution she would have stated her intention differently.

Sometimes the client sees quite clearly, from what happens in the constellation, that his stated intention comes predominantly from his survival self, and in that moment sees that the current constellation has nowhere else to go with this particular intention. This can constitute an increased awareness of his survival strategies. From this point arises the possibility of an intention for the next constellation, at another time, that comes from a more healthy orientation. I would not generally consider changing the intention at this point and re-starting the constellation.

Some clients, particularly if they are familiar with this way of working, will go for an intention that in reality is over ambitious (but not 'wrong' even so). For example, a client who hasn't really seen the nature of his symbiotic trauma has a stated intention of "I want to love myself and be whole". In the constellation then he may see absolutely clearly how much he *doesn't* love himself, and in fact how incapable of loving anyone his mother was, all of which doesn't mean that the intention is fulfilled, but it does mean that a very big step towards it has been taken, and that is likely to be enough.

Ending the constellation for the representatives

In my experience the representatives usually don't need any particular process to let go of their representation, except sometimes when the constellation has been particularly complex and involved some very difficult and emotionally laden representations. In such circumstances the representatives themselves usually know if something extra is needed. At times the client himself may wish to thank those who have represented. I tend not to make rules about this, and leave it to each person's choice. It is sometimes the case that a person is chosen as a representative for someone whose issues are similar to his. This has intriguing possibilities for the representative in relation to his own situation, but may at the same time leave him confused and unable to let go of the representation after the constellation is finished. In general I tend to think that if someone has difficulty letting go of a representation it is usually because of just such a situation, and it is helpful for the person to consider this.

7.10 Contact and Connection

> "Eye contact, although it occurs over a gap of yards, is not a metaphor. When we meet the gaze of another, two nervous systems achieve a palpable and intimate apposition."
> *(Lewis et al, 2000)*

It is intriguing when watching a constellation in process, to see the effect and power of eye contact between people. It is two nervous systems coming into closeness ("apposition"). It is a closeness that we find hard to put into words, but we know by our ability, or inability, to look deeply into the eyes of another, exactly how powerful this can be. We also know, if we think about it, when another looks at us, directly into our eyes, whether he or she does actually perceive us, or not. We know what that real spark of contact is, how at times it may make us feel embarrassed, self-conscious, even ashamed, causing us to need to hide from such contact. At the same time perhaps we have also that experience of really being seen by another, as the most including and valuing, moving and inexplicable moment, the power of which often instantaneously causes us to look away rather than be able to bask in it. Real contact is not a hard stare, daring the other to look away. It is soft and tentative, warm and shy, vulnerable and strong at the same time.

In my demonstrations I often do a little exercise to show this basic phenomenon of contact. I ask for two volunteers and place them in the space some distance apart, facing away from each other. Both know that the other is there, but in this first instance they do not see each other. I ask each what their current experience is (remember, there is no subject for this 'constellation', no client, no intention). Frequently their experience is one of curiosity about the other (and what I am about to do), sometimes a bit anxious or fearful, often to do with the idea of something going on behind them that they cannot see. I then turn one person slightly towards the other, so that if she looks straight ahead the figure of the other would be within the extreme periphery of her vision; she can see the other but, provided she doesn't turn her head, only just. I then turn the other in the same way, so that both have the other in their peripheral vision. Their experiences now tend to turn to curiosity; they usually feel better, and easier, because at least they can see where the other is, and to an extent what is happening. They both also know that they can, if they want, turn their head and see the other directly, although I generally ask them to stay with the peripheral vision for the moment.

Then I turn one so that she faces the other directly, but of course the other is still facing away. And then finally I turn the second person to face the first, usually about three or four feet apart.

As they make eye contact for the first time in this exercise, there is always a palpable impact, even if only for a moment. Often both flush in their faces, perhaps becoming tearful, start to breathe more deeply, soften, smile, even laugh. Sometimes after this initial moment one or both may succumb to embarrassment or shyness, and look away, but the flush of pleasure is still there. Rarely is it otherwise. Try it for yourself with two of your friends. Take time over it and watch carefully what happens.

Those who witness this experiment also feel it; here we have mirror neurones hard at work. For all of us, as we watch, this is usually a pleasurable and moving experience. The clearer our own perception is, the more we are able to recognise truth by the emotional effect it has on us. It is true that one can see fear in another's eyes, suspicion, sadness, anger, and we know it, which is also often why we may avoid eye contact, as too intimately revealing of ourselves.

Such is the power of contact. The eyes have been called the windows to the soul, and there certainly is a sense of vulnerability about someone being able to see into our eyes, as if we feel they can, indeed, see to the very depths of our soul.

Trauma tends to draw a veil over the eyes of the traumatised person, so eye contact becomes difficult, even impossible, and even if made is usually uncomfortable. Looking into the eyes of a severely traumatised person is often an experience of looking through a veil, as if the real person is hard to find there. In fact this supports the idea that only a traumatised person can hurt another, because to an extent the traumatised person does not see the other clearly. To make such eye contact as I describe in the exercise above would seem to me to make harming the other person impossible.

In the process of the constellation of the intention, integration of the split off parts of the self comes when such eye contact between the client and another part of herself (perhaps her 'intention') can be made, and a warm and loving relationship can be forthcoming. Hence the helpfulness of the constellations process: to have another real being represent that other part of myself allows me to experience a moment of contact with that person as that other part of myself. Ruppert has called this a "falling in love with the self".[61]

---

[61] Personal communication.

This kind of contact cannot be made to happen; it can only happen when all the right conditions are in place. In the coming together of the client and another part of herself there are often issues of trust and mistrust to be dealt with, as I have said before, and these issues are part of the process of clearing the way for good contact. When it does happen between the client and another part of herself the work, for now, is done.

8

Working with the Constellation

"By avoiding a one-sided outlook we gain a much deeper
insight into the structure and function of the . . .
individual . . ." *(Perls, 1969)*

As may now be obvious, working with trauma requires a sensitivity to issues of power that flows through to every moment of one's work. It requires discipline, and an eye for reality and clarity in the face of confusion and obfuscation. And it requires us to walk a path between understanding trauma from a good theoretical framework and a persistent openness to the new and unexpected, a fluid movement between knowing and not knowing, with a reasonable ability to be comfortable with both. The therapist cannot know everything, and it is not for her to do so; the client's own discoveries are his most valuable ones.

8.1 A Phenomenological Approach

"The [therapist] strives to occupy the neutral territory between
the poles, the "center" of the polarity, where both poles can
be perceived and both can be understood without regard to
either pole being preferred over the other, that is, with
creative indifference." *(Stevenson, 2004)*

"A phenomenological approach is one that gives primacy to
the 'isness' of phenomena, the here and now subjective experience and observation of phenomena stripped of analysis and
interpretation." *(Broughton, 2012)*

Trauma is about power, and powerlessness. And herein lies a strong reason why a non-directive and phenomenologically-oriented approach to the facilitation of the constellation is useful when working with trauma. The authority for what happens must always be with the client, simply because here and now the client is *not* a victim, is *not* powerless. Even though, because of her underlying trauma, her defining experience may well be of powerlessness, in effect this is simply not true in the present moment. Describing what can be seen, commenting on that, even offering an interpretation from a theoretical understanding of what is seen is one thing; telling the client definitively what is so and what is not is yet another.

The phenomenological approach is a means of studying consciousness as it is experienced in oneself or in someone else; a description of the givens of immediate experience. It is an attempt to capture experience in process as it is lived in the moment, through description before subjecting it to conceptual analysis and interpretation. In the phenomenological approach experience is described directly without undue interpretation. Conceptualisation and interpretation remove us from direct subjective experience, often turning the phenomenon into something other than it actually is.

Taking a phenomenological approach to one's work is an aspiration, not an absolute. On the one hand I am looking at what I see and hear in the constellation from the perspective of my theoretical framework; on the other, I strive to maintain a stance of openness and curiosity towards the new. To rely too much on the theory may mean that the therapist misses something important, because the particular theoretical lens is too rigidly adhered to and doesn't provide the space for something new. But at the same time a theoretical framework that makes sense provides a means of understanding what one sees.

Working from a phenomenological perspective, the phenomenological approach, has three principles:[62]

1. **Epoché** – the word 'epoché' comes from the original Greek 'epokhe' meaning suspension. So this principle means a suspension of ideas/beliefs, so that any interpretations will be lightly held, are easily reversible if necessary and therefore more adequate. This is not an elimination of one's ideas, biases or beliefs (which is impossible), but an awareness of the existence of such ideas and biases as perhaps conditioning the perception, and a willingness to hold them lightly, with an openness to the here and now emerging phenomena.
2. **Description** of phenomena before interpretation, description being less likely to be tinged with personal biases.
3. **Equalisation** (also known as 'horizontalization') of phenomena: valuing all phenomena that arise in the process equally until such time as it becomes evident what is important and what is not. This means not excluding anything that occurs until such time as it proves itself to be unimportant.

In this way the therapist can work with the constellation in an experimental way, where each intervention or inclusion of further representatives is in the nature of a question to the constellation, that by its answer provides more information.

8.2 Trauma Emotions and Survival Emotions

There is a difference between emotional expression that relieves and resolves trauma, and emotional expression that avoids and maintains the status quo of the split off trauma. These two types of emotional expression have been called 'primary feelings', associated with a movement towards

---

[62] Based on the work of Ernesto Spinelli: *The Interpreted World: An Introduction to Phenomenological Psychology* (1989), quoted from an article by Mark A Fairfield in *Gestalt Review (Fairfield, 2004)*

engagement, and 'secondary feelings', associated with a movement away from, or avoidance of, engagement. (Franke, 2003)

Emotions are a fundamental way in which we know how we feel about something, our relationship to it. They have often been described as 'positive' or 'negative', such categorisation being based on whether the particular emotion makes us generally feel good or bad. However, all emotions are important and useful for what they tell us about our perceived situation, our relationship to our immediate environment, whether animate or inanimate. "Emotions are thought to be related to certain activities in brain areas that direct our attention, motivate our behavior [sic], and determine the significance of what is going on around us." (Wikipedia). This is as good a definition as I can find.

Emotions originate in the body, emerging into awareness, at which point we can make a cognitive interpretation, and name it a particular emotion. If we are able to give our emotions space to be experienced, and value and trust them, they can tell us the truth of our relationship with a particular situation or stimulus. A traumatised person is much less likely to trust their feelings since their psyche is split, and the split-off feelings are unconsciously deemed wrong, dangerous and to be avoided at all costs. The symbiotically entangled person will be confused about his feelings since his feelings are likely to be merged with those of others. So, many people are frightened of their feelings, do not trust them and work hard to control them by all the means available through their survival strategies.

The following are generally considered to be our basic emotions:

- **Fear** tells us that we are under threat, that we are vulnerable and the environment is dangerous for some reason, prompting us to look for ways to save or protect ourselves. Terror is an extreme form of fear connected with the experience that one's actual life is under

195

immediate serious threat. It is therefore a primary emotion of trauma and is, in itself, a feared emotion: we are terrified of our terror.

- **Anger** as a primary emotion tells us that we need to protect ourselves, not necessarily from something actually dangerous. Anger tells us we need to set boundaries, differentiate ourselves from something that is not good for us, say "no" to something, express displeasure at something. Anger often accompanies other emotions, or even takes the place of them; we may feel angry with something that has scared us or caused us physical or emotional pain. Anger is also often an 'instead-of' emotion, frequently expressed as aggression, as a means of not feeling other feelings that we find unpleasant, painful or frightening, most commonly fear or grief. Anger in this sense is often the emotion of perpetration: acting with aggression towards another is a way of not feeling one's own trauma feelings of terror or grief.
- **Sadness** and **grief** tell us that we have lost, or are in the process of losing, something or someone that is dear to us, that we have a close emotional bond to.
- **Joy** tells us that all is well, we are safe, what is happening around us is good for us, enjoyable and pleasurable. We are comfortable and at ease with our situation. It is also a response to an inner sense of wellbeing/ exhilaration, which may not necessarily be immediately related to the environment.

Some writers on emotions will add:

- **Disgust** which functions to protect us from ingesting something harmful. This is primitively related to poisonous or otherwise harmful foods, but also relates to harmful, 'poisonous' or 'disgusting' experiences. It is often accompanied by nausea. Experiences of disgust and nausea are common in incidents of unpleasant, inappropriate and abusive sexual contact.

There are more complex emotional experiences that have a morally moderating and protective function, such as shame and guilt. There is often confusion about the difference between shame and guilt and the meanings of both often seem to overlap. Here I am attempting to make some distinction between them:

- **Shame,** in its healthy form, may inform us of our cultural and social wrong-doing, but the experience of shame usually involves a profound sense of exposure and humiliation to do with our sense of self, our very being. The person is exposed as *being* wrong, rather than just to have acted wrongly. The shamed person feels an acute desire not to exist. The norms for 'right' and 'wrong' in a family may be distorted, and shame and humiliation are often used as an aggressive weapon by the more powerful. In a family that has become founded on culturally and socially unacceptable activities, such as incest, violence or sexual abuse, shame abounds but can never be addressed or acknowledged, because to do so would call into question the foundations of the family, and would require people to experience their unresolved trauma.
- **Guilt,** in its healthy form, also tells us of our cultural and social wrong-doing, but is more often thought of as a feeling of having betrayed or let ourselves down by our behaviour and actions, by our *doing*. Guilt can also become distorted in a family that has much to feel guilty about. It tends to be more connected with actions that harm another. Guilt can also be used as a manipulative weapon: an avoidance of one's own guilt is often managed by making others feel guilty instead, as in a display of helpless and resigned 'martyrdom'.

And then there is love:

- **Love** is a particular emotion that has many functions, the most prominent of which are bonding and attachment. It is the emotion that prompts procreation, parenting, social and community effectiveness and collaboration, healthy symbiosis and relationship. Falling in love, in my view, is a particular kind of love that includes lust and may be a means of securing procreation and strong coupling that benefits the offspring. Falling in love has a kind of compulsive intense madness about it that, when one eventually falls out of love leaves one surprised at the intensity, and often longing for the same feeling again.

All emotions exist on a continuum. For example, fear can range from terror to mild unease; anger can range from rage to contempt, mild irritation, frustration or grumpiness; grief can range from extreme grief to mild sadness and sense of loss; joy can range from ecstasy to contentment. These words that I have used are examples and there are many other emotional terms that can be included.

One learns in therapy the skill of differentiating one's feelings as to whether one feels cross, angry, irritated, frustrated or aggrieved for example. Our emotional lives are deeply nuanced: the more integrated we become the less frightening our emotions are to us; the more we come to trust what we feel, the more subtle our use of emotional language.

Our emotions are, in the first instance, informative of our relationship to a situation, and in the second instance they move us to expression as the means of showing how we are affected and of discharging accumulated energy connected with the emotion. In some situations (i.e. anger or fear) our feelings are oriented towards effecting change. The emotions connected with trauma are strong, their expression is clear and primal, without moderation or modification, and their function is resolution and change. The emotional expressions that come from our survival self are moderated, modified, confused and indistinct, but may still be loud and commanding of attention. Their function is avoidance and maintenance of the split psychological structure.

Primary Emotional Expression

The properties of primary emotions are:

- The emotional expression may be strong, is always clear and over quite quickly, rarely more than a few minutes.
- The expression is accompanied by a movement towards connection with the self, another person or situation, rather than a movement to avoid connection.
- They flow freely, are voiced clearly and there is no sense of interruption.
- They are sometimes quite subtle, even quiet, as in a particularly deep breath or sigh, and relaxation in the body.
- Expression arises from the belly rather than higher up in the body, is fully supported by the breath and involves the whole body; the body becomes in the moment of expression an integrated whole.
- The emotion can be clearly defined as grief, anger, rage, terror, fear, love or joy.
- They enable the person to move on, and allow for change.
- The emotion expressed and the intensity of expression is congruent with the situation.
- Witnesses resonate with the feelings and are moved, and will feel the emotion in themselves almost as if their own: primary emotional expression in another stimulates our mirror neurones and limbic resonance.
- Once expressed the emotion is past and, while it may occur again, as for example with the ongoing process of grieving, each incident will be whole and satisfying in itself.
- Primary emotions cannot be forced.

Secondary (survival) Emotional Expression

Secondary emotional expression avoids true contact with what is needed, and is a substitute for and protection from the primary expression, and therefore is usually the emotional expression of the survival self. Secondary emotions are often 'instead-of' emotions, taking the place of experiencing the primary feelings, because the primary feelings are too frightening in that moment.

The feelings shown are ambiguous and derivative such as frustration and irritation (instead of anger), depression and melancholy (instead of grief), some forms of aggression (instead of rage), anxiety and panic (instead of terror and fear). Love is expressed as need, enthralment or slavish loyalty. Misery, petulance, self-pity, melancholy and endlessly welling tears are all typical expressions of secondary feelings. The experience is as if the feelings never resolve, never go anywhere and remain hopelessly entrenched and persistent; they are the emotional expression of symbiotic entanglement and survival.

Properties of secondary emotional expression:

- The purpose is to defend the person from feeling the deeper, primary feelings.
- They inhibit change and maintain the status quo of the psychological splits.
- They result in a movement away from engagement, and tend to make others want to move away from the person.
- The expression doesn't peak and seems without ending, and sometimes may continue for a long time without experience of resolution.
- They are not definable as a clear emotion such as grief, anger, fear or love, but usually a confusion of several.
- They appear to originate high up in the body, often in the throat, which may feel constricted, and they do not engage the whole body. Breathing is likely to be shallow, even stopped, or interrupted, gulped and panicky.
- They are often not congruent with the actual situation.

- They generally do not evoke resonance in witnesses; on the contrary often evoke impatience and frustration.
- They feel and are repetitive.

In my view, the resolution of trauma must, at some point, include a release and expression of the original trauma feelings by the client herself. There are many steps to this, and many constellations may be involved. Over time, in the constellation, the real trauma feelings may be seen and expressed by representatives of parts of the client, and by the client herself, sometimes only for a moment, and often confused with survival emotions. The emotional expressions of the client, or lack thereof, are useful diagnostically for the therapist, providing a direct indication of how safe and able to face her trauma the client is in the present moment.

A client, Bridget, in a constellation, while facing her 'intention', was very restless in her body. She stretched and moved and contorted her body, as if trying to relax it or let some tension go. At the same time she was very emotional, scrunching up her eyes and crying. Only momentarily did she make eye contact with her 'intention', and then quickly went back to crying and rubbing her eyes and moving her body. Her 'intention' was quite still and solid, and kept trying to make contact with Bridget, but nothing more happened. At times Bridget would seem to express strong emotion that, while involving effort and what looked like catharsis, didn't seem to change the overall process between her and her 'intention'. It seemed to me as if she tried to get something out of her that couldn't come, and I thought then "I wonder who this emotion really belongs to?" After I had asked her a bit more about her mother and her background, she included representatives for her mother, her grandmother and her great grandmother. The mother moved right away from the client, the grandmother faced in a different direction and the great grandmother started to turn around in circles looking at the ceiling. Then we put in a representative for the emotions and feelings that did not belong to Bridget. After a while this representative said she felt like she had a scream in her legs, but in her chest she felt anxiety and agitation, but could not express it. She also said that she felt most connected to the mother, but also the grand mother and great grandmother.

From this moment Bridget was more able to make contact with her 'intention', and eventually they moved further away and Bridget stopped crying and was able to be just with her 'intention'.

If the feelings that a person keeps trying to express are not her own feelings she cannot resolve them. In this example Bridget's emotions were through symbiotic entanglement with the mother's, and maybe also the grandmother's and even great grandmother's unexpressed terror (the scream) and suppressed feelings (the anxiety). The child in such a family will be unable to distinguish which feelings are really hers and will continue to attempt to resolve an emotional experience that isn't hers by continued emotional catharsis. The child tries to resolve the parent's emotional trauma, which, since it is not really hers, is not possible. A suggestion to the client in such a situation is to say to her 'intention' "We need to find out which feelings are ours, and express those, and leave our mother's feelings with her." This idea accomplishes several things: the client has a concept that perhaps the feelings she feels are not hers, and she may then find that this helps her to connect with her own feelings, which she may then be able to express in a resolving way; it provides the notion that she can be separate, or more separate from her mother; and it confirms to her that she can be an autonomous feeling person herself. To have the idea that her feelings may be confused with her mother's already empowers the person to make such distinctions. Endless attempted catharsis that doesn't resolve may lead the therapist to consider such confusion, and including the necessary representatives may show this distinction.

8.3 Working with the Survival Self

> "As a therapist, I do not want to be used by a patient's
> survival self so that the psychotherapy becomes a
> consolidation of the split rather than an integration."
> *(Ruppert, 2011)*

The strategies of survival involve illusion, self-deception and avoidance as the means of protecting the person from the reality of the trauma and maintaining the silencing of the trauma. The therapist needs to be able to step aside from being with the client in a way that may become a consolidation of the client's splits.

Julia is a young woman in her thirties. She smiles and talks a lot, and seems very engaging. Having done several constellations she had decided on an intention worded as follows: "I want to understand really who I am." She said that she felt confused by herself, and often felt very frightened, and was not sure what she was frightened of. She was the sixth and youngest child in her family. She said that her mother had always been anxious, and apart from the fact that her mother's mother had been quite a hard and cold woman she didn't know much about her mother's family. Her father had seemed more accessible, but her childhood experience was of having been bullied and shoved around by everyone.

As soon as she was placed, Julia's 'intention' seemed very distressed. She reported feeling confused, at one moment feeling like an old man and at another feeling like a woman, and another feeling like a small child. This is likely to indicate a symbiotic confusion with others in the constellation, so we included representatives for Julia's mother and father, and subsequently their parents, Julia's grandparents. As these people joined the constellation Julia's 'intention' became more distressed, but more clearly a distressed child than confused with others. Meanwhile Julia kept coming up with stories about people in her family, turning to me and telling me more and more information, and then trying to soothe her 'intention', but not really seeing her 'intention's' distress. The other representatives of her parents and grandparents showed very clearly that there was much distress in the family, and no one related well to anyone else.

203

Suddenly Julia's 'intention' started to cry and said "I can't bear it anymore, no one tells the truth, everything is just tales about themselves . . .", and then to Julia "You just tell more and more stories and no one sees me, you don't take any real notice of me." The 'intention' then curled up and sobbed. Julia kept trying to look after and soothe her 'intention'. We included a representative for 'the stories', and this representative stood quietly in the middle of the room looking at Julia and her 'intention'. Immediately the 'intention' quietened, and looked at Julia and said: "We can't listen to any more stories, it is too much for us". Julia found this very difficult to hear, and she couldn't look at her 'intention', but the 'intention' felt much stronger and started to look clearly at Julia, saying "We have to stop living the stories." Finally Julia turned to me and said: "All my life has been stories, I really don't know what is true any more and I don't know what anything is without the stories. I hang onto the stories because I'm so frightened that if I don't, nothing will mean anything any more . . ." She started to cry. I suggested she say this to her 'intention', which she did, but she still found it difficult to look at her 'intention'.

This moment of seeing such a profound truth is often very disorienting, and so it was for Julia, so we ended the constellation there. To see the whole framework of one's family and one's life as having been based on the avoidance of trauma by the construction of distracting stories to explain things is disorienting, and for some moments, even some days, this can feel like having the rug pulled out from underneath one's feet. Nevertheless, usually there is also a sense of hope that comes from a moment of having faced a truth. The following day, in the group, Julia said she felt shocked, but clearer and somehow different in a way that she couldn't quite put into words.

It is the survival self that finds it hard to look into the truth, and the struggle between the healthy self and the survival self is always present. It is the therapist's job to recognise the client's aversion to looking at the truth, understand it, and not collude with it. During the above constellation Julia's struggle between her healthy self and her survival self was evident throughout. Her difficulty in looking at her 'intention' at the end showed this clearly.

The 'intention' had reached a place where it could not any longer avoid the truth and the distress that goes with it, but for Julia to look at this was still very hard.

To work effectively the therapist needs to realise how completely terrifying it is likely to be for a child to exist in a family that never faces the truth, and instead tells delusional stories. How does the child find anything solid to rely on? Little is real, and yet a child needs some sense of reality to feel safe. If there is none the child cannot feel safe, and that is a trauma. In the confusion of Julia's trauma, her survival self also ignores her own distress (her 'intention'), because to really see it and feel it is too terrifying at that moment. If the therapist understands this, he can see the avoiding survival strategies, not collude with them, but also see clearly the client's current need for these strategies to 'survive' this moment, which in a sense will parallel the original trauma situation. If Julia cannot look at her 'intention' it is because she has seen something that has dislodged her perception of herself and her life, and to look at her distress at that moment seems too much. Better to end the constellation here rather than try to push further and risk an unhelpful retraumatisation.

The Survival Self and Transference

Much traditional psychotherapy is oriented around the phenomenon of transference, which is a Freudian term used to describe the unconscious assignment to others of feelings and attitudes associated with significant figures from the person's early life. The transferential interpretation is that the client behaves towards the therapist as if he were a significant person from the client's early life, usually the mother or father. Working 'with the transference' is the primary method of psychoanalysis and psychodynamic therapy and involves a process that ranges from interpreting the transference back to the client, to accepting that the client is going to behave in this way towards the therapist until he or she has worked through whatever the relevant material is, and is able to relate to the therapist as the person that he actually is. Often the approach is a combination of these two.

However, I take the view that since unresolved trauma is held unconscious, often by means of secrets, subterfuge and self deception, the therapist, when working with trauma, must always work with reality as it is in the moment. What I mean by this is that, although the phenomenon of the transferred material interpreted as 'transference' is real to the client, it does not relate to the therapist as he actually is. Both methods of working with transference mentioned above seem to me to be incongruent with an understanding of trauma and the aim of supporting integration and autonomy: interpreting the transference back to the client tends to transfer authority for the therapy to the therapist, making him the arbiter of the reality of the client, while not confronting the transference colludes with the delusion and is likely to become "a consolidation of the client's splits rather than an integration" (Ruppert, 2011).

Transference as a phenomenon happens, but it is an expression of the survival self, not the healthy self. If this is understood by the therapist there could be an argument in favour of interpreting to the client his survival strategies in light of the transferred experience. However, in my view this still puts authority in the hands of the therapist, and as such might be unhelpful. These decisions are ones that the therapist must make in the particular moment.

The healthy self is able to make clear contact with another, whereas the survival self avoids contact and projects ideas and illusions onto the other. Ideally the trauma constellations therapist recognises this and does not engage with such survival projections, but stays with the here-and-now reality, maintaining a sense of separateness (therapist's autonomy) and side-stepping the transferred material. To designate the therapist too much as a 'helper' (which immediately affects the power balance between therapist and client) lays him open to a sense of inappropriate responsibility for the client, thereby causing him to lose his autonomy and become vulnerable to collusion with the client's survival self:

"With psychotherapists who strongly take on a helping role, there is a tendency to protect the client from his trauma feelings. Here the therapist may change the subject, comfort the client or try to calm him down whenever he starts to feel his fear, anger or pain, i.e. his trauma feelings. In this instance the therapist is reacting from her own survival self, which also wants to prevent the therapist's own trauma from surfacing."
(Ruppert, 2011)

Resonance or Counter-Transference?

Within the traditions of psychotherapy, as well as the phenomenon of 'transference', there are also the designations of 'counter-transference' and 'projective identification'. All these terms roughly cover the phenomenon of the transfer of experiences from one person to another and the resulting effects. My thinking is that the transference phenomenon is the same as the 'representative experience' in a constellation, but with an explanation that differs from the one we favour in the constellations process (see also Chapter 4 on the brain system).

So, while 'transference' covers the supposed transfer by the client of their experience of their mother or father or other significant person onto the therapist, counter-transference was originally termed to cover the therapist's own unresolved unconscious issues that may be stimulated by the client's behaviour. If the therapist does not become conscious of this, she may behave back to the client from her counter-transference experience, her own issues and needs, rather than from a clear, unentangled place. This leads to an increasingly entangled and collusive relationship if not addressed. This is often how couples relate to each other, as I shall discuss in the chapter on couples-work (Chapter 10).

Latterly counter-transference has been redefined to include the phenomenon of the therapist's experiences as a form of attunement to the client's state. In other words the therapist's experiences while in the company of the client, may be interpreted as coming from unresolved personal issues of the therapist, but once made conscious for the therapist may also give valuable diagnostic information about the client.

The distinction is important: if I have strong feelings when sitting with the client that are clearly not resonance feelings (as when the client is overcome with primary emotional feelings that move me), then I must suspect survival mode in him, *and suspect it also of myself*. If it were not the case I could sit with a client in his survival mode, recognising it, without having any strong reaction myself. The reaction in myself comes from my entanglement with the client's survival mode, which must mean that my own survival mode is activated. A distinction that may help here is that a *reaction* is like a knee-jerk action, a non-considered answer to a stimulus, whereas a *response* comes from a sense of separateness and autonomy, is usually to a degree a considered and responsible answer to the stimulus,[63] and includes an awareness of the broader context of the unfolding event. This ability to respond rather than react is indicative of our freedom from entanglement, and was stated as such by the American existential psychologist, Rollo May, in the 1970s:

> "Human freedom involves our capacity to pause between the stimulus and response and, in that pause, to choose the one response toward which we wish to throw our weight."
> *(May, 1975)*

In the end the work goes well if the therapist remains unentangled and unaffected by anything the client does from her survival self. If the therapist does feel a strong reaction in the sense described above, it is helpful to notice it, recognise it for what it is, and internally step aside from it. The more the therapist is aware of her own vulnerability to being restimulated, the easier it will be to maintain this place.

---

[63] The trauma startle response that comes from the ancient, reptilian brain is a quick and unconsidered reaction rather than actually a response, even though it is called a response. In that situation of course the reaction is, hopefully, what contributes to saving the person. It needs to be quick, sharp, and without any time for consideration.

If the therapist understands the terrifying nature of trauma feelings, and the function of the survival self as a natural instinctual reaction to trauma, to a great extent he will be able to avoid such a situation. I have developed one simple rule for myself that helps: Never, ever, argue with the client. The argument posed by the client is usually energised by his survival needs, and if the client's survival self is active then the therapist knows that the client's anxiety is heightened. The therapist may be right in his contention (and he may not), but the message from the client is clear: whatever it is, it is too much for the client for now. For the therapist to engage with such argument is likely to entangle him in the client's inner confused and conflicted process. This is particularly the case when victim-perpetrator dynamics are at play; it is extremely easy for the therapist to be drawn into these dynamics and become entangled with the client's process, acting in a persecutory manner towards the client, and at the same time feeling victimised by the client. The forces at play are at times very strong, but the therapist can remember: if the survival strategies of the client are strongly activated, the client's trauma is re-stimulated, her trust in the therapist and the situation in that moment is diminished, and to try to go further may not be useful or even possible.

8.4 Working with Symbiotic Trauma and Symbiotic Entanglement

It is hard to say what we are likely to see in the constellations process. Often in the course of working with a person the work may focus on a pre-birth time, as in the following example:

In a group, Mary's intention was that she wanted to be able to be a better mother to her children. In the constellation Mary's 'intention' immediately felt contorted in her body, very restricted, and with her eyes closed. Over the next few minutes, as Mary watched her 'intention', the representative went down onto the floor and seemed to be trying to wind her legs around her body as if to take up as little space as possible. Mary sat down with the representative and tried to help, but the 'intention' seemed not to trust her ... when Mary tried to move closer to the 'intention', the 'intention' got very anxious. The representative said it felt as though they were worlds apart. Mary then started to talk about how her mother told her that she had felt very ambivalent about having children. Her own mother (the client's grandmother) had been in a violent marriage and had had several abortions, and the client's mother herself had got pregnant by mistake, had been disowned by her mother and had not wanted to go through with the pregnancy. Mary added that her mother was very cut off and there was some notion that she had been abused as a child. She continued to say, while crying, that she felt very confused with her mother and was confused about whether she had been abused or not herself. She chose a representative for her mother, who found her own place, facing the 'intention' and stared at her without feelings. The 'mother' said she felt nothing, and felt like she had no relationship with anyone. The 'intention' then said she felt as though she had never been born, as if she was still scrunched up inside, too large but frightened of moving. She said: "it's as if you [Mary] were born but I stayed here." Mary then said that her mother told her that her birth had been very overdue, and very hard for the mother. After a little while Mary and her 'intention' were able to talk to each other and sit close, but as yet without touching. We stopped there.

The reason we stopped there was because Mary herself felt she had done enough. She had seen how disconnected her mother was, and had been able to distinguish between herself and her mother, and had made a connection as it would seem with a part of herself that had not wanted to be born. She felt that this showed her how difficult it was for her to be a mother to her own children and connect with them. The process must take its time, and to attempt to take this further at this time would have been too much for Mary.

In my experience of working with the constellations process in this way, this is not unusual. In utero trauma, which may be caused by such ambivalence on the part of the mother towards her unborn child, seems at times to cause the child to be ambivalent about being born: a part of the self is split off, and remains as if still unborn. When people are able to see another person represent this terrified and reluctant part of themselves it often explains many things about their experience of themselves over the whole of their life. How is one to engage fully with life if one is split and alienated from part of oneself at such an early stage? While most constellations do not spontaneously and immediately go to this depth, it is not hard to see the seeds of this dilemma in many constellations. For some it seems this is the starting place for their healing, and some people's first constellation goes to this level; for others it seems that they need to see the symbiotic entanglement first in order to glimpse the seriousness of what they are dealing with; the survival self cannot allow the person to venture to this place yet.

I have thought that there is a general direction of healing whereby the person first of all needs to see how entangled she is with the traumatised system, and to see how traumatised her mother and/or father was, before she can really start to engage with her splits. For many, until this point, they have continually expended all their energy in trying to get good contact with their parents, oblivious to the impossibility of this; all their relationships (including with their therapist) in some way are attempts to get from the mother the good, loving connection that the mother could not make, and so become repetitive failures. The illusion here is that the answer is external to the self, that someone else must provide her with what she lacks. This is encapsulated in the phrase: "I wish my mother had been different." It is such a hard thing to take on that she wasn't and couldn't be, and nothing can ever be done about that. The survival self resists this perception because to allow it means that the person must experience the devastating feelings that this idea protects her from. There is, and never was, anything the child could do to change the state of the mother, but for many the delusion persists: "If I can just figure out what would change her, how I could help her, heal her, save her from her pain, then everything will be alright and I can have the happy childhood I didn't get."

There is a point in this process that is often a moment of devastation and despair for the client, when she can really see for the first time how impossible it was, and when she realises how alone she is (and in a sense always was), how confused with others' traumas and how much she doesn't really know who she is separate from this. It isn't an easy moment for anyone, and for some it may take several constellations to really see it. However, as one client wrote to me:

"I am coming to realise just how entangled I am with my mother, to the point where I literally cannot tell what are my thoughts and feelings and which are hers. It's really discon- certing to become conscious of the extent of our entanglement – although much better I'm sure to be starting to discover the real cause of my frequent distress, rather than battling along with it as best I can in the dark ... I feel at once completely overwhelmed and terrified, and at the same time strangely reassured and comforted by this process – it's bizarre!"

As this client says, within that moment of experiencing the overwhelming terror there is also always the seed of hope. As another client put it:

"Although I feel terribly disoriented and frightened, I also realise how much I have never been able to trust myself ... in fact I have never really known who I really am, and I now think for the first time I can find out who I am and what in myself I can trust and what is confused with others ... and that feels such an enormous relief and reassuring."

There are many routes to self-integration, and many steps along the way; indeed there are many 'integrations' that become part of the overall integration of the self. Symbiotic trauma by its nature is confused with symbiotic entanglement, because it is the mother's own symbiotic entanglement and her own traumas that underlie the attachment trauma (except perhaps in cases of adoption or other early separation). However, I do see in many people's journey that there comes a point, maybe several such points, where the very simple relationship with the self becomes the only thing that matters. These are often intensely moving moments, as the person can finally see herself as she is, distinct from the trials and traumas of her parents, purely and simply trustworthy and good. Herein lies real hope for a real future.

8.5 Adoption and other Separations

"Adopted children are self-invented because we have to be;
there is an absence, a void, a question mark at the very
beginning of our lives. A crucial part of our story is
gone, and violently, like a bomb in the womb."
(Winterson, 2010)

"[The] baby explodes into an unknown world that is only
knowable through some kind of a story . . . adoption drops
you into the story after it has started. It's like reading a book
with the first few pages missing. It's like arriving after curtain
up. The feeling that something is missing never, ever leaves
you – and it can't, and it shouldn't, because something
is missing." *(Winterson, 2010)*

Adoption or any other post natal extended or permanent separation must always incur an attachment trauma in my view. How could it be otherwise? The connection with the mother that has developed over the nine months in the womb, through the shared experience of the birth and whatever time the child does spend with the mother before being separated, is lost, broken. What must that be like for this vulnerable child?

Regardless of the reasons for the separation, which may well be intended for the child's benefit, it seems to me such a separation must cause an attachment trauma. Even if the child has to be put into intensive care for his survival, or separated from the mother because her life is under threat, the separation is going to be a massive moment of loss, confusion and fear for the child. No one can explain anything to the child at this early stage; the child is on his own to deal with something he has no means to make sense of. This is different from any in utero traumatisation or imprinting of the mother's split psyche which may have happened before the child is separated from the mother. We do not really know the deeper impact of such things. Does the adopted child already have an internalised symbiotic confusion with her real mother? How then does the child adapt to the psyches of the adoptive parents? There are many questions yet to be answered.

In the constellations process I have seen the client have a moment of extreme disorientation when the constellation contains representatives for both biological parents and adoptive parents as if, although the knowledge of adoption was there, somehow the reality of there being other, biological, real parents, hadn't really penetrated. I have seen the client show psychological confusion with her mother's mental/emotional state, even though she had been removed from her mother's care just a few days after her birth. I have worked with people whose lifelong sense of disorientation and self-confusion, never previously verbalised, appears in stark reality as they stand in their constellation with representatives for their biological parents.

For the mother, giving up a child is likely to be a situation of confusion and disorientation. Illegitimacy has been a major stigma in western society until very recently, and many adoptions in the 20th century were accompanied, for the mother, with feelings of shame, of being coerced by her family, socially ostracised and, within all of this, helpless. In the 1950s many young pregnant girls were sent to institutions for the duration of their pregnancy and the birth, after which the child was taken away. How do these impending feelings of the mother also affect the child? We don't know, but within the constellations process we may see vestiges of what it might have been like.

> Sheila's constellation showed, through the 'intention's' trans-fixed fascination with her biological mother's mother, how an entanglement can form in utero. Sheila had been taken from her mother pretty much straight after her birth and put in an incubator, after which she was given to her adoptive parents.

214

The 'intention' in the constellation experienced sadness and a sense of fear whenever the representative for the biological mother looked at her or came close. Sheila found it very hard to look at her 'mother' and her 'intention', and kept distracting herself. When we included a representative for the baby Sheila who had been given away Sheila burst into tears, went to the 'baby' and held onto her tightly sobbing. Meanwhile the 'intention' finally could look away from the mother, towards Sheila and the 'baby'.

In terms of working with the constellations process, the information that a client gives in the opening session, whether about the circumstances of his birth, being taken from his mother into an incubator or other such separation, and adoption (whether official and legal, or unofficially by another family member) is important. The therapist will decide in collaboration with the client, in response to what happens in the constellation, when and if to include the relevant representatives.

Isabel knew that she had been adopted. She had always known, her adoptive parents taking the view that they shouldn't keep it a secret and that it was better to tell the child as soon as she could understand. Isabel didn't remember being told, she had just always known. She knew nothing about her mother, and she had never felt any need to find out. Her adoptive parents had not told her anything more. As she told me this information it was just facts, the story of her life. There was no emotion in the telling, and during the rest of the interview she used the words 'my mother' and 'my father' for her adoptive parents. These adoptive parents had been "very good" to her, and she felt grateful. She said she loved her 'mother' and 'father' (meaning her adoptive parents) and that they felt like her parents. Isabel's intention was to be able to relate better to her husband and her children.

In the constellation we included both sets of parents. Isabel felt quite disoriented, while her 'intention' felt no interest in the adoptive parents but compelled towards the biological mother. The adoptive parents seemed to have more of a connection with each other than with Isabel or her 'intention'. The biological mother said she felt very weak and it was unbearable to look at

215

either Isabel or her 'intention'. The biological father walked to the opposite end of the room and faced away, but said later that he felt he was not allowed to turn, that he wasn't allowed to look at Isabel. For Isabel the experience was startling, to have her biological mother and father embodied was very confusing she said, as she had never really considered them as real. In relation to her original intention, she understood that somehow she had always felt ungrounded and slightly unreal, and that this impacted on her relationships with her husband and her children. This was enough for her in that moment.

Death of the mother in childbirth

If the mother dies in childbirth (or when the child is still very young), this then is a complex situation, where the child loses his mother, and also has to contend with the resulting emotional environment. Who cares for the child? If it is the father or other close family member, does the child then, with all his other symbiotic trials, spend his early years in an atmosphere of expressed or unexpressed grief? How does the father look at this child? Is the child confused with the death of the mother, even subtly seen as the cause of it, by the father? Or does the father perhaps take refuge and solace from the child? How does this affect the bonding ability of child and father? Of course the loss of the mother results in a symbiotic trauma, but how is this made more complex by the attitudes and abilities of those who take on the care of the child? How also might this affect the relationship between the infant and any siblings? These are all complex questions, the answers to which may emerge in the constellations process.

David's mother had died shortly after he was born, and he described himself as depressed and constantly preoccupied with death. His father had married shortly after his mother's death, and his stepmother had brought him and his two older brothers up. David said he felt that he hardly knew his father, who was alcoholic, and although his stepmother had been kind and looked after him and his brothers well, after she had a child herself David felt she had ignored him. David's intention for the constellation was to find a good relationship, and find happiness. In the constellation David's 'intention' went to the opposite side of the room and sat down on the floor facing the wall. David look shocked and asked his 'intention' what was going on. The 'intention' replied that he felt alone, isolated and almost overwhelmed with sadness and grief ... he couldn't bear to face into the room. When we included the 'father' he stood like a statue and stared into the distance. When we included a representative for David's mother she said she felt lost and confused and didn't know who anyone was ... but David's 'intention' was able to turn around and look at her. After a while the 'intention' went over to the mother and started to cry, even though the 'mother' only attended to him in a desultory fashion. David stood at the edge of the circle, overcome with emotion and very attentive to his 'intention' even though he felt he could not go towards the 'intention'. This felt enough for David. He didn't feel he could go to his 'intention' at this stage, but realised just how much emotion was tied up in him over the loss of his mother.

8.6 Working with Children

I don't work with children, not because I don't think it possible to work in this way, but because I never have and I prefer to work with the parents. In my view children's behaviours are the symptoms that point towards the parents' issues. Children do not choose the atmosphere and environment in which they are born and grow up. I do not believe that any child is inherently bad or badly behaved; more to the point they are doing their best in the face of their own attachment trauma and their entanglement with the parents' unresolved traumas and the emotional environment in which they find themselves, and must remain. Although in my opinion the parents cannot heal the traumas of their children, they can, by resolving their own traumas, make the space in which the children grow clearer and less entangled with historical traumas. The more the mother strengthens her healthy aspect and diminishes her need for survival strategies, the more the child is able to have a realistic and healthy relationship with his mother, which must, in turn, strengthen his own healthy part. The child then has a better chance of growing up in the best possible circumstances, given the original context, and additionally will perceive the parents' process of healing, and take courage from this to deal with his own trauma as an adult. As a client wrote to me:

> "Since doing this work and becoming clearer about just how entangled I have been with my mother's unresolved stuff I am finding that my relationship with my son [4 years old] is becoming much easier. I realise that he has sparked so much in me that isn't to do with him, and I am now finding it so much easier to be with him . . . simply with him as a child . . . and he also has changed. He doesn't wet the bed any more and he listens to me in a way he never did before. I realise now that he was reacting to my panic and terror . . . now I don't feel it so much he seems to relax."

It is possible that the more serious behavioural difficulties of children, diagnoses such as ADHD or other 'attention deficit disorders', have as their underlying cause the parents' unresolved traumas. If the parents are always maintaining their splits, oscillating between a kind of love and suppressed terror, and relating from survival strategies, the child has formed his attachment to this, and can only relate to his mother and father through his own survival strategies. It may be that ADHD comes from the child's desperate attempts to survive in a severely traumatised, anxious and entangled family, where suppressed panic and anxiety are all he knows. His aggression and disruptive behaviour may be his means of protecting himself from his confusion with his parent's panic.

I know from discussions with colleagues that working with children is especially difficult if the parents have designated the child as the problem and refuse to seek help for themselves. The therapist in this situation is required to send the child back into a family environment that doesn't change, but remains a repeatedly traumatising one. Perhaps in such a situation, the very best the therapist can do is show the child that there are other options for relationship, that adults do and can behave differently from his parents. One colleague I know refuses to work with a child unless the parents also seek help. For myself, if someone approaches me wanting me to work with her child, I say that I prefer to work with the parents and see if she can agree to that.

With regard to doing constellations work with the child, I think this is entirely possible. Children are unlikely to have any difficulty working with the constellations process, even less than some adults, because they are likely to be less conditioned and more open to the playful and experimental aspect of the process. Working with trauma constellations with children is an area for research.

8.7 Incest and Child Abuse

"The history of childhood is a nightmare from which we have only recently begun to awaken. The further back in history one goes, the lower the level of child care, and the more likely children are to be killed, abandoned, beaten, terrorized, and sexually abused." (de Mause, 1974)

This is the opening statement from de Mause's book *The History of Childhood* published in 1974. It seems that today we are, for the first time in our western history, beginning to understand children and respect their rights. His account of the history of parents' relationship to their children is horrifying and shocking. However, even in our more enlightened time many children suffer terrible abuse in their only possible home.

It seems that incest and child abuse are systemic issues, in that such acts are usually re-enacted over several generations (Fromm, 2012; Schore, 2012, de Mause, 1974). Such distorted family dynamics are the nature of the traumatised bonded system in Ruppert's schema of types of trauma (see Chapter 1.3). In this view it makes sense to think that, for a person to perpetrate such aberrant acts, their ability to relate to and empathise with their victim is seriously impaired, such impairment being caused by the dissociation and distortion of perception resulting from severe traumatisation. The proposal here then is that it can only be traumatised people who perpetrate such abusive acts, and it is a traumatised system that does not see or overlooks such aberrant behaviours. This is not an excuse but an explanation. It is well understood that sexual abuse, domestic violence and child abuse are usually re-enacted across several generations, seen as the result of the child experiencing such behaviour as the norm for childhood relating, and thence replicating the behaviour in their adult relating (Egeland, Jacobvitz & Sroufe, 1988). In a traumatised bonding system, even if incest or other child abuses are not overtly enacted on the person, my work has shown that the atmosphere of the system is imbued with such abuse, never discussed or openly acknowledged. System members who may restrain their actions, are nevertheless influenced by such thoughts and feelings in all their relationships, particularly with their own child. It is a system based on perpetrator/victim dynamics, where the system members are deeply and unconsciously entangled and may not know how to be otherwise.

While there are many from such a family, perhaps directly abused themselves, who as adults manage to act differently with their partner and children, nevertheless they will hold their own unresolved unconscious trauma, which may restrict their ability to be really open and loving with their children. It would seem likely that they consciously and unconsciously must hold part of themselves back from relationship. I would also propose that there will always be an underlying early attachment trauma, since to be born into such a family must presuppose that the parents have suffered some trauma themselves, and so are compromised in their ability to provide a safe attachment for their child.

I have worked with many clients who fear that they have been sexually abused but have no memory or other evidence. My experience of working with such people is that, if they have actually been abused, at some point the memories will emerge in a way that the client feels sure of, whereas if not the person's fears may be located in their symbiotic entanglement with others earlier in the system who have been so exposed. In the close and intimate process of attachment, the child cannot separate herself from her mother's psychological state, and if the mother herself has suffered abuse, her child will not be able to differentiate her feelings from those unresolved feelings of the abused mother.

It is also often the case that those who come from systems that are seriously traumatised over several generations tend to be drawn to others who are similarly traumatised. The danger of perpetuation is compounded by dissociation and confusion, if not by enactment (Egeland & Susman-Stillman, 1996). An important question to consider is: why does this woman find herself married to an abuser, or vice versa: why does this man come into relationship with a woman who has been abused or is abusive herself? In my experiences of couples work (which I will discuss more in a later chapter), I have seen many relationships which have as their basis a repetition of the dynamics of symbiotic trauma, on both sides. People are drawn to each other for many, complex reasons, most of which originate with symbiotic trauma and entanglement.

Incest is difficult to work with, because of its quiet, private, dark, secretive and systemic nature: everyone within the system is in some way unconsciously, or consciously, involved, and everyone is therefore somehow the perpetrator *and* the victim of the incest. Apart from the actual abuser and abused, everyone else may have their own particular involvement: the child who isn't actually abused but unconsciously knows, and keeps quiet because if she spoke out she would be betraying the systemic 'contract' of silence and collusion, and she may hope to avoid being abused herself. To betray such a 'contract' is terrifying for the child because his or her safety paradoxically depends on the family. She has grown from an infant in this family, and as abusive as it may be, her bonding with it makes any betrayal of the family very personally threatening. She has lived her whole life in such a confusion of values it is unlikely she can see through this to take such a step.

Or the child who actually desires the abuse because in this confused family, that appears to be the means of obtaining some 'loving' contact. Or the child who, for safety, sides unconsciously or consciously with the abuser because the symbiotic contract in this family is that the abuser may do what he or she likes. The boy child who knows, and copies the father by abusing his sisters; or who fears he will be abused as well and becomes confused about his sexual identity. Or the boy who desires sex with the mother because of his confusion about the nature of the relationship and the expression of connection in this system.

All members of the system may become both victim and perpetrator. The mother, who may not know about the abuse because she herself is traumatised, and so is dissociated and does not recognise the signals; or who, having come from an abusive family herself, also abuses her children, or who lives out a violent and abusive relationship with her husband; or the mother who sees the abuse, and because her own traumatised self is so distorted, she relinquishes her daughter to be abused by her husband, rather than be abused (raped) herself; or, because she comes from a sexually traumatised system herself, in her confused sexuality she is excited that her husband abuses her daughter.

The abuser perpetrates from his own painfully abused part. He (or she) cannot bear to feel his traumatised victim self, and so acts to make others feel that instead. A person becomes a perpetrator because he has been a victim of perpetration him or herself. I don't think there is any such thing as a person who is just evil; I believe that what one might call an 'evil person' is one who comes from a family traumatised over several, even many, generations.

Working with the constellation of a person who comes from a traumatised bonded system is complex. More often than not the process is severely restricted in the beginning, as the person (and the constellation) manifests the embargo on talking about anything that endangers the guarding of the unspoken secret. To do the necessary work requires the person to face and speak about the unspeakable, which is often experienced as an extreme betrayal of the family, and a severe threat to the person's own safety; speaking out in this family is experienced as life-threatening. A member of such a family may view family members as kind and loving, and yet somewhere she also knows this is not the truth. Coming to own this can take time. I had a client whose main issue was that she had never had a relationship with anyone, and all her constellations for quite a while were oriented around wanting to be in a relationship and her difficulties with this. At the same time she admitted having no memory of her childhood at all up to the age of 16, although insisting that apart from her mother being quite strict, there was nothing wrong. However, it is not usual at all for someone to have no childhood memories. It was very hard for her to move away from the issue of current relationship as the problem, to having an interest in her childhood difficulties. To focus on the present day relationship issue was, in effect, a distraction from the underlying issues. It took her many constellations until she was ready to see the confusion and trauma in her family's background.

> Charlotte's sister had committed suicide the previous year and while Charlotte had been very shocked, what preoccupied her most was the fact that the signals had been there that her sister was vulnerable but she hadn't realised what the implications were. Her intention was to value herself as she thought she should. The representative for her 'intention' immediately closed her eyes and looked very shaky and fragile. When Charlotte went close to her 'intention' it became clear that the 'intention' was frightened of Charlotte. When we included a representative for Charlotte's mother, this representative said she felt sick, vulnerable and very scared. Meanwhile Charlotte looked at this representative for her mother with obvious rage and accusation. Charlotte then told of many ways in which her mother had tortured her as a child, and said that she felt absolute rage towards her. We included the mother's mother

and grandmother, and all expressed feelings of disgust, nausea, fear, rage and other physical symptoms. Charlotte then said that she thought the mother within her wanted to torture her own inner child (referring to her 'intention').

It became obvious that in order to survive the tortures of her mother (who had obviously been tortured herself) Charlotte had repeated the perpetration within herself: she behaved similarly to her 'traumatised' child self, as a way of surviving her mother's treatment. She was confused with her mother's rage at the grandmother, and found the only solution in becoming a perpetrator herself to her victimised (traumatised) self. In this way the perpetrator/victim dynamics within a traumatised bonding system become the internalised self dynamics as a survival strategy so as not to feel the strong feelings of her trauma.

Many complex feelings are involved in such cases: confused systemic feelings such as shame, guilt, hate, contempt, murderous rage, violation and violence. Distinguishing which such feelings are one's own and which belong to others takes time and many constellations, and requires a sense of safety and trust in the therapist and the process.

In the end a symbiotic trauma will become apparent, but it may take time and clarification of the symbiotic entanglements before the client can come to this point. Along the way, as the client separates and integrates different splits within herself, strengthening her healthy self and lessening her need for her survival strategies, she will also always to an extent be addressing the underlying trauma of attachment.

8.8 Trauma and the Body

> "... [trauma] therapy needs to consist of helping people to be
> in their bodies and to understand their bodily sensations. And
> this is certainly not something that any of the traditional
> psychotherapies, that we have all been taught, help people to
> do very well." *(van der Kolk, 1998)*

> "Trauma is a psychophysical experience, even when the
> traumatic event causes no direct bodily harm."
> *(Rothschild, 2000)*

The mind inhabits the body, and the body is a reflection of the
mind. The psychological splits that happen in a trauma do not
happen separately from the body. They are held in the body
and by the body; by the millions of small muscular contrac-
tions, many of which, after the trauma is past, do not release
or relax back into their original state. Our body, to someone
who can read it such as an experienced osteopath, chiropractor
or physiotherapist, is a reflection of our trauma history. The
body bears the burden[64] of the psychological processes of
trauma, and trauma work must in this sense be bodywork.

This has consequences in relation to our thinking about
physical illnesses: how much might a physical symptom
actually be a symptom of the stress of trauma survival? How
much may the physical ailment be a strategy of survival that,
over time, has coalesced from the psychological and physical
stresses of maintaining the splits into a gross detectable illness?
It is possible and useful to consider the potential contribution
of unresolved trauma in any physical ailments, even if the
particular illness is generally thought of as a genetically transmitted condition.

The issue of genetics versus the emotional and psychological effects of traumatic events seems not clear yet from the
scientific perspective. I would propose that what may seem to

---

[64] This is the title of an excellent book on the topic of the physiology of trauma
by Robert C Scaer *(Scaer, 2001)*

be a simple genetic inheritance may have its origins in a traumatic event, the survival of which caused a particular form of psycho-physiological compromise that may in itself reflexively feed back into the genetic system. Epigenetics is the study of how events and experiences may influence and alter the DNA expression. Apparently our DNA structure does not easily change, but how it performs and expresses itself does. Usually these alterations are discussed in terms of chemical changes, but I think it is unhelpful only to think in terms of chemical changes and imbalances. If a high stress and subsequent trauma event causes the body to produce all sorts of hormonal (chemical) changes, which in the resulting survival mode may continue to be produced, then it would seem that we must think that these chemical changes may be those that cause the DNA expression to alter. In other words, if the organism after the trauma has fixed itself in a certain way of being (the survival mode), this may then cause a continuing chemical change that becomes the status quo. Just as children may adopt the same behavioural survival strategies as their parents, they may also have the same chemical changes resulting in the same physical illnesses.

Physical symptoms, just like psychological symptoms, should not be ignored; they are natural warnings that something is wrong, alerting us to attend to ourselves, and ignoring them is another version of avoidance. We may not want to hear the messages behind the alarm, but at the same time we ignore them at our peril.

The Constellations Process as Bodywork

Most trauma therapists now accept that trauma work must include the body (Levine, 1997, 2008, 2010, Rothschild, 2000, van der Kolk, 1994). The constellations process is a body work: it requires the client, and the representatives, to get out of their seat and stand up; and in standing, immediately we are more connected with our body. To stand and choose representatives, walking around as they are placed in the room, immediately puts the client much more in touch with her own body, and the constellations process shows, in the body movements, configurations and contortions of the representatives, how things are in that part of the psyche. Often when a representative is chosen and placed you can see her shake her body slightly, often looking down, seeming to go inside, to connect with her bodily self in order to know herself as this representation. The client often does likewise.

The information that emerges from the body, if attended to, trusted and valued, is less easily manipulated into delusions and stories. Like our emotions, the body has a truth and honesty that cannot be denied. It is the thinking mind that creates stories, interpretations and ideas about things, the body and emotional self cannot. The mind interprets the body and emotions, and will do so according to its current belief system, but that may not be the truth. A highly traumatised person finds inhabiting her body painful and frightening, and her survival self will switch off these physical and emotional sources of information in an attempt not to feel, the mind then interpreting what is left in its own way, with the stories arising from the survival self. In such a way trauma creates a split between mind and body. Such survival interpretations of the body and emotional experiences, then, are likely to misinterpret what may be a clear alarm signal, ignoring the physical emergency. The traumatised person is unlikely to trust her physical experiences, just as she does not trust her emotional experiences, and so she does not trust herself. Through symbiotic entanglement, many of her physical sensations, just as her emotional experiences, may not in effect come from her own experience, but may be the residues of the physical trauma experiences of others. With increased understanding and clarity, these physical experiences and symptoms that arise from entanglement with others' traumatic experience are likely to dissipate and even disappear, and the person will gradually come to be in relationship with her body and her emotions, increasing her trust in herself.

Trauma feelings engage the whole body. We do not emerge from trauma without such emotional expression at some point, which relieves the psyche and the body of long-held tensions and structures. Integration is not an intellectual idea, it is a physical experience of becoming whole, of merging with, or reclaiming and taking in, of feeling (in the body) more real, more oneself, more present and more whole.

8.9 Trauma in the Elderly

As we get older, physically our available strength and energy naturally diminish. The split psychological structure is held in place by muscular contraction in the body, and over a prolonged period of time this contraction exhausts the physical reserves. The combination of diminishing strength and physical exhaustion renders the older person's ability to keep trauma unconscious severely compromised. This means that there is an increasing danger of the trauma feelings and experiences breaking through. It is my opinion that this probably underlies some of the illnesses particular to the elderly such as dementia and perhaps even Alzheimer's, where, in effect, the person retreats into mental confusion and dissociation as a last ditch effort to maintain the split. It is a further survival strategy to enable the person to dissociate from the frightening feelings. In some cases the dementia is a means to express some of the feelings that can no longer be held at bay, without having to take conscious responsibility for them. Such outbursts of rage or violence that sometimes occur can be put down to the dementia, without the recognition that they may be valid feelings of long-held unresolved trauma that the person can no longer split off and suppress.

My mother, not long before she died, succumbed to dementia. I didn't understand then as I would now, but her dementia allowed her to enact much earlier trauma experiences, and release many feelings that had been bound up within her for a very long time. At one point she became a danger to my father, as her inhibitions against certain acts disappeared, leaving only her raw rage, terror and confusion.

After my mother died, my father, then well into his

eighties, was devastated, and as a result could no longer hold onto trauma feelings attached to dreadful experiences from before the second world war when he was based in what is now northern Pakistan. He was a young air force pilot at the time, having recently graduated from Cranwell air officers' college. Never mind the experiences he had when in Pakistan, they are not mine to tell; but he did tell them to me, in a rush of despair, rage, fear and confusion. No longer could he hold onto it all, and sadly, he died in the middle of this process; not a peaceful or easy death.

8.10 Facts and Fiction

What happens in a constellation cannot be taken to be the factual truth, unless appropriately corroborated by the client. We have to be extremely careful, especially when working with trauma, as to what we credit as 'truth'. A constellation may 'show' that someone's mother has been sexually abused by her own father, but we cannot then give this information the virtue of fact unless the client confirms it as so, because she knows it. Many people have come to me having done a constellation before elsewhere, sometimes deeply disturbed by something that emerged in a constellation that was credited as truth by the facilitator. For me this is irresponsible on the part of the facilitator and invests him/her with far too much power as the arbiter of truth.

Setting up the trauma field in the constellation may show that there *is* trauma in the ancestral line by the level of dissociation, confusion and chaos in the constellation, which the client can either confirm or not. If confirmed, that information may have to be enough if the client does not know what the trauma actually was. The representatives will show trauma behaviour and describe experiences that are the symptoms of traumatisation. The client also, in describing her mother or father will portray trauma phenomena in the description of their behaviour, for example, "my mother was always very controlling and controlled", or "my mother was never really there ... she always seemed detached or distracted and never stood up to my father." To resolve personal trauma the client does not need to know the exact nature of the ancestral trauma; she only needs to know that there *was* trauma and that this affected the bonding ability of her mother, which in turn caused a symbiotic trauma for her.

There is a danger that psychotherapy and constellations work can become a kind of archaeological excavation where the client is set on a path towards knowing everything about what happened in their family's past. This in itself becomes an unnecessary distraction from dealing with their own unresolved trauma. Also, if, for example, a mother was abused and chooses not to talk about it, her choice deserves to be respected. I do not see any of us as having any rights over such intensely personal details of others' lives, and I would never encourage anyone to ask. If the client does choose to ask, that is up to him or her; and if the mother (or whoever else) chooses not to answer, that is up to them. In my view the client has to live with that and get on with healing her own inner trauma without the re-entangling distraction of making her healing dependent on her mother divulging her own pain and suffering. Making one's healing dependent on another doing something first, whether the mother or father, husband or partner or child, only re-entangles the person in others' traumas and deflects him away from his journey towards autonomy.

At the same time, sometimes the constellation shows something that confirms to the client what he has always known ... this is a process whereby, symbolically, the constellation triggers some unconscious awareness in the client, bringing clearly into focus something that has been in the mists of his unconscious all along. In the end the truth must reside with the client ... what works for him, what resonates for him as he is able to see it right now is the only thing that matters in resolving his trauma.

8.11 Group Processing

I ran therapy groups for over ten years and in that environment the interpersonal processes of participants and the therapist are the focus of the work. However, as a constellations therapist, my focus is very different.

If process issues do appear in the group I do not participate; to do so changes my role, encourages such processing, and will usually serve as a distraction from the work of resolving trauma. The processes that may occur between participants, the differences, arguments and irritations that seem to require attention, are issues of relationship, which are likely to have as their causal roots the effects of symbiotic trauma and entanglement, and to address them at the level of group process in my view is not ultimately useful for this work. For the therapist to begin to facilitate such processes is likely to entangle him in the arguments. If these issues do arise in the group I will wait until people are finished, which usually happens quite quickly. The intervention of the therapist in such issues is likely to prolong the process, so in my view it is better to wait it out and then suggest we get back to the work.

It is a myth that all differences can find a good resolution; sometimes we just have to acknowledge our difference and let go of the illusion that we can come to a good and mutually loving place with each other. A question I have of such well-worked through and apparent resolutions is: what has been missed, overlooked, forgotten or compromised, and to what extent might this resolution be influenced by survival modes?

In fact, in general, such incidents are few in the constellations group. There are various reasons for this: one is that such differences and irritations seem to melt away in the process of being a representative in or witness of another's constellation. Sometimes people actually get chosen to represent roles that somehow replicate the argument that was brewing in the group, and then the issue may be addressed unconciously in the representation as part of the process of the constellation. Another reason is that the work of the constellation is a work of service, where participants offer themselves willingly to represent in each others' constellations, and this takes their relationship with each other immediately to a deeper and more connected level, where such irritations are more likely to dissolve and disappear.

There is a communality that develops in the constellations group, where everyone realises that we are all in the same boat, that we all have suffered to some extent, that trauma is not the differentiating factor but the common factor, and to see another as, at a particular point in their lives, the victim of trauma, takes one's perception and understanding to a level beyond the more superficial and entangling irritations. In addition, as participants come to understand the role of survival strategies, their meaning and function, and become aware of, and unashamed of, their own strategies, they tend to feel increasingly compassionate towards themselves and towards others.

9

The Individual Constellation

The private session can seem an impossibility due to the lack of a group of people to act as representatives, but it isn't so. Working in the private session has its own complexities, but I do not see it as being any less useful or productive than the group, and for some people in some situations it is infinitely preferable. Private session work is a major part of my practice, and some people who come to see me privately may never go into a group.

The reasons why people opt for a private session are many: for some the idea of being in a group is too intimidating, and the fear of being shamed and exposed in front of unknown people is too much. Some fear that their issues and situation are so complex that they cannot think of how to manage them in a group setting; or they fear they will have to compete for time which may re-trigger feelings of vulnerability; or the idea of having to be a representative for another person at this stage is too much. Some people come to a private session first and then, when they have gained a bit of confidence in the process and me, feel more able to go into a group session. At least 50% of my practice happens in the private sessions, and I see people make great changes in their lives through such work alone.

In an individual session the therapist will take the role of the 'intention' in the constellation. The initial interview, the clarifying process, is pretty much the same as in the group, and once achieved the client will set the therapist up in the room as her 'intention', and then place herself in relation to the 'intention', just as previously discussed.

The transition from being the 'therapist' to being a representative for the 'intention', and back again later in the process, requires clarity in the therapist so as not to confuse the client and himself. On the surface it can be quite disorienting for the client to have her therapist make such a switch in roles, and some more intimate moments later in the constellation may have to be truncated because it may be too confusing for the person. Sensitivity on the part of the therapist as to what is possible in this regard is extremely important, along with maintaining a clarity as to 'who', so to speak, he is being for the client in any moment. Throughout the process I try to maintain clarity within me as to whether any particular thought, idea or statement I have comes from the representation I am being, or from myself as the therapist. If I am not clear I say so, including my own uncertainty, in service of keeping nothing hidden. To make the therapist's process transparent to the client, even the therapist's confusion and lack of clarity, improves the process for the client and heightens her trust in the therapist and the process, since nothing is hidden from her. Such transparency maintains the perspective of the client as the prime motivating force in the work, and the prime meaning-maker.

It is a complex undertaking for the therapist to represent the 'intention' and be the therapist, sometimes almost at the same time, and it takes practice. Speaking slowly and deliberately helps; keeping the whole process slow, making clear statements, even if statements of confusion; all of this will help the overall process be as clear as possible to the client. It is well to remember that in the constellations process, when the client looks at the therapist she sees the therapist's face ... and for someone to whom the whole process perhaps is new, it may be a supreme challenge for her to stay in touch with who you are representing for her in that moment, and everything you can do, even if it seems superfluous, helps maintain the clarity. However, some people do find it intuitively easier and have no difficulty with making these distinctions.

Many people I see are new to me, and may have no knowledge of constellations. They need to have some opportunity to make a relationship with me, and this starts from the moment they get in touch to make the appointment. In my view it helps (and I have had feedback from clients that this is so) to have an efficient appointment-making process, that includes the new client receiving a letter (perhaps by email) giving all necessary directions to the workplace, information about trains, parking etc, what the cost is, and how and when this is to be paid. People will assess you and your work from the moment they come into contact with you, whether via your webpage or other advertising. Most 'referrals' in my experience are made through word of mouth from friends and personal contacts, so it is always worth bearing in mind that your work is your best advertisement.

On arrival it helps to feel welcomed and put at ease. I am aware that the client is usually anxious and uneasy; she is right to be suspicious and careful, and I respect that. I and what I do are on trial, and while this doesn't mean I should compromise myself or what I do, it does mean that I should keep this in my awareness. In most cases the invitation to the client to say what she wants initiates a period of time where she talks about the things that are difficult in her life. I say little during this time, but try to remain as present and attentive as I can as she gains confidence in me and in herself. Since the whole operation is new to her, even though I may start off by asking her what she wants, it is unusual that she will answer this question in the beginning. But the initial stages follow pretty much the same course as for the group constellation (see chapter 7.2).

At the point at which we are ready to do the constellation I emphasise that I don't know what will emerge, but suggest we just begin the process and see what happens. If this is her first introduction to the constellations process I try and keep it very simple and have modest expectations of what will happen. If she has a reasonably good experience of being with me this first time, and sees something useful that is new, this increases her confidence and trust in me and the process, and herself in this new situation.

I invite her to stand up with me, ask her to tell me her intention again as a way of enrolling me, and then place me as her 'intention' somewhere in the room. I then ask her to place herself somewhere in relation to her 'intention', and suggest that we both quietly focus on our experience for a few moments. I tell her that after a short while I will start to say what my experience is. I am always the first one to do this, especially if the person is new to the process. In this way I can show her, in a sense, how to focus on her experience. I include everything I can, with any hesitations or uncertainties as my experience evolves. In this first phase while telling her my experience, which may be useful to her, I am also, in effect, teaching her how to be a representative of herself.

As an experienced representative myself, my offerings are quite detailed, and may include an experience of being split myself, or perhaps that I am feeling conflicting and confusing experiences. I offer all of this as best I can. At times I include a reference to being her 'intention' as in, for example: "standing here as your 'intention' I feel rather shaky and weak ..." This keeps her aware of what I am representing. As her 'intention' I am also representing a part of her, and often at some point I will include this reference as well, as in "with all of this I feel as though I am part of you, perhaps a young part ... yes, if I ask myself how old I feel, I feel about five years old ..." This then introduces the idea that as well as her 'intention' I embody some part of herself. All of this helps to orient her in the face of what may seem a rather weird and unusual process. If I don't feel as though I am a part of her I will, of course, include that information. For the 'intention' not to feel a part of the client is likely to be indicative of systemic entanglements.

At some point I will ask her (and this is from the 'therapist' place) to say something of her experience and, perhaps, any strong reactions she has had to anything I have said. This gives her an orientation as to what she can say, and often the first things she will say will be her reactions to what I have said. Many people are unfamiliar with describing their own experience, and so I do not expect people to be able to do this immediately. But most people, even from a more cognitive place, will be able to say something about their reaction to what the therapist has said. The most common responses at this stage from the client are to the things that I have said that make sense to her, or are familiar experiences to her. This does not necessarily invalidate anything else I have said, but it does show what aspect of what I have said the client can relate to at this moment.

This process, going back and forth, may continue for a while. As she says things from her perspective, I as the 'intention' notice any effect these things have on me, and share these with her.

At some point there usually seems little more to add, and the constellation may seem to have come to a stop, or an impasse. Then I suggest we come out, put down markers for where we have stood (which may have shifted from the beginning position if either of us have moved), and sit down to discuss what has happened so far.

The markers I use are pieces of felt of various colours cut into circles to represent females, and squares to represent males, about nine inches square or diameter. All pieces of felt also have a triangular notch, which indicates which way the person marked is facing:

Female   Male
Examples of markers I use.

We place markers for the client and for the 'intention' and then sit down.

From here on the process is similar to that described above for the constellation in the group. I stay in contact with the client as she talks about what has happened so far. Very often the most prominent thing at this stage is that I, as the 'intention', have reported experiences that the client knows well, and this in itself is usually exciting and interesting for her. Here is one advantage of the private session: the therapist, who is an experienced representative, is skilled at phenomenological reporting of experience. Often this doesn't happen so clearly in the group unless the representative is seasoned and used to the work, and for the client the experience of having someone else tell her in quite a lot of detail about feelings and experiences that she recognises as her own is an intriguing phenomenon for her.

From here she can include further markers as more information about the 'trauma field' surfaces, and so we proceed. In time we may have quite a complex field, much information will have surfaced, and a pattern will have evolved, perhaps like the following example:

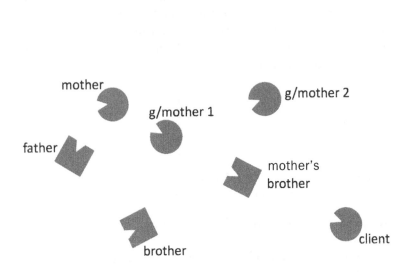

Without any information about the 'story', there are some interesting points we can see in this particular constellation:

- the distance between the client and her 'intention';
- the fact that they can hardly see each other (if the representatives were real people);
- the fact that the 'traumatised field' is between them, separating them;
- the fact that no one looks at the client, or the 'intention';
- the fact that no one really looks at anyone else – no real contact is made;
- in terms of symbiotic trauma, the mother is a long way from the client and looks in a completely different direction;
- in terms of potential symbiotic entanglement, the closest person to the client is the mother's brother, and the person directly between the client and her 'intention' is grandmother 2 (the father's mother);
- the client is closer to the traumatised field than the 'intention', and looks towards the traumatised field, whereas the intention looks in the direction of the client (even though, because of grandmother 2, she wouldn't be able to see the client properly).

A constellation such as the above example, will have developed from information given by the client, and will prompt questions from both therapist and client. Here is another advantage and difference of the individual session: you have a constellation that offers an easy patterning to see, and in which you don't have many representatives sharing their experiences and moving around as may happen in a group. In a way it makes it simpler, but you lack the wealth of information from the representatives. However, some of this may well emerge from the discussion between the therapist and client.

Just to see some of the complexity of the expanded field may be enough for the client. Most of us envision our problems within the smaller scale of 'myself and my problem'.

With the constellations process we are expanding the field, sometimes to encompass several generations, and this in itself changes the client's perspective of the context of herself and her problem. To make connections between the mother's alcoholic grandfather and her own subdued and fearful nature, changes the client's perception of her early attachment and subsequent relationship to her mother. To see the impact of the loss of a child on a mother and on the surviving child, by how the marker for the mother faces away from the surviving child, with a close focus on the lost child, shifts one's perception. The patterns that emerge as markers are added to the constellation can be extremely helpful in understanding the dynamics of one's family. For example, in a picture such as this:

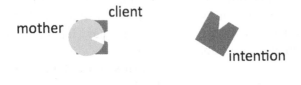

mother / client / intention

grandmother / grandmother's dead son

The client's intention is to be able to separate from his mother. He is sixty-two years old and his mother is dead, but he still feels like she is breathing down his neck. When he came to include the marker for his mother he placed it on top of the marker for himself. His mother's mother had lost her eldest son while pregnant with the client's mother. A hypothesis at this point is that his grandmother was so absorbed with the death of her son that she had no ability to relate to the new child, his mother, who therefore had suffered a symbiotic trauma. On the birth of her child she unconsciously looked for the symbiotic attachment she had missed with her mother in her relationship with her newborn son. He saw this in the pattern of the constellation he had set up. As the 'intention' my experience had been, before he placed the marker for the mother, that I couldn't look at him.

At this point I observed how, when working with markers it was possible to place the mother on top of the marker for himself, and speculated on how that configuration might be replicated with people as representatives, as one might in a group. He replied that the mother would be holding him from behind in a vice-like grip that would hurt and restrict his breathing. As he said this he became very emotional and said "I feel really angry and want to throw her off." He picked up the marker for his mother and threw it to one side. Then he said that he didn't want to feel angry with her because he could see that it wasn't her fault. I observed that he didn't actually look angry, but more assertive, as one has to in making autonomous boundaries for oneself.

I do not usually suggest we stand on any markers of the 'trauma field', since to do so may confuse the work, and invite entanglement. This is similar to not working with the 'trauma field' representatives in the group constellation.

I may sometimes ask the client whether she thinks any of the markers, if they were real people representing, might move, or how they might feel. For example, I may say: "I just thought of what would be happening if these were real people representing your family members; what do you think might be happening?" This can often elicit interesting responses, such as some family members moving, a particular sense of how one might feel and so on.

I regard part of my function as educative: I am interested in discussing trauma and encouraging people to think about how it manifests in their lives. I may well invite the client to think about how vulnerable she must have been as a new baby arriving in the environment in which she did. I talk about what it might have been like in the womb before she was born and how non-separate she would have been from her mother, and how she may have absorbed the traumas her mother held. These ideas are new to most people but at the same time make sense and open their eyes to their vulnerability at that time.

Talking about these things often also elicits more information and memories for the client. To discuss this time of extreme vulnerability frequently elicits thoughts about themselves that they have never told anyone before. Often a client has said something like: "You know, I've always felt an acute awareness of death," or "All my life I've never been quite sure if I wanted to live," or "I always knew that my mother was traumatised, that she was frightened of life, but I never thought about it like this." I think that because I understand trauma as I do, a space is created in which people can more easily approach things about themselves that they have never dared to before.

At the end of the session I suggest the client go away and see how the constellation evolves within her, and when (and if) she feels ready to make a further step she can make another appointment. I rarely suggest booking another appointment at the time because I prefer to leave the client to make her own decisions as to when she comes, and how frequently. Often what emerges in the session needs time to settle, and for the person to consider it and get used to it. Everyone has their own pace and rhythm when resolving their trauma, and I prefer to leave such decisions to the client.

When a person comes on a reasonably regular basis, perhaps once a month for a while, I do not feel that I should remember, or retain in any exact way, information about her family background. I personally don't keep notes. I prefer to approach the person anew each time, and hear the story of her family she tells on that particular day. It may be quite different from the one she told the previous time. In the same way, even though she may be setting up a constellation of the same people repeatedly, it will never be the same configuration. Each constellation recounts a different perspective located within a different intention and with a different degree of clarity. A phenomenological approach does not in my view require the therapist to retain details of what has been said before. Of course often during the process of the later work, details will surface in the therapist's memory, but again I tend to trust that what does surface is what should surface at this particular moment.

10

Working with Couples

"Trauma fosters illusions, particularly in our ability to love
and to be loved." *(Broughton, 2011)*

The strategy for working with couples[65] that I have developed
grows out of the awareness that symbiotic trauma lays the
foundations for our ability to be in relationship. Having spent
many years working as a conventional couples therapist, I now
work very differently. I do not engage with the current relational processes between the couple, as I would have in the
past.

When a new couple comes I explain my thinking about
couples work, and invite them each, separately, to say
something about why they have come. I don't assume that what
each wants out of the session concurs with what the other
wants. This also paves the way for whoever is going to do a
constellation to develop their intention.

If the couple talk to each other, or start to argue together,
I tend to wait quietly until they are ready to continue. In my
view their present day relating styles will have their roots in
symbiotic trauma and entanglement, and for the therapist to
begin to engage with this day to day relating distracts from the
important and needed work of the constellation.

---

[65] This applies to married couples, partnerships and can also apply to close
friendships.

244

If a discussion between them is prolonged or becomes heated, I may interrupt and make it clear that I don't work that way (processing their interaction), and while I am happy to wait until they are ready, it is up to them how they choose to use the time. I will do a constellation with one of them, but I will not engage in the present process.

The way I work with couples and partners is to do a personal constellation with one, while the other watches and witnesses. This has several advantages:

- the witnessing partner sees some of the underlying symbiotic trauma and entanglements of his or her partner, thereby increasing his or her understanding of the partner;
- the witnessing partner also sees that much of the partner's more difficult relating style is rooted in a time long before the witnessing partner came on the scene, and in this sense is not so much to do with him or her. This can often feel a relief to the witnessing partner because he sees what happens between them is not his fault, but due to much deeper and older issues.
- the witnessing partner will also see the ways in which his processes and life issues parallel and entangle with those of his partner;
- the working partner gains support from the witnessing partner's presence, and from his ability to see something profound that explains the working partner to the witnessing partner in a new way;
- there comes a parity between the couple, where each can see that neither is at fault. The ability of both to be intimate together has been severely compromised long before they met.

At the end of the constellation the witnessing partner is often as moved or enlightened by what he or she has seen as the working partner, and they may then together talk about their relationship with new insight.

Basics of couple dynamics

People choose to be with another in an intimate relationship based on many criteria, which are most likely clouded by their survival strategies of traumatisation and symbiotic entanglement. Becoming intimate is emotional, and feeling any emotion will also surface unresolved feelings such as those split off from consciousness as a result of trauma. Intimacy with another is a situation of vulnerability, and vulnerability is also the prime condition of a trauma situation, so the potential for a retraumatisation within intimate partnerships is high. This retraumatisation is likely to manifest as low-grade anxiety or panic of the suppressed trauma feelings, causing the person to feel compelled to withdraw or push their partner away.

For the traumatised person, as much as intimacy is yearned for, it is likely to feel threatening. The partner then becomes a threat. We can only come into true intimacy with another, without feeling threatened or the compulsion to withdraw, if we can see the other clearly without going into our splits. I would say that we can only be in a good clear relationship with another if we are in a good, clear and loving relationship with ourself, when we work with our psychologically split psyche. Rather than blame the other for their deficiencies, we need to understand the complexity of the partnership, where on the one hand we may feel safe, but on the other that very safety may feel threatening. Very often the 'deficiencies' we see in our partner will mirror the situation of our early attachment traumatisation. At an unconscious level we ask our partner to protect us from our symbiotic trauma and entanglements, at the same time as they are re-enacted. The unconscious contract of most couples is based on two conflicting and impossible quests:

> "I need you to protect me from my trauma, and I will protect you from yours."

> "I must relive my trauma with and through you, and I will relive yours with you."

The work of the couple who desire a better relationship is for each to address their own trauma, thereby coming into good, loving relationship with the self. Then each can see the other clearly for who he or she really is, and approach the other from a place of love of oneself.

My couples sessions are usually two hours long, unless the couple specifically request more time. Within a two hour session it is usually only possible to do one constellation, but I think this is useful, because even the one constellation often gives them both a considerable amount to go on, and they can then book the next appointment for the other constellation.

Part 3

Other Issues

11

Trauma Constellations and Family Constellations

Ruppert's ideas have caused considerable controversy within the Family Constellations field, and the topic of the differences between the two has resulted in confusion and misunderstanding. Ruppert's work *is* challenging to the traditional Family Constellations approach. For those who are interested I will try and clarify the important differences between the two.

The primary theoretical challenges that Ruppert's work presents to conventional Family Constellations (hereafter referred to as FC) are:

1. The main aim of FC is to reconcile the client with her family, primarily her parents. *In Ruppert's view such reconciliation is not possible if the parents are traumatised, and if they weren't it wouldn't be necessary. Such enacted 'reconciliation' will encourage and strengthen the symbiotic entanglements, and deflects from resolving the individual's own trauma.*

2. In FC the reconciliation between the client and her parents in the constellation happens by encouraging the client to connect with her 'parents' using rituals such as bowing and other modes of honouring, statements that diminish the status of the client to "just a child" in relation to her parents. *Again this encourages and strengthens the entanglement and dependency, and dimin-*

251

ishes autonomy. Such rituals are done with representatives, not the real parents, and so it cannot be assumed to affect the real parents, or change or heal their split psyches. No one can heal anyone else's trauma.

3. The aims of FC often includes resolving issues to do with earlier family members, even those long since dead. *This perpetuates illusions and strays into the unreal, which will support and exacerbate survival strategies and entanglement. It also colludes with deflecting away from the client's own trauma by focusing on others in the system, and puts an emphasis on the person's internal healing being dependent on the healing of others.*

4. The changes in demeanour of representatives of family members, such as parents or grandparents, that occur during the constellation, from distressed (traumatised) to a more benevolent, engaged and loving attitude, is sometimes deemed to be real in FC. In other words they are deemed to be an 'also truth' about the person represented, even if long-since dead. *Our view is that this has no basis in reality beyond the constellation, and so plays into survival modes and strengthens entanglement. The representatives are just representatives and it cannot be assumed to have any affect on the real people.*

5. 'Reconciliation' with parents and ancestors in the constellations process undermines the developing autonomy of the person, as it encourages her to continue to look outside of herself, to others, for her own internal healing. This perpetuates her dependency on others changing in order that she can change. The idea that those long since dead can be healed by the work of people in the present encourages illusions and a pseudo authority of the client as being responsible for the wellbeing of her ancestors.

To encapsulate, in our view Family Constellations increases symbiotic entanglement and the person's dependency on others, thereby undermining her autonomy.

A second set of arguments for me have to do with the facilitation of the constellation and the approach of the therapist that subtly (and at times not so subtly) assumes authority over the client's constellation. In Family Constellations the facilitator is the one who must know what is needed and what the best resolution is. In this way facilitation is usually directive and managerial:

1. In FC the facilitator chooses who is represented in the constellation, thereby in the first instance being the person who knows and authorises the constellation. Whereas with the constellation of the intention, the stated intention arises clearly from the client, and the constellation always starts in the same way, with the client and a representative for her 'intention', thereby diminishing the therapist's influence.

2. In FC the client is 'given' (by the facilitator) a sideline role in the beginning (having a representative for herself in the constellation), so is less involved and kept out of the constellation until such time as the facilitator deems it right to include her. The facilitator assumes the authority for the judgement of when this happens.

3. In FC the facilitator moves representatives according to his idea of what should happen, usually with reference to the principles of the 'orders of love'. This diminishes the potential for the representatives to trust themselves and the facilitator, which may have an influence on the client's ability to trust the process, and also perpetuates the facilitator's authority for what happens and how. This does not support the client's move to autonomy.

4. In some instances in FC the client is coerced (this has been accepted practice by many working with family constellations) to do or say things that the facilitator thinks necessary, such as bowing, statements of honouring, diminishing of importance, etc, without an experimental or proposing attitude on the part of the facilitator. The facilitator here is thought to 'know what is

best'. This can often lead to a culture of shaming the person into such actions.

5. In FC the facilitator's aim is to re-order the constellation's representatives according to a deemed 'correct order'; again the facilitator is the one who 'knows' what is right.

6. Many FC facilitators do not fully understand trauma and may be oblivious to the dangers of retraumatisation. This is not the case with all; there is a growing awareness of the existence of trauma, but not necessarily along the same lines as presented here.

7. Work with the 'interrupted reaching out movement' (symbiotic trauma) in FC is a situation where the facilitator (usually) takes on the role of the mother and encourages the client to enact the interrupted movement to reach out for the mother. This reinforces the illusion that somewhere, sometime my mother will be there for me as she should have been, which strengthens the entanglement. It is a kind of re-parenting which in itself is illusory.

Though the effect of Family Constellations is often moving and satisfying in the moment, nevertheless there is a question about how long this lasts and what difference it makes in the person's life. But above all I do not see how such work can resolve the internal fragmentation resulting from trauma, nor how it can maintain safety in the face of such usurpation of power and authority by the facilitator, and nor how it works to support the person's movement to being more autonomous and self-authorising and less dependent. There is a difference between healthy interdependence and an unrealistic and unhelpful dependency.

I worked with Family Constellations for ten years, and I wrote a book that was primarily based on understanding the topic. There are few things that I now criticise that I did not do myself during that time. The shift from Family Constellations to the work that I now do was not an easy shift for me, and took six years overall.

12

Trauma Constellations and Psychotherapy

The work of trauma constellations presents several challenges to the conventional practice of psychotherapy, both theoretically and practically, and I will deal with these topics separately.

Theoretical considerations

Trauma as a general topic has been, as we have seen, rather more avoided than focused on for the last hundred years, and is only now beginning to be seen as a more central issue, particularly with the inclusion of the DSM IV diagnostic category of PTSD, the work of Peter Levine, Babette Rothschild, Pat Ogden and colleagues, Bessel van der Kolk and colleagues, Allan Schore and colleagues, and the emergence of techniques such as EMDR and EFT that seem to relieve the pressures of trauma. However, generally trauma is only considered in terms of rememberable (i.e. later) trauma and post trauma symptomatology. Additionally, although the concept of psychological splitting has been in the frame since the mid 19th century, it also isn't a mainstream psychotherapeutic concept in the sense in which Ruppert proposes.[66]

---

[66] There is currently a resurgence of interest in the work of Pierre Janet as referenced by Onno van der Hart and B Friedman (1989)

Neither of the perspectives of symbiotic trauma or symbiotic entanglement are in the mainstream of psychotherapeutic considerations, even though attachment and child development theory have been around since the 1950s. Psychotherapy generally does not hold a transgenerational perspective of the client, and since attachment trauma happens in the pre-verbal phase of life, and is therefore difficult to access as a topic for discussion, psychotherapists rarely make these topics a sufficient focus. It is only with the recent findings of neuroscience that some are beginning to understand the potential of early attachment as a trauma, particularly for someone who might be assessed as having a disorganised attachment. However, as I have said before, I have had many clients who would be diagnosed as having a secure attachment but who, in the constellation, are found, even so, to have a trauma of attachment. Understanding the ideas of the split, fragmented psyche, and the potential affect on the child (even within the womb) of having a split and dissociated mother is not within the general psychotherapy frame yet.

It is rare for a conventional psychotherapist to think of the client further back than his relationship with his parents within the client's life, and most therapists think of their clients only in terms of present life events, that is those events that occurred within the lifetime of the client. Since access to pre-verbal memory is difficult, psychotherapy has tended to rely on explicit memory and free association as the sources of issues for discussion, and while the circumstances of prior generations may be available, if the therapist doesn't enquire, the client is unlikely to volunteer it. The client will follow the therapist's frame of reference. To include a transgenerational perspective, and an understanding of the reality of the traumatic implications of very early life, requires a shift in perception that the profession in general has yet to make.

Apart from this, the stumbling blocks in my view are a lack of inclusion of the body in the therapy (too strong a focus on talking), too strong a focus on the relationship between the client and the therapist, and an absence of a consciousness of the power issues of traumatisation. This last is due to a lack of a real understanding of trauma. To analyse and interpret the client's experience back to him assumes an authority that encourages a dependence on the perspective of another about myself, rather than my own.

To take these topics in turn:

Trauma is held in the body and by the body, just as much as in the psyche and by the psyche. The body/mind separation has been as much a feature of mainstream psychotherapy as it has been in science and medicine. It is a completely different thing to involve the body in the therapy in some way as we do in the constellations process. Sitting and talking are more likely to disconnect us from our body than connect us, and so could be seen as a collusion with trauma avoidance. Some therapies, such as Gestalt, do include ideas of body process, but in my view this is often relegated to the background, perhaps because of a lack of understanding of trauma. Once one realises that the dynamics of trauma can only be addressed fully through the body, one has to allow the body to be more figural. Van der Kolk considers that a primary focus on the relationship as the psychotherapeutic frame may contribute to an avoidance of the physiological experiences of trauma:

> "Clients may look for 'relationship' in therapy because they can't stand what they feel in their own bodies – as long as the therapist is with them, they can distract themselves from their inner experience. The 'felt sense' has become a minefield, and clinging to others is one way of avoiding the intolerable sensations within . . ." *(van der Kolk in Sykes Wylie, 2004)*

Too much emphasis on the relationship between the client and the therapist can confuse the issue of integration of fragmentations: who is the therapist being for the client in the work of integrating her splits? And how do internal fragmentations then integrate? In the constellations process the representative for the 'intention' is clearly representing another part of the client's self, and the work can proceed accordingly, whereas the conventional therapist, with only the ideas of transference and projection available, is unlikely to consider her experiences when with the client within the frame of a representation of some part of the client. In fact the therapist is likely to represent unconsciously many opposing and confusing impulses that could be seen in the light of the constellations process as parts of the client and confusions with other earlier traumas (entanglement). This raises the question as to what exactly transference is. Thinking within the frame of the possibilities of the constellation, we could say that transference is the spontaneous representation by the therapist of an unstated, and so unclear, 'intention' of the client, with all that we have seen that this can include. With such a proposal we would see the phenomenon of the transference in quite a different light. To me transference and the representative experience are the same phenomenon, interpreted differently.

Additionally, a strong emphasis on the therapeutic relationship between the client and the therapist implies that healing occurs within this relationship (as a laboratory, so to speak, for all other relationships). Part of this idea is that the client can revisit, and 'redo', certain aspects of her history that have remained painfully unresolved. For me this can easily stray into an illusionary avoidance of the reality: the therapist can never replace the traumatised mother, but the invitation for this in the relationship is strong. It may also increase a dependence on the external and have little effect on internal integration and increase of self-trust.

Finally, psychotherapy generally orients itself around the idea of 'helping'. Helping means many things, but even the designation of 'helper' can skew the power relationship between therapist and client. However, the term is less important than what actually happens between the therapist and client. Unless the therapist really understands the extreme vulnerability of the trauma situation, particularly vis a vis the very early stages of life, the delicacy of the power imbalance between therapist and client will be given insufficient attention. Further, the only way in which one can develop such sensitivity is by exploring one's own trauma, particularly one's own symbiotic trauma, and this requires the awareness of the possibility of such work, as set out in this book.

Practical considerations

The methodology of the trauma constellation presents several practical considerations, the main one of which is how to structure one's practice, and I will describe my own process of restructuring my practice as a way of discussing this.

When I first started to work with the constellations process (at that time with Family Constellations), I was particularly interested to discover how best to work in the individual one-to-one session, and I set about exploring the possibilities. Over time the main problem I encountered was this: when I did a constellation in a therapy session, it always surfaced so much useful information and shifts in perspective for the client that, at the subsequent session a week later, there was never very much to do. We did, of course, talk about what had happened in the constellation session, in fact often that was the only thing the client wanted to talk about, but in subsequent sessions I found that the client was usually not ready to explore anything else, and it also became apparent that continuing to discuss the constellation was not of interest to her either. It seemed that there was nothing of any urgency for the client to be interested in.

For a while I would do a constellation in my assessment sessions with prospective clients, using markers as described in chapter 9 above, as a kind of mutual diagnostic tool. It would help me to understand the client's family, and it was always very interesting for the client.[67] However, what I also found was that sometimes for the next six months the client was continually referring back to this original constellation, using it as a reference point, but also demonstrating that even that short exercise had had a profound effect.

[67] Bearing in mind that this was never just an exercise of setting something up, but always for me informed by a trans-generational perspective as found in Family Constellations, which was what I was doing at the time.

Over a period of some four years, while I continued to see clients weekly, I gradually started to do one-off constellations sessions for people who came to me specifically for that work. This seemed to go well: a client would come for an hour-and-a-half session (I had realised that the constellations session had to be longer than fifty minutes), do a constellation, and leave. I left it to the person as to whether they came back or not.

As I started to get known for this work more people started to come for the constellations sessions and it became a larger part of my practice. Around this time I came to the view that the constellations work I was doing was more effective (and, I own, for me more interesting) than the usual therapy work. In fact I began to feel very uncomfortable in the conventional therapy sessions because I started to question the whole concept of relational weekly therapy, and so I stopped.[68] Additionally, as my work became more informed by Ruppert's model, with trauma the focus, clients began to want to see me more regularly, but I still left this frequency up to the client. As I understood the power dynamics of trauma better, and relinquished the central relational emphasis of the therapy, it seemed more appropriate for the client to decide when to come and how frequently.

Overall this process has taken twelve years, and currently my practice is run along these lines. The shift in perception and practice outlined here is considerable, hence the twelve years.

---

[68] This of course had a big, and slightly frightening, impact on my financial situation.

Conclusion

One step at a time . . .

It *is* possible to resolve our trauma. We are not helpless now, and we can come to understand the multi-generational stresses on our parents, and thence on us, and let go of our desire to blame, hold to account or accuse. To see our existence in this way engenders a true compassion that comes from real understanding and clarity. We can feel, and survive feeling, our early experiences of despair, disappointment, betrayal and disillusion. We can absorb our feelings of momentary terror, and thereby develop a more peaceful and stable psyche. We are each responsible for ourselves, and to work to integrate our splits and resolve our own trauma is an extremely personal and self-responsible venture. While it may seem shocking initially to realise that the person I thought I was is mostly a construction of a survival self, it can also be a moment of exhilaration, because there is also the realisation that perhaps I really am a person who is okay, well adjusted, worth loving and caring for, able to be in loving relationships, worthy of respect, value and dignity, and capable of fulfilling my best talents and potential. For others to see me so, however, I must first see it myself, not as a managed and imposed strategy of 'positive thinking', but as an embodied and undeniable reality, something I just know with the whole of myself as being true. From there, I will not put myself, or allow others to put me, in situations that compromise or misuse me. I am then able to make good, respecting and respectful, loving relationships; I am able to be with my partner as a partner, my child as a mother, my friends as a friend, rather than as a frightened traumatised and confused child.

When one first comes up against the thinking expressed in this book, one can feel overwhelmed by the consequences of such a perspective. Our global society avoids seeing the consequences of trauma. Many of our political and personal acts create and/or repeat trauma situations. If we collectively understood the consequences of trauma we would have to re-think many of our established societal ways of working and being. In America, for example, maternity leave is limited to a few weeks, and while in the UK it is considerably longer, many of us put our children into play school and nurseries very young, and women often go back to work quite soon after their child is born. Our welfare systems do not understand just how important it is to support mothers and fathers to be with their children, how much these early stages of their lives will impact on the future of nations and communities. We need to consider this in the light of symbiotic trauma and entanglement, and understand the role that the mother's and father's psychological state has. If we understood the transgenerational impact of trauma we would have to re-think much of our international politics, certainly how to deal with international and national conflicts, wars and refugee situations. We would have to re-think our schooling, our child-minding, how we relate to childhood abuse and abusers, to perpetrators, and to victims, how we think about our criminal justice systems, how we manage our hospitals and our health and maternity issues, our social services, our politics, our police services, and our psychotherapy. This may not be in our life-time, but that doesn't mean it isn't, even so, worth thinking about for the greater good.

The human spirit has survived for thousands of years despite dreadful traumatisations from war and inter-personal conflict, from diseases and natural disasters, and despite the many more concealed domestic and childhood abuses and deprivations. We are still here, having found the means to survive, but those means have also resulted in the perpetuation of trauma. Today we have so much suffering from the results of trauma: the scale of psychological suffering, the proliferation of disorders and addictions, the daily traumatisation of millions who cannot find enough to eat, somewhere to sleep, or even a place to feel safe.

Personal healing is a profound political act; it is the most powerful political act we can undertake, much more so than demonstrating on the streets, because by healing ourselves we gain the clarity of vision to see what the appropriate action is in any situation in which we find ourselves. Our ability to make good, productive relationships improves, and our ability to act autonomously with courage and commitment, clear of symbiotic entanglements, shines through. We can develop a healthy attitude towards others and towards the political and global issues we personally and collectively face. Our real responsibility in any situation is more clear and so, more easily accomplished.

The task is enormous; but we can only address it one step at a time, to try to do more entangles us further. And the first step must always be myself ...

Appendix

DSM IV 309:81: Post Traumatic Stress Disorder

Diagnostic criteria for PTSD include a history of exposure to a traumatic event meeting two criteria and symptoms from each of three symptom clusters: intrusive recollections, avoidant/numbing symptoms, and hyper-arousal symptoms. A fifth criterion concerns duration of symptoms and a sixth assesses functioning.

Criterion A: stressor
The person has been exposed to a traumatic event in which both of the following have been present:

1. The person has experienced, witnessed, or been confronted with an event or events that involve actual or threatened death or serious injury, or a threat to the physical integrity of oneself or others.
2. The person's response involved intense fear, helplessness, or horror. Note: in children, it may be expressed instead by disorganized or agitated behavior.

Criterion B: intrusive recollection

The traumatic event is persistently re-experienced in at least **one** of the following ways:

1. Recurrent and intrusive distressing recollections of the event, including images, thoughts, or perceptions. Note: in young children, repetitive play may occur in which themes or aspects of the trauma are expressed.
2. Recurrent distressing dreams of the event. Note: in children, there may be frightening dreams without recognizable content.
3. Acting or feeling as if the traumatic event were recurring (includes a sense of reliving the experience, illusions, hallucinations, and dissociative flashback episodes, including those that occur upon awakening or when intoxicated). Note: in children, trauma-specific reenactment may occur.
4. Intense psychological distress at exposure to internal or external cues that symbolize or resemble an aspect of the traumatic event.
5. Physiologic reactivity upon exposure to internal or external cues that symbolize or resemble an aspect of the traumatic event.

Criterion C: avoidant/numbing

Persistent avoidance of stimuli associated with the trauma and numbing of general responsiveness (not present before the trauma), as indicated by at least **three** of the following:

1. Efforts to avoid thoughts, feelings, or conversations associated with the trauma
2. Efforts to avoid activities, places, or people that arouse recollections of the trauma
3. Inability to recall an important aspect of the trauma
4. Markedly diminished interest or participation in significant activities
5. Feeling of detachment or estrangement from others

6. Restricted range of affect (e.g., unable to have loving feelings)
7. Sense of foreshortened future (e.g., does not expect to have a career, marriage, children, or a normal life span)

Criterion D: hyper-arousal
Persistent symptoms of increasing arousal (not present before the trauma), indicated by at least **two** of the following:

1. Difficulty falling or staying asleep
2. Irritability or outbursts of anger
3. Difficulty concentrating
4. Hyper-vigilance
5. Exaggerated startle response

Criterion E: duration
Duration of the disturbance (symptoms in B, C, and D) is more than one month.

Criterion F: functional significance
The disturbance causes clinically significant distress or impairment in social, occupational, or other important areas of functioning.

Specify if:
Acute: if duration of symptoms is less than three months
Chronic: if duration of symptoms is three months or more

Specify if:
With or Without delay onset: Onset of symptoms at least six months after the stressor

References

Alford, C.F. (1992). *The Psychoanalytic Theory of Greek Tragedy*. Yale University Press, USA.

Blakeslee, S. (2006). *Cells that read Minds*. New York Times, Science, January 10, 2006.

Blaney, P. H. & Millon, T. (2008). *Oxford Textbook of Psychopathology*. Oxford University Press.

Bowlby, J. (1949). 'The Study and Reduction of Group Tensions in the Family', in Human Relations, 2 (2) (April).

Bowlby, J. (1958). 'The Nature of the Child's Tie to His Mother'. International Journal of Psycho-Analysis, London.

Bowlby, J. (1969). *Attachment and loss: Vol. I: Attachment*. New York: Basic Books.

Bowlby, J. (1973). *Attachment and loss: Vol. II: Separation: Anxiety and Anger*. New York: Basic Books.

Bowlby, J. (1980). *Attachment and loss: Vol. III: Loss*. New York: Basic Books.

Bowlby, J. (1988). *A Secure Base: Clinical Applications of Attachment Theory*. Routledge, London.

Brook, J. A. (1991). *Freud and Splitting*. http://http-server.carleton.ca/ ~ abrook/SPLTTING.htm. Department of Philosophy, Carleton University, Ottawa, Canada.

Broughton, V. (2010). *In The Presence of Many: Reflections on Constellations Emphasising the Individual Context*, Green Balloon Publishing, Steyning, UK.

Broughton, V. (2010b). 'In Conversation with Franz Ruppert,

In The Spotlight Series', The Knowing Field International Constellations Journal, Issue 16, June 2010. Frome, UK.

Broughton, V. (2011). 'Love's Illusions: Symbiotic Entanglement and the transgenerational Nature of Trauma'. Self & Society Forum for Contemporary Psychology, Vol. 38, No. 3, 2011, UK.

Broughton, V. (2012). 'Gestalt, Phenomenology and Trauma-Oriented Constellations'. The Knowing Field International Constellations Journal, Issue 19, January 2012, Frome. UK.

Broughton, V. (2013). 'Trauma Constellations with a Gestalt Perspective', due to be published in The British Gestalt Journal, 2013, Vol. 22, No. 2, UK.

de Mause, L. (1974). *The History of Childhood*, edited by de Mause. Rowan & Littlefield, USA.

Egeland, B. & Susman-Stillman, A. (1996). 'Dissociation as a Mediator of Child Abuse across Generations', in Journal of Child Abuse and Neglect, Vol. 20, No. 11.

Egeland, B., Jacobvitz, D. & Sroufe, L.A. (1988). *Breaking the Cycle of Abuse in Child Development*, Mother and Child Research Project, University of Minnesota.

Etherington, K. (2003). *Trauma, the Body and Transformation: A Narrative Enquiry*. Jessica Kingsley, London.

Fairfield, M. A. (2004). 'Gestalt Groups Revisited: A Phenomenological Approach'. In Gestalt Review, Vol. 8.

Farrow, T. and Woodruff, P., (2007). *Empathy in Mental Illness*. Cambridge University Press.

Franke, U. (2003). 'In My Mind's Eye: Family Constellations in Individual Therapy and Counselling'. Carl-Auer-Systeme Verlag, Germany.

Freud, A. (1949). 'Certain types and stages of social maladjustment'. Searchlights on Delinquency, ed. **K. R. Eissler.** Imago Publishing, London.

Freud, A. (1954). 'Psycho-analysis and Education'. Psycho-Anal., Study of the Child, 6.

Freud, S. (1922). *Beyond the Pleasure Principle*. International Psychoanalytic Press.

Freud, S. (1933). *New Introductory Lectures on Psycho-analysis*, Penguin, New York.

Freud, S. (1962). 'The Aetiology of Hysteria' (1896), in Standard Edition, Volume 3, translated by J. Strachey. Hogarth Press, London.

Freud, S. (1922). *Beyond the Pleasure Principle*, in *Sigmund Freud: Beyond the Pleasure Principle and Other Writings* (2003). Penguin, USA.

Freud, S. (1931). *The Interpretation of Dreams*, Kindle edition.

Friedland, M. J. (2004). *Treating Psychological Trauma and PTSD*. The Guildford Press.

Fromm, M. G. (2012). *Lost in Transmission: Studies of Trauma Across Generations*. Karnac Books Ltd, London, UK.

Gerhardt, S. (2004). *Why Love Matters: How Affection Shapes a Baby's Brain*. Routledge, UK.

Glenn, M., Jaffe, J., Segal, J. *Trauma, Attachment, and Stress Disorders: Rethinking and Reworking Developmental Issues*. www.healingresources.info.

Goleman, D. (1995). *Emotional Intelligence: Why It Can Matter More Than IQ*. Bantam, New York.

Grogan, J. (2012). *Encountering America: Sixties Psychology, Counterculture and the Movement that Shaped the Modern Self*. Harper Perennial, USA.

Grossman, D. (2009). *On Killing: The Psychological Cost of Learning to Kill in War and Society*. E-Rights/E-Read, New York, USA.

Hart, D. & Sussman, R. (2008). *Man the Hunted: Primates, Predators and Human Evolution*. Westview, USA.

Herman, J. L. (1992). *Trauma and Recovery: The aftermath of Violence from Domestic Abuse to Political Terror*. Basic Books, New York.

Holmes, J. (1993). *John Bowlby & Attachment Theory*. Routledge, London.

Kalsched, D. (1996). *The Inner World of Trauma: Archetypal Defenses of the Personal Spirit*. Routledge, London.

Kardiner, A., & Spiegel, H. (1947). *War Stress and Neurotic Illness.* New York.

Keysers, C. (2011). *The Empathic Brain: How the discovery of Mirror Neurons changes our understanding of human nature.* Amazon Kindle edition.

Landy, H.J., & Keith, L.G. (1998). 'The Vanishing Twin: A Review', in Human Reproduction Update, Vol. 4, No. 2. Published by European Society for Human Reproduction and Embryology.

Levine, P., with Frederick, A. (1997). *Waking the Tiger: Healing trauma.* North Atlantic Books, USA.

Levine, P., & Kline, M. (2008). *Trauma-Proofing Your Kids.* North Atlantic Books, USA.

Levine, P. (2008a). *Healing Trauma: A Pioneering Program for Restoring the Wisdom of Your Body.* Sounds True Inc., USA.

Levine, P. (2010). *In an Unspoken Voice: How the Body Releases Trauma and Restores Goodness.* North Atlantic Books, USA.

Lewis, T., Amini, F. & Lannon, R. (2000). *A General Theory of Love.* Vintage Books, Random House, New York, USA.

Linton, K. R., (2003). 'Knowing by Heart: Cellular Memory in Heart Transplants', in Montgomery College Student Journal of Science & Mathematics, Vol. 2, September 2003.

MacLean, P. (1990). *The Triune Brain in Evolution.* Plenum Publishing Corporation, New York, 1990.

Masson, J. (1984). 'Freud and the Seduction Theory: A Challenge to the Foundations of Psychoanalysis'. The Atlantic Monthly, February, 1984.

Masson, J. (2012, first published 1984). *The Assault on Truth: Freud's Suppression of the Seduction Theory.* Untreed Reads Publishing.

McGilchrist, I. (2010). *The Master and his Emissary: The Divided Brain and the Making of the Western World.* Yale University Press, USA.

May, R. (1965). 'Intentionality, the Heart of Human Will'. Journal of Humanistic Psychology, Vol. 5, No. 2, 1965.

May, R. (1975). *The Courage to Create*. Norton, USA.

Miller, A. (1987). *For Your Own Good: The roots of violence in child-rearing*. Virago Press, London.

Miller, A. (2012). *The Drama of Being a Child: The Search for the True Self*. Virago Press, London.

Naparstek, B. (2006). *Post-Traumatic Stress Disorder: Reduce and Overcome the Symptoms of PTSD*. Piatkus, London, UK.

Ogden, P., Minton, K., Pain, C., (2006). *Trauma and the Body: A Sensorimotor Approach to Psychotherapy*. W.W. Norton, UK.

Perls, F. (1969). *The Gestalt Approach and Eyewitness to Therapy*. Science and Behavior Books, USA.

Pert, C. B., (1999). *The Molecules of Emotion: Why you Feel the Way you Feel*. Pocket Books, Simon & Schuster Inc., London, UK.

Price, J. L. (2005). 'Free Will versus Survival: Brain systems that underlie intrinsic constraints on behavior'. Journal of Comparative Neurology, 493, in Schore, A. N. (2012).

Rizzolatti, G., Fadiga, L., Fogassi, L. & Gallese, V. (2002). 'From mirror neurons to imitation: facts and speculations'. In Meltzoff, A. & Prinz, W. (eds.), The Imitative Mind. Cambridge University Press, Cambridge.

Rizzolatti, G. & Craighero, L., (2004). *The Mirror-Neuron System*, in Annual Review of Neruoscience, 27.

Rosenberg, K. R. and Trevathan, W. R. (2006). *The Evolution of Human Birth*, in *Evolution: A Scientific American Reader*. University of Chicago Press, Chicago, USA.

Rothschild, B. (2000). *The Body Remembers: The psychophysiology of Trauma and Trauma Treatment*. Norton, London.

Ruppert, F. (2008). *Trauma, Bonding & Family Constellations: Understanding and Healing Injuries of the Soul*. English translation edited by V. Broughton. Green Balloon Publishing, Steyning, UK.

Ruppert, F. (2011). *Splits in the Soul: Integrating Traumatic Experiences.* English translation edited by V. Broughton. Green Balloon Publishing, Steyning, UK.

Ruppert, F. (2012). *Symbiosis and Autonomy: Symbiotic Trauma and Love Beyond Entanglements.* English translation edited by V. Broughton. Green Balloon Publishing, Steyning, UK.

Ruppert, F. (2012a). 'Constellation Work Based on Bonding and Trauma and how they differ from Traditional Family Constellations'. The Knowing Field International Constellations Journal, Issue 19.

Scaer, R.C. (2001). *The Body Bears the Burden: Trauma, Dissociation and Disease.* The Haworth Medical Press, USA.

Schore, A. N. (1994). *Affect Regulation and the Origin of the Self: The Neurobiology of Emotioned Development.* Lawrence Erlbaum, UK.

Schore, A. N. (2012). *The Science of the Art of Psychotherapy.* Norton & Company, New York and London.

Schore, A. N. (2012a). London lecture notes, *The Science of the Art of Psychotherapy.* London October, 2012.

Shay, J. (1994). *Achilles in Vietnam: Combat Trauma and the Undoing of Character.* Scribner, New York.

Shay, J. (2002). *Odysseus in America: Combat Trauma and the Trials of Homecoming.* Scribner, New York.

Shutz, L. (2005). 'Neuropsychology Review', in **Schore, A. N.** (2012)

Siegel, D.J. (2010). *The Mindful Therapist: A Clinician's Guide to Mindsight and Neural Integration.* Norton Publishing, New York, USA.

Sparrer, I. (2007). *Miracle, Solution and System: Solution-focused systemic structural constellations for therapy and organisational change.* Solution Books, Cheltenham, UK.

Stein, P.T., Kendall, J. (2004). *Psychological Trauma and the Developing Brain: Neurologically based interventions for troubled children.* Routledge, New York.

Stevenson, H. (2004). *Paradox: A Gestalt Theory of Change.* The Cleveland Consulting Group, Cleveland, USA.

Stolorow, R. D. (2007). *Trauma and Human Existence: Autobiographical, Psychoanalytic and Philosophical Reflections*. Psychoanalytic Inquiry Book Series, Vol. 23.

Sulak, L.E., Dodson, M.G. (1896). 'The Vanishing Twin: Pathologic Confirmation of an Ultrasonographic Phenomenon'. Obstetrics & Gynecology 68.

Sykes Wylie, M. (2004). 'The Limits of Talk: Bessel van der Kolk wants to Transform the Treatment of Trauma'. The Psychotherapy Networker, January/February 2004.

Terr, L. (1991). 'Childhood Traumas: An Outline and overview'. American Journal of Psychiatry, 1, 10–20.

van der Hart, O., Nijenuis, E.R.S., Steele, K. (2006). *The Haunted Self: Structural Dissociation and the Treatment of Chronic Traumatisation*. Norton, New York.

van der Hart, O. & Friedman, B. (1989). 'A reader's guide to Pierre Janet on dissociation: A Neglected Intellectual Heritage'. Journal of Trauma and Dissociation.

van der Kolk, B. (1994). *The Body Keeps the Score: Memory and the Evolving Psychobiology of Post Traumatic Stress*. Harvard Review of Psychiatry 1(5).

van der Kolk, B. A., McFarlane, A. C., Weisaeth, L. (1996). *Traumatic Stress: The effects of Overwhelming Experience on Mind, Body and Society*. The Guildford Press, New York & London.

van der Kolk, B. A. (2007a). 'The History of Trauma in Psychiatry', in *Handbook of PTSD: Science and Practice*. Edited by Friedman, M.J., Keane, T.M., Resick, P.A. Guildford Press, New York.

van der Kolk, B.A. & Van der Hart, O. (1989). 'Pierre Janet and the Breakdown of Adaptation in Psychological Trauma'. American Journal of Psychiatry, 146 (12) December, 1989.

van der Kolk, B.A. (1998). 'Neurobiology, attachment and trauma'. Presentation at Annual Meeting of the International Society for Traumatic Stress Studies, Washington DC.

Wieland, S. (1997). *Hearing the Internal Trauma: Working with Children and Adolescents Who have been Sexually Abused*. Sage, California.

Weingarten, K. (2004). *Common Shock: Witnessing Violence Every Day.* New American Library, New York.

Whitfield, C.L. (1995). *Memory and Abuse: Remembering and Healing the Effects of Trauma.* Health Communications Inc. Florida, USA.

Winnicott, C. (1977). *Communicating with Children II.* Social Work Today, Vol. 8 (26) 1997.

Winnicott, D. W. (2000). *The Child, The Family and the Outside World.* Penguin.

Winterson, J. (2011). *Why Be Happy When You Could Be Normal?* Jonathan Cape, London.

Zepinic, V. (2011). *Hidden Scars: Understanding and Treating Complex Trauma.* Xlibris Corp. USA.

Index

Green Balloon Publishing

Other publications from Green Balloon

Vivian Broughton

In the Presence of Many: Reflections on Constellations emphasising the Individual Context, 2010, 305 pages.

Becoming your true self: a handbook for the journey from trauma to healthy autonomy, late 2013.

~~~~~

Franz Ruppert

Trauma, Bonding & Family Constellations: Understanding and Healing Injuries of the Soul, 2008, 335 pages.

Splits in the Soul: Integrating Traumatic Experiences, 2011, 285 pages.

Symbiosis & Autonomy: Symbiotic Trauma and Love Beyond Entanglement, 2012, 294 pages.

Trauma, Anxiety and Love: On the path to Healthy Autonomy – how constellations can be helpful, due 2014.

Green Balloon Publishing, 42 Goring Road, Steyning, BN44 3GF
01903 814489
info@greenballoonbooks.co.uk

www.greenballoonbooks.co.uk

Green Balloon Publishing

Due for publication autumn 2013

---

vivian broughton

becoming your true self

A handbook for the journey from trauma to healthy autonomy

In this book Vivian takes us on the journey towards healthy autonomy by giving a simple account of the theories of multi-generational trauma of Franz Ruppert, along with ideas and proposals for ways in which individuals can support their therapeutic progress.

This book is for personal explorers, individual seekers after to psychological and emotional health and anyone interested in understanding themselves better.

Using diagrams and drawings, Vivian offers complex ideas in simple terms, an enjoyable account of the place of trauma in all our lives.

Green Balloon Publishing, 42 Goring Road, Steyning, BN44 3GF
01903 814489
info@greenballoonbooks.co.uk

www.greenballoonbooks.co.uk

Green Balloon Publishing

Due for publication spring 2014

Franz Ruppert

Trauma, Anxiety and Love

On the path to healthy autonomy –
How constellations can be helpful.

In this, Franz Ruppert's latest book, he gives a résumé of his theoretical and practical developments on the topics of trauma, belonging and psychological disturbance and disorder over the last 20 years. An extraordinary journey of research, discovery, and innovative thinking, Ruppert's work is likely to change how psychiatric diagnoses are made, how we work in psychotherapy and our perception of ourselves and each other. Building on the revolutionary developments of John Bowlby in the 1950s, and extending their implications to the field of trauma, Ruppert's work changes our perception and understanding of what trauma is, how it works and affects all of our lives, and the long reach trauma has across generations individually, socially, politically and globally.

Green Balloon Publishing, 42 Goring Road,
Steyning, BN44 3GF
01903 814489
info@greenballoonbooks.co.uk

www.greenballoonbooks.co.uk

Lightning Source UK Ltd.
Milton Keynes UK
UKOW06f0930310315

248832UK00015B/517/P